Multinational Companies and the Third World

LOUIS TURNER

ALLEN LANE

First published in the United States by Hill and Wang in 1973
Published in Great Britain in 1974

Allen Lane
A Division of Penguin Books Ltd
21 John Street, London WC1N 2BT

ISBN 0 7139 0326 0

Reproduced photo-litho in Great Britain by
J. W. Arrowsmith Ltd., Bristol 3.

CONTENTS

INTRODUCTION

THIS book is about the confrontation of multinational companies and the Third World. This clash is not just a matter of economics but has important social and political implications as well. It is, for instance, impossible to deal with the tourist industry—one of the Third World's most promising money-spinners—without looking at its impact on primitive societies. Equally, the subject of multinational companies and Southern Africa is impossible to discuss without asking political and moral questions; even if one sticks to issues like "What has been the economic impact of multinational companies on the Third World?" it is impossible to answer without making major assumptions about what would have happened if the companies had never invested, or if they had been used for only part of a project. In any case, economists continually disagree about the value of sheer "growth," arguing that it may be achieved at the cost of other social benefits. I have, therefore, tried in this book to reflect most of the major issues raised by multinational investment in the Third World and have illustrated the main themes by telling stories, filling in historical backgrounds, and discussing the role of the personalities who have influenced events.

The two key terms are used very loosely. "Third World" is neater than most of the alternatives, such as "less developed countries," "LDC's," "underdeveloped countries," "developing countries." Most of these terms are cumbersome and downright confusing when used as the opposite of the so-called "developed economies" of the West. "Third World" here will refer to most of the countries of Africa, Asia, and Latin America. However, South Africa (discussed in Chapter 9) and various European countries like Spain, Portugal, and Southern Italy do have many problems in common with Third World countries. Communist states like Bulgaria and Rumania, which are also faced with similar development problems, have not been included in the analysis. But in my discussion of tourism it would have been ridiculous not to have included Yugoslavia, so in my blanket use of the term, I make no assumptions about these countries other than that they are relatively poor compared to North America and Europe. I certainly do not use the term to imply that the countries on these continents form a cohesive group. In practice they possess a wide spectrum of political and economic systems, approaches to development, and attitudes toward international politics. They are united only by poverty.

I have used "multinational" very loosely to designate companies that for any reason are interested in Third World countries. I make no assumptions about the number of plants they have in countries around the world or the relative international outlook of their managers. In most cases "multinational" is used as a synonym for "company." Apart from the fact that "multinational" is the topical term, it is understood on both sides of the Atlantic, while words like "company," "corporation," or "firm" are not nearly as international in their acceptance. In some cases the term is used to describe companies with only the slightest interest in international operations but that accidentally impinge on a Third World country. At the other end of the continuum we are describing organizations that, in their ability to take the globe as their plaything, are a totally new phenomenon. (For a more general description, see my previous book, *Invisible Empires*.)

On the whole, this book has been written from behind a desk in England. I've set foot in four Third World countries, but only for brief periods. The backbone comes from academic work, fleshed out with interviews and correspondence with some forty companies involved with the Third World. However, a large part of whatever life there is in this book comes from newspapers and journals, which I have devoured voraciously. It is very difficult to do anything ambitious in this field without having access to an extremely wide range of journals. I was lucky to have use of the Royal Institute of International Affairs' library in London, which is excellent, and I found it chastening to discover how often journalists raised crucial issues years before academic authorities had begun their analyses.

I would like to give due thanks to a number of key journals, which are listed in the order of the number of times I cited them: *Financial Times, Far Eastern Economic Review, Latin America, African Development, The Guardian, Business Week, The Times, Economist* (cited an equal number of times), *Observer, The New York Times,* and *The Christian Science Monitor* (London edition). I would also like to thank all those public officials, managers, academics, and trade-union officials who took the time to see me or correspond, especially Walter Goldstein, Gyorgy Adam, Robin Murray, Terry Lacey, and Joseph Nye; also the librarians of Salford University, Singapore Polytechnic, the Institute of Development Studies, Sussex, and the Salzburg Seminar in American Studies.

The sections on trade-union reactions to the runaway company owe much to a grant from the EEC Institute for University Studies which allowed me to visit the United States.

The book as a whole is dedicated to the Swinton Commune—past and present; Jean—my favorite newshound; and my filing system, without whom this book could not have been written.

Finally, the bulk of the niggling, boring work was done by John Ash and Jutta Greaves. Barbara Evans did the typing and Paul Neville did the general assisting, proofreading, and indexing. Thanks to you all.

LOUIS TURNER

Department of Sociology
Government and Administration
Salford University

1 : : *Coming of Age*

Give us the right atmosphere and we will sow towns and cities in place of theories. We will show you how to achieve in peace a fuller independence than can be won on the battlefield or across the negotiating table. Without sacrificing your ancient traditions, we will carry forward the historical revolution in the way people everywhere long for.
Eugene R. Black, former president of the World Bank[1]

Capitalism is the extraordinary belief that the nastiest of men for the nastiest of motives will somehow work for the benefit of us all.
Attributed to John Maynard Keynes

THE 1970's will be a tough period for all companies. Minority groups, political activists, environmentalists, and regulatory government agencies are not likely to fade away. It is less obvious that the governments of the Third World will consolidate the major gains they have been winning from the multinational companies in the late 1960's and early 1970's. In oil, in mining, even in manufacturing industries, Third World governments are on the offensive against companies that for decades have had things their own way.

The 1970–1 Oil Crisis

In 1960 few people in the oil industry had worries about the future. Seven companies dominated the industry, and they felt so confident that they responded to a slowdown in the world market by cutting the prices they paid the producing governments for their crude oil. There was immediate uproar, but it was another ten years before the governments got these prices raised again—however, the situation came to a head in late 1970 and early 1971. No one in the oil industry will be the same again.

The changing balance of power between governments and companies can best be illustrated by the experience of Libya. In 1960 it was ruled by King Idris, a conservative, whose reputation rested on his role in heading the resistance to the much-hated Italians during the Second World War. Promising oil discoveries had been made in the late 1950's by Western companies, allowed in by the king on extremely generous terms compared with those demanded elsewhere in the oil-producing world. Production started in 1961, and Libya, a poor country with few natural resources, moved rapidly into the position of the world's third largest oil-exporting country, upon whom Western Europe depended for a full third of its oil supplies.

It did not take long for the other oil-producing governments (who were now joined in an organization called OPEC— Organization of Petroleum Exporting Countries)—to see that King Idris was being overgenerous to the companies based in Libya. So, under heavy pressure, in 1965 Libya persuaded the companies to accept terms that were in line with those offered elsewhere.

King Idris himself was becoming increasingly conservative and was far too pro-Western for younger Libyans, who looked toward the more radical leadership of Egypt's President Gamal Abdel Nasser. In 1969, while undergoing treatment in a Turkish spa, King Idris was deposed by a group of young officers led by Colonel Muammar el-Qaddafi, who was then aged twenty-seven. For an initial period the new regime concentrated on rooting out the corruption that was rife under Idris, on ousting the British and Americans from military bases on Libyan soil, on expelling Italian technicians and what remained of the Jewish community, on removing foreign-language signs even from the airport, and on banning alcohol. Qaddafi and his colleagues then turned their attention to the oil companies. They stopped playing the game by the rules.

In May 1970 a bulldozer engaged in cable-laying work for

the Syrian telephone company (later reports say it was a farmer) somehow managed to puncture the Trans-Arabian Pipeline (Tapline), which was used to transport oil from Saudi Arabia to the Mediterranean, thus bypassing the closed Suez Canal. The actual circumstances of this incident are obscure, but the crucial point was that Syria refused to allow the pipeline to be repaired for another nine months. Europe, which was already suffering from the closure of the Suez Canal since the 1967 Arab-Israeli war, found itself even more dependent on Libyan oil, its only major source on the European side of the canal. The Saudi Arabian oil would have to come to Europe around South Africa at a time when tanker charges were mounting at an alarming rate. Libya put on the pressure.

During May and June of that year, Libya forced the oil companies on its soil to cut back production, thus tightening the squeeze on Europe. At the same time the government started negotiations with the weakest companies, and in September Occidental Petroleum, one of the smaller firms in the industry, not only conceded an increase in the posted price (the figure from which governments' revenues are determined) but also granted the government 58 percent of that price as its share. By the end of the month, the other companies in Libya had followed Occidental's lead, and the government revenue from oil was boosted by about 30 percent.

There followed seven months of escalating demands from all over the oil world that left the companies shattered. The Shah of Iran was able to use the Libyan deal as a lever in his own negotiations, and his success was followed by pressures from the remaining producing countries, leading to a series of ad hoc deals. Then, in December, all the OPEC countries met to coordinate further demands. This was a significant meeting, when the producing governments realized that they had the companies on the run. They therefore decided that the governments from the producing area in the Gulf of Persia would negotiate as a bloc with the oil industry. In January 1971 the Libyans came back to the companies saying that the previous autumn's bargain had merely compensated for the previous exploitation the country had suffered at the hands of the oil companies. "Now," they asked, "how about giving us some more money on top of that?"

The companies were thunderstruck. First, Libya had to be pinned down to an agreement that would stick for some time. This would be difficult, since Libya's financial reserves were strong enough for it to survive without any oil revenues for almost a year, while the industry would find it extremely difficult to replace Libya's three million barrels a day. Second, the industry had to counter the Libyan tactic of picking on the smaller companies. It had to stamp out any possibility that Libya and the governments east of Suez might start a series of "leapfrogging" negotiations in which the concessions given, for example to Libya, would automatically be demanded by the rest. Behind the companies, the consuming governments were deeply concerned, since any further concessions would damage their balance of payments. These governments therefore allowed the companies to ignore the usual antitrust restraints by coming together to decide on a common negotiating stand and to discuss ways of helping their smaller brethren should the Libyans, in particular, continue to try picking the companies off one at a time.

In the negotiations that followed, the producing governments demanded more money in the form of higher posted prices and other fringe allowances. The companies, though obviously trying to limit the size of any such concessions, were chiefly aiming at agreements that would be guaranteed for five years and that would not be undermined by any leapfrogging claims. The east-of-Suez states proved more amenable than Libya, but finally, by April 1971, all the major OPEC governments had agreed to deals that were to last for a five-year period. In return, the companies had conceded payments to governments that, in the case of Libya, were about 80 percent higher than they had been twelve months previously.

It was an expensive settlement, and the cynics asked whether the five-year guarantee was worth the paper it was written on. By autumn 1971 it was already clear that the contracts, specified in United States dollars, would have to be renegotiated to compensate for the fall in the value of the dollar. More seriously, a drive for government participation in the production activities of the companies was under way with the blessings of OPEC. Thus, even if the prices paid to the governments did remain as agreed for five years, most objective observers of the industry accepted that the firms would have to let producing governments take at least a 20 percent share in their production activities—maybe more in countries like Libya.

Whatever concessions they are forced to make over oil production, there is no doubt that the companies will survive. They will remain firmly in control of marketing, refining, and, to a lesser extent, the transportation of oil, since their know-how in these matters is far greater than that of the producing governments. As long as most of these governments are highly dependent on their regular checks from the companies, it is in their interest to push the companies only so far. Both sides still need each other, though the terms of the often unwilling partnership are steadily moving in favor of the governments. In the meantime, the companies are diversifying out of oil as fast as they can, although oil will still provide their major source of income for the immediate future. They now claim to be in the "energy," not "oil," business, and are buying up coal mines and moving into nuclear power. Some are capitalizing on their exploration and production know-how, and are instigating more general mining. Others are capitalizing on extensive landholdings in America by creating new towns.

Since the "golden age" of the early 1960's, the companies have been losing ground, either on their rate of return on oil investments or on the proportion of the non-Communist world's crude-oil production, refining, or marketing that is in their hands. They are still large, important, and powerful, but their influence is on the wane. An era is ending.

On the other hand, life looks good for the producing countries. Unlike other Third World countries, their economies rest on a product that more developed economies need desperately, and in quantities that mean that any short-run attempts to find substitutes are doomed to failure. It may well be that nuclear power will eventually supersede the demand for oil. It may also be that new sources of oil from countries like Nigeria or

Indonesia, or from new areas like Alaska and the North Sea, will lead to a glut in production, causing falling prices and therefore giving greater bargaining power to the companies. But this seems unlikely. Annual discoveries on the scale of the Alaskan and North Sea operations are needed if the long-term growth rate in world consumption of 5–10 percent is to be met. In the meantime everything is going their way, and countries like Libya, which in 1960 were of little importance, have set an example, with a mixture of nationalism and really tough bargaining that has shaken the industry. However, the success of the 1970–1 negotiations should be placed in a wider perspective to show that, although important to the companies and to the producing governments, the actual achievement is minimal.

In 1969 the seven leading oil companies paid $4.2 billion to

Declining role of the oil "majors" outside
North America and the Communist countries.[2]

	% 1963	% 1968
CRUDE OIL PRODUCTION		
"Majors"	82.1	77.9
"Independents"	9.3	13.1
Governments	8.6	9.0
REFINING		
"Majors"	65.3	60.9
"Independents"	21.1	23.1
Governments	13.6	16.0
MARKETING		
"Majors"	62.6	55.6
"Independents"	26.8	30.8
Governments	10.6	13.6

"Majors" are the seven giants: Standard Oil of New Jersey, Royal Dutch/Shell, Mobil, Gulf, Standard Oil of California, British Petroleum, Texaco. "Independents": all other non-governmental groups but including the Compagnie Française des Pétroles.

the producing governments in the Eastern hemisphere. The 1970–1 negotiations have raised this figure by another $2.9 billion or so, but for an industry where everything has recently been running in favor of the producing countries, these figures are still ridiculously low. Here are some comparisons:

1. Despite cries that the developed economies will be bank-rupted if the greedy oil producers continue their demands, the producing government's "take" of the final selling price of a gallon of gasoline at the beginning of 1971 was 12.5 percent, compared with the consuming government, which was taking 45 percent in taxes for itself.[3] In other words, the governments of countries like Britain, the United States, West Germany, etc., are doing roughly four times as well in revenue from the final product as the producing governments like Libya, Iran, Kuwait, etc.
2. In 1971 the after-tax profits of America's five most profitable companies (General Motors, Exxon, Ford, IBM, and Texaco) came to $6 billion. This is more than the producing govern-ments' income from oil in the same year.

We are dealing here with figures that, though important to the Third World, are trivial when compared to the strength of the developed economies. Robert McNamara, the current president of the World Bank, quotes a figure that puts the whole aid pro-gram in a similar perspective.[4] The annual flow of aid comes to just under $13 billion per annum, which he compares with the $180 billion the world spends annually on armaments. Even more important to this book is to compare *private direct in-vestment* in the Third World, which was a mere $2.5 billion dollars in 1969.[5] When compared to the profits of the five companies just mentioned, this figure is peanuts. We should never forget this disproportionate scale.

Latin America and the Rise of the Andean Pact

If oil were the only industry losing ground to Third World governments, private-enterprise enthusiasts need not be too worried. It is, after all, the only industry the Third World possesses that is essential to the growth of the developed nations. Private enterprise, however, has been losing power on a wider front. In the late 1950's most businessmen assumed that Latin America was still under the control of the United States government and was therefore a fairly safe area to invest in. Some of them paused for thought after the riots that accompanied the tour of Latin America in 1958 by Richard Nixon, then U.S. Vice-President. But it was not until Fidel Castro's success in Cuba in 1959 that the worries began in earnest, though another ten years would pass before the façade finally cracked.

The American government's main attempt to see that Castro's Marxism did not contaminate the rest of the continent was the Alliance for Progress, which was signed in 1961 by the United States and all Latin American governments except Cuba's. The deal was that the United States would provide official aid and private investment, while the Latin American governments carried out reforms that would allow these funds to be used effectively. Thus, the United States government expected the Latin Americans to forge ahead with land reforms, progressive taxation schemes, vastly improved educational systems, and so on. It never crossed anyone's mind in public that the first conservative citadel to be stormed might be Latin America's passive acceptance of foreign private investment.

For a while, everything continued smoothly. Brazilian politicians at this time inclined perhaps too far to the left, and in 1964 a military regime replaced them. Since then, Brazil has given foreign firms a reasonably free hand. On the west coast of the continent, Chile produced a much-vaunted reformist politician, President Eduardo Frei Montalva, who was elevated into a symbol of the alliance. He carried out reforms on a piecemeal basis, and in return, Chile became the fourth largest recipient of UN aid in the world, after India, Pakistan, and Egypt. Of course, as we shall see, this did not stop Chile from electing as Frei's successor in 1970 the continent's first democratically elected Marxist head of state, Dr. Salvador Allende.

However, Frei and his counterpart to the north, Peru's President Fernando Belaúnde Terry, were both involved in disputes with foreign companies that were to explode by the end of the decade. Chile's economy rests almost entirely on copper, and it and Zambia are the two largest sources of copper in the world. However, 90 percent of this crucial sector of the economy was in the hands of companies that were subsidiaries of two United States companies, Kennecott Copper, and Anaconda and Andes Copper Mining. Frei realized that political opinion in Chile would no longer accept this foreign stranglehold and devised the policy of "Chileanization," whereby the state would buy into the two companies. This policy got bogged down in Congress (Frei was careful to follow the constitution) and when ratified was only partially successful. Kennecott went along with the scheme and sold 51 percent of its main mine to the government, but Anaconda worked hard to permit the government a mere 25 percent of the company's third, and smallest, mine, keeping 100 percent control over the mines that mattered. There things stuck, since Frei moved slowly (one of the reasons why his party was rejected in the 1970 elections) and the companies did not feel particularly threatened.

The breakthrough, however, came in Peru, and unexpectedly in the form of a populist military coup. The civilian president, Belaúnde, had got embroiled in a long-running dispute with International Petroleum Corporation (IPC), a subsidiary of Standard Oil of New Jersey, the oil giant. The dispute was complicated because IPC had titles that gave it, alone among the oil companies, ownership of the surface and subsoil of its Peruvian oil field. The government was trying to make a bargain by which the ownership would be handed back to Peru, in return for IPC being granted a more normal and acceptable concession. A deal was struck and for a while it was interpreted as a victory for Peru. But then a scandal blew up over a page missing in the contract's text that suggested that the company was being given the right to hedge against inflation, which the average Peruvian just had to suffer. Belaúnde's party, Accion Popular, split, and with an imminent presidential election, there was a good chance that a well-known radical candidate might be elected. However, the military moved in and suspended civilian rule.

This all happened according to the Latin American formula; however, the incoming government expropriated IPC's Peruvian assets, nationalized the sugar industry (kicking out W. R. Grace, Inc., one of the largest United States investors in Latin America), instituted controls on the banking and fishing industry, expropriated ranches owned by Cerro (a United States mining company), and the telephone system run by the world's largest conglomerate, International Telephone and Telegraph Corporation (ITT), and even clawed back some of the foreign exchange that less patriotic Peruvians had stashed away in foreign bank accounts.

There had been one or two previous examples of populist military coups (Argentina's Perón and Egypt's Nasser), but this one, as well as being unexpected, acted as a catalyst for a large part of Latin America, until, during the summer of 1971, only Brazil seemed to be left as a major upholder of the right of foreign investors to go where they pleased and do what they wanted.

The most important aspect of the regime of General Juan Velasco Alvarado was that Peru got away with it. The sky did not fall on his head when he started tampering with the rights of United States investment. In fact, every threat by the American government only strengthened the regime's hold on the nation, since the military were able to show themselves true Peruvians threatened by the hemispheric giant. The United States was in a quandary since the junta was anything but Communist, and therefore the wilder threats to cut off all aid were never carried out.

In the meantime, there had been attempts to instigate various schemes of regional economic integration, the most important being the formation of the Latin American Free Trade Association (LAFTA). Such common markets cannot work without a fair amount of give and take, especially by the larger countries. Unfortunately for LAFTA, the larger countries involved (Brazil and Argentina) soon lost interest, so that the smaller countries (Peru, Chile, Bolivia, Ecuador, Colombia) decided to get together in a subgrouping, which was to be known as the Andean Pact (formed in 1969). This might have proved ineffectual, except that the Peruvian nationalists found an ally in Allende, who was elected president of Chile toward the end of 1970. He immediately moved in on the copper companies, which Frei had only partly tackled, and nationalized them.

The nationalization of the Chilean copper mines might not have greatly affected the supporters of free enterprise, but the Andean Pact went further, drawing up a charter on foreign investment to which all five member countries subscribed. This surprised outside observers, who felt that Colombia and Ecuador would be unwilling to join any pact that might frighten off new investment. Certain sectors, like the steel industry and banks, would be totally forbidden to foreign investors, while in all others foreigners could take only a minority shareholding. In particular, existing firms would have fifteen years at the most to come up with the necessary local participation, while Peru wanted it to be found much faster.

The impact of the nationalizations in Peru and Chile was traumatic. Other countries followed suit, like Bolivia, which nationalized Gulf Oil's assets. But the companies were possibly most disturbed by the realization that a country like Chile could democratically elect a Marxist president, who would then work with other countries to formulate terms seriously affecting private investment—by imposing limits on equity participation and repatriation—and get away with it.

Many United States firms now feel that the whole continent is disintegrating. Where they once trusted the ability of the United States government to keep affairs running smoothly, they now see formerly servile governments lining up to join any Latin American or world organization not dominated by large, aggressive American delegations. The military regime of Argentina is flirting with the Andean Group. It is even possible that Castro's Cuba will be allowed into the mainstream of Latin American official life after a decade in the wilderness. Only Brazil is left as a reminder of those legendary days when local regimes bent over backward not to antagonize foreign investors. It is still possible that Brazil's current boom may lure the weaker members away from the Andean Pact; however, it is unlikely that Brazil's laissez-faire policies will survive. The 1950's and early 1960's saw the emergence of economic nationalism. It has been suggested that the younger Brazilian officers will be affected by the Peruvian model and that in the medium term the military may become more xenophobic, discriminating far more heavily in favor of Brazilian enterprise. For instance, the current regime, under President Emilio Garrastazú Medici, has tangled hard with the Americans about its claim to extend Brazilian control over the first two hundred miles of territorial water—a dispute that unites Brazil with Andean Pact countries like Peru and Ecuador.

Whatever the future policy of Brazil and the Andean Pact, many firms have already decided to pull out (the technical term for this is "divestment"). Thus W. R. Grace, a company that has always been heavily involved in the continent through sugar, ranching, shipping, and mining interests, has been steadily withdrawing. Its 1970 annual report shows that it has completely divested in Chile and Ecuador, and is substantially reducing investments in Brazil, Colombia, Central America, and Peru. Other firms, like General Motors and Ford, have withdrawn from assembly operations in Peru and Chile, though this kind of withdrawal is not very difficult for them, since the business involved is minimal by their standards and is relatively unimportant for the countries involved: their problem is too many auto plants, not too few.

Decisions not to invest in the first place could prove more critical. *Business Week* reported that Argentina was probably about to lose $300 million in new investments from firms like Dow Chemical, General Motors, Ford, Exxon, and Kodak.[6] Earlier in the year the Council of the Americas (the major lobby of United States firms investing in Latin America) claimed that eighty-four projects backed by United States money were currently held up as a result of the Andean Pact. This announcement apparently worked against the United States position in Colombia, where domestic business had been hostile to Andean Pact policies on foreign investment but felt this statement by the council was a blatant attempt to interfere with internal domestic politics. As a result, Colombia swung behind the Andean declaration at a time when it might possibly have dug in its heels over the position it was being required to take.

As with the oil industry, we find that foreign investors in Latin America consider the 1960's to have been a decade in which everything moved against them. Established wisdoms have been challenged. Existing power structures, if not changing in any major way, have moved heavily against the foreign investor, thus disappointing United States dreams that surrounded the Alliance for Progress. Will those dreams ever be resurrected?

How Much Sympathy for the Multinationals?

Most multinational managers feel genuinely bitter about what is happening to their companies in the Third World. They feel betrayed and are very reluctant to admit that the Third World may have a case. It is, however, difficult to feel much sympathy for them. Some of their number behaved abominably, even by the lax standards of the bygone era of the robber barons. Even the better-behaved firms involved with the Third World acted callously, if we judge them by today's business standards. They bribed officials, they failed to train local nationals with any urgency, they "fiddled" their accounts so that poverty-stricken countries were further weakened by massive outflows of precious foreign exchange, and when there were disputes with local interests, they would get as much diplomatic help from their home country as possible. Even today many of the complaints against the activities of genuinely well-meaning companies have considerable justification, and no company should do business in the Third World without at least being aware of the types of activities that cause resentment.

However, the process of being "beastly" to the multinationals can go too far if it ignores the genuine contributions they can make to a development program. There is, therefore, a significant cost attached to any policy that aims to do without multinational investment—but this cost can sometimes be justified. There is a perfectly valid trade-off to be made between national susceptibilities and sheer economic efficiency. Some governments argue further that such investment goes into sectors that make an equitable economic policy harder to achieve. Thus, a country like Cuba deliberately excludes investments from multinational companies in the hope of achieving a more just and equitable domestic society. Supporters of the multinationals point to the glaring inefficiencies that can be found in such relatively autarchic regimes, but they miss the point. Economic nationalism is an idea whose time seems to have come; it may well be an important part of the nation-building process. Less time should be spent on regretting that the days of passive Third World governments are over; more should be turned to analyzing the mature relationship that will evolve between genuinely independent Third World governments and multinational companies.

Notes

For full bibliographical details of items cited in the notes, refer to the Bibliography on pp. 275–87.

1. Daniel, *Private Investment,* p. 1.
2. Chandler, "The Myth of Oil Power," p. 712.
3. *Financial Times,* February 4, 1971.
4. It is common to include private investment and export credits as a form of aid. This inflates the totals found in the statistics, but a number of commentators refuse to accept such investment as a true form of aid.
5. UNCTAD, *Handbook of International Trade, Supplement 1970,* Table 5.2.
6. *Business Week,* September 4, 1971.

2 : : *The Bad Old Days of Naked Force*

BUSINESS apologists normally try to shrug off the bad old days in which their predecessors plundered the Third World. "Of course," they say, "there were excesses in the past, but to-day . . ." If we ignore the implications that businesses have been behaving impeccably in recent years, it is doubtful if we should yet ignore this era. It would be ridiculous to hold today's managers morally responsible for the earlier activities of their firms. On the other hand, we know nothing about the scars left by some of the worst excesses. It may well be that the virulence of today's economic nationalism in many parts of the world is at least in part conditioned by memories (admittedly often the result of propaganda) of the times when foreign companies were very much on top.

The Imperial Era

Pure greed by no means explains everything about the drive for empires (viz. Charles Kindleberger's demolition job).[1] Certainly, it was mostly straight economics that drove the early merchant-adventurers after spice, gold, sugar, slaves, etc.; but by the late 1800's the picture was very much more complicated than that. The mobs who poured into the British streets to celebrate the relief of Mafeking, or the American citizens who thrilled to the exploits of Teddy Roosevelt's Roughriders in Cuba, were re-sponding in a much more personal way than was called for if the only significance of these events was that British or Ameri-can firms would now find it easier to make money in South Africa and Cuba. In fact, there was a messianic drive, partly religious but mostly nationalistic, that ran parallel to the cruder economic motives of many of those who were actually out in the field. So, by the time of the 1884 Berlin conference, in which twelve European powers, Turkey, and the United States drew up the ground rules for one last scramble for the unclaimed parts of the globe, the whole imperial drive had become highly complex.

The vast majority of the business adventurers who scoured the globe for opportunities beside the soldiers and the missionaries were in it solely for the cash. There were, however, more complex characters like Cecil Rhodes, the developer of South Africa's gold and diamond industries, who in his early and more euphoric days once wrote that he wanted to monopolize the diamond industry, paint the map of Africa red (i.e. British), restore the United States to the British Empire, "square the Pope," and found a secret society that would control the world or even annex the planets (the pioneering Rhodes scholarship scheme partly had its roots in this mystical ideal).[2]

These adventurers found plenty of opportunities. Rapid urbanization in Europe and America meant there was a demand for cattle and wheat (Canada, Australia, Argentina, Uruguay); bananas (Central America and the Caribbean); coffee, tea, and cocoa (Brazil, India, Ceylon, and West Africa); while the parallel industrialization unleashed a growing demand for raw materials like nitrate (Peru, Chile); rubber (Brazil for a while, then Malaya); tin (Malaya); and copper (Chile, Northern Rhodesia). And then, of course, demand for gold and diamonds proved insatiable as ever, thus providing the economic base for South Africa. These were rough-and-ready days, in which profits were large for those who could successfully satisfy demands back in Europe or North America. Many adventurers failed, but the stakes were high enough to make all of them pretty careless of the natives (generally non-white).

The British Empire, whatever its other faults, tried to keep its industrialists on a tight rein. With varying degrees of haste, the government would take some form of direct control of territories that companies had opened up for them. Thus, India passed from the hands of the East India Company in the 1850's, and other areas like Nigeria and the Rhodesias were later removed from their commercial guardians. Colonial administration tended to be staffed by younger sons of the traditional, landed upper classes who, as Colin Cross points out,[3] considered any form of trade disreputable and could not be guaranteed to back their British business colleagues in disputes with native interests. There were also the missionaries, a thorn in the flesh of the businessmen, whom they viewed as corrupters of native society.

This mix of interests could lead to some strange and complex relationships, as can be seen in Cecil Rhodes's negotiations for mining rights in Matabeleland, which will also help to describe how a number of companies achieved extensive territorial and economic concessions throughout the world. Rhodes was a gold and diamond magnate who, starting from South Africa, was obsessed with the need to drive to the north. Since legal formalities had to be observed, he had to get the agreement of various chieftains, one of whom was Lobengula, king of the Matabele (Matabeleland covered roughly the area we know now as Rhodesia). When Rhodes's delegation of representatives reached Lobengula's headquarters at Bulawayo, they found four similar delegations, a bunch of cutthroat European camp followers, a missionary who translated for Lobengula, and, later, the Anglican Bishop of Bloemfontein, who wanted permission to proselytize among the wretched Lobengula's followers in the North. This was a fairly typical retinue for any important African chieftain, at least one of whom drank himself to death on champagne while rivals quarreled over concessions. With Lobengula were also a couple of Boers who were trying to forge his mark. The king probably had only the vaguest idea of what he was signing away when he eventually made a deal with Rhodes's men, who promised money, guns, ammunition, and a gunboat (African kings came a bit more expensive than Red Indian chieftains, but their fate was the same). The king probably thought he was just signing a document giving Rhodes's British South Africa Company the right to dig a hole on Matabele territory. When it was pointed out that it gave the company the right to dig large numbers of holes, he became more concerned, but it was too late, and the two Matabele wars were

pathetic attempts to redress the balance. But the contract was
not enough, and Rhodes had to get a charter from London on
the basis of Lobengula's agreement that would give his company political as well as economic control. Eventually, despite
some setbacks as the missionaries tried to quash the bid, the
charter came through, and Rhodes managed to add some other
territories to form a state that he modestly dedicated to himself.

It was upon such treaties (others were even more nefarious)
that most of the Central African mining empires were constructed. Even if Latin America was economically and politically
more sophisticated than Africa, the ease with which concessions
could be purchased from local rulers was much the same, and
the ethics of the foreigners no more admirable. Latin America
differed from the rest of the world in one important respect—
there were no colonial authorities from the imperial power to
act as a foil between companies and the local nationals, since
the United States chose (in theory) to respect Latin American
political independence. It was only when governments became
unsatisfactory that the Marines went in. Thus it was that much
of the local hatred Latin Americans built up in this period was
aimed specifically at the companies that were the chief symbol
of foreign domination. So, although in Africa there were firms
like the United Africa Company (part of the Unilever group),
which dominated the Nigerian economy just as much as United
Fruit dominated the banana republics, the United Africa Company was only part of British colonial rule in Nigeria, and in
the drive for Nigerian independence, anti-British feelings were
directed most logically at the official colonial administration,
and only secondarily at the company. In Latin America there
was no such buffer force, so that there was a direct clash between firms and local citizens.

Finally, we should remember that the businessmen who came
south from the United States were from the same generation of
businessmen as the railroad tycoons, men like Andrew Carnegie, who were to become known as the "robber barons." It
is one of the tragic paradoxes of history that Teddy Roosevelt,
who did sterling work in helping to curb the worst excesses of

these entrepreneurs, gave a lead to their first cousins south of the border by following a Latin American policy of the utmost cynicism. The Colombians were "jack rabbits," and the people of Bogota "contemptible little creatures." It is not surprising, therefore, that United States businessmen were able to get away with practices in Latin America that would have been banned or at least disparaged in the United States. Some men were so bad one almost ends up admiring them. There was William Walker, who started his career by trying to conquer Lower California. A year later (1855) he muscled in on Commodore Cornelius Vanderbilt's operations in Nicaragua (Vanderbilt was planning an Atlantic–Pacific canal). A couple of the latter's subordinates gave Walker $20,000 of Vanderbilt's money, with which he tried to conquer Nicaragua, which was very nearly admitted into the Union as a slave state. He was eventually kicked out by Vanderbilt, but was by then a popular hero. Later on he declared himself president of El Salvador, Honduras, and Nicaragua, legalizing slavery. The British Navy eventually executed him.[4]

On the whole, this was not a noble era. Admittedly, a number of cities had gas lighting installed; there was a certain amount of competition (between the Americans and the British) to get railways built; and the continent was linked to the United States and Europe by steamship lines. But often this was at the cost of putting money into the pockets of people only slightly more savory than Walker, and at the cost of virtually bankrupting the countries concerned, as they ran into difficulties paying the interest on the loans they had raised to pay for the gas or the locomotives in the first place. It was in this environment that United Fruit grew.

United Fruit

We must produce a disembowelment of the incipient economy of this country in order to increase and help our aims. We have to prolong its tragic, tormented and revolutionary life; the wind must only blow on our sails and the water must only wet our keel.[5]

United Fruit grows bananas ("Chiquita" bananas in the United

States; "Fyffes" in Britain). In the course of this business it has owned plantations, railroads, towns, ports, shipping lines, private armies, and politicians. Even if it had behaved in an exemplary fashion, it would have been hated, but its behavior until just recently made it a particularly easy prey.

The company was formed in 1899 by the merger of two banana empires, one of which had started with Boston shipping, the other with railroad promotion in Costa Rica. Gradually it spread through Central America, and the feel of these early days can be gotten from United Fruit's entry into Honduras, when a business associate organized an invasion (1910) in order to pre-empt a bid that might have brought J. Pierpont Morgan into the country's affairs. Money for a yacht, a case of rifles, three thousand rounds of ammunition, and a machine gun for a mercenary called Machine Gun Malony were all that were needed. The United States consul arbitrated for the anti-Pierpont Morgan faction, and United Fruit got its entrance to Honduras.

It was not normally necessary to resort to such tactics, since the company's power rested ultimately on the fact that by owning the railroads within the country and the shipping line to take the bananas to the United States, it could break any opposition, be it independent planters within the banana republics (Honduras, Guatemala, Costa Rica, El Salvador, Nicaragua) or rival American companies. It was particularly easy to achieve this kind of monopoly since bananas are perishable and the company could always ensure that those from troublesome producers would be slowed down in transit, or even be rejected as of inferior quality if independent planters were selling to United Fruit. In Costa Rica, the company once had to drive out Atlantic Fruit, which was trying to purchase bananas there. Bananas left on railway platforms for Atlantic were chopped to pieces with machetes on the order of United Fruit officers. Train shipments were delayed and legal claims were instigated against Atlantic Fruit's bananas, thus triggering court embargoes; but since they were perishable, the producers would desperately turn them over to United Fruit, who would then ship them north. If the company could behave this ruthlessly with its own kind, local citizens had no chance.

Over the years, the company did concede wage increases and higher shares of its profits to local governments, and build schools, experimental farms, and clinics. However, just when the company was beginning to live down its earlier excesses, which included the use of armed bands to intimidate militant workers (during a strike in Honduras in 1931 company planes flew the workers' leaders into neighboring El Salvador), the 1954 Guatemala coup rekindled suspicions. Jacobo Arbenz Guzmán, a reformist president, enacted a land-reform program in 1952 that hit the company hard. Both John Foster Dulles, the U.S. Secretary of State, and his brother Allen Dulles, then head of the CIA, had strong connections with the company. There were other complicating factors, which included the allegation that Arbenz had been going to Czechoslovakia for arms, and a coup took place in which the CIA was heavily involved. United Fruit apologists deny that their company was actively implicated. Clearly, however, the company was one of the chief beneficiaries, and there is no evidence that it was opposed to the outcome. Even as late as 1960 it was again implicated in a basically political dispute. The company still owns the Tropical Radio Telegraph Company, which is the chief international communications company in Central America. During a revolt in Guatemala in 1960 the Ydigoras regime used this network to communicate with Washington. The badly coded messages were monitored and deciphered throughout Latin America, which did not improve the company's already tarnished image.

The situation today seems to be more respectable. After a merger, the company has camouflaged itself with the name United Brands. The United States antitrust authorities hit the company with a judgment in 1958 that has been forcing it to be very much more circumspect. It has had to sell its shares in its Central American railway interests and, in September 1970, was trying to make a deal with another United States agricultural company, Del Monte, whereby the latter would buy

United Fruit banana-producing properties in Guatemala. In the meantime, it has been diversifying into plantains (a variety of banana that can be cooked), oil palm, peanuts, and plastics. It has been moving heavily away from direct ownership of production facilities and is relying more heavily on "associate producers" to supply its North American markets.

All the same, *El Pulpo* (the Octopus), as the company has been familiarly known, is still inevitably involved in disputes where it virtually has the power to make life-or-death decisions for national economies. A typical dispute was the Jamaican banana war of 1970-1 in which one of United Fruit's subsidiaries, Fyffes, was involved.

There is at present a world glut resulting from the expansion of banana growing in new sources like Taiwan, the Ivory Coast, and the Canary Islands, many of whom are producing fruit at prices that can knock out industries in higher-cost areas like Jamaica. These relatively inefficient industries are often bolstered by ex-colonial powers who reserve given proportions of their markets for the product of their ex-colonies. Britain has such an arrangement with Jamaica, which has the right to provide half the British market. The industry is independent and is the fourth largest on the island, employing 80,000 people at a time when overall unemployment is around 16–25 percent. Fyffes had a contract to sell 75 percent of its production, but the company decided to break the agreement, arguing that it wanted more freedom to supply the British market from other sources. The company's basic argument (which is not really disputed) was that the Jamaican industry was inefficient. The bananas being exported to Britain were of low quality, and as a result the British consumer was tending to turn away from the fruit altogether. Fyffes was losing money on its Jamaican trading, had other more promising sources, and wanted to wriggle out of its obligations.

Britain was extremely concerned, since this state of affairs could well have led to the destruction of the Jamaican industry and provoked further controversy over government policy. Closer examination suggested that Fyffes's case was by no means watertight. For instance, it was charging noticeably more for freight than a British firm (Geest Industries) was from some other Caribbean islands. And Geest had accepted a much more active role in stimulating the growers into adopting better practices. There were also some puzzling aspects to Fyffes's gradings of the quality of bananas it accepted (a Jamaican competitor, Jamaican Producers, used laxer gradings but was still more profitable than Fyffes).

Eventually a compromise solution was produced in which Fyffes agreed to raise its payments to Jamaica and to help assemble a team of technical advisers who would help the industry achieve its targets. A critical omission, however, was that Fyffes was still free to supply part of the British market from cheaper sources, such as Surinam, the Ivory Coast, and the Canary Islands.

This unstable compromise may well set a precedent for an increasing number of agreements. It is clear that whatever productivity increases are made, the Jamaican industry is now uncompetitive at the existing level of Jamaican wages. The key to the industry's survival lies not with United Fruit but with the British government. Should the company desert Jamaica, other arrangements could be made to get the fruit to the protected market in Britain. But if the British government decided to buy from the cheapest sources, then nothing, not even a United Fruit run by a band of angels, could keep the industry alive as an exporting entity. Where governments are heavily involved, as in this case, the companies are mere middlemen who can play minor roles with varying degrees of constructiveness. However, where the producing countries have no guardian to preserve their markets, the companies can play God, deciding to allow one nation's industry to decline for the benefit of another nation's more profitable one. This becomes a much more complex issue, which will be discussed in Chapter 7.

Liberia and Firestone

Companies in other parts of the world have dominated their host economies as United Fruit has done. Firestone, for instance was invited into Liberia in the 1920's at a time when the goverment, descended from freed American slaves, was facing bankruptcy. Its experience with European loans had been disastrous (the first president to arrange one was subsequently lynched), so it thought that a loan offered to it by Firestone might loosen its dependence on Europe. The company was granted the right to introduce extensive rubber plantations, which, even in 1970, Firestone claimed were the largest in the world. However, the loan involved a virtual reorganization of the Liberian government's control over finance. It acquired an American financial adviser, who was to be nominated by the U.S. President, and a number of American subordinate advisers and auditors who had extensive powers. The company controlled the only local bank, and the government was not permitted to raise any new debts, either external or internal, without the permission of these Americans. The company also held all the most important distributorships of United States and European consumer goods and could even influence the price of rice, the staple item in the Liberian diet. Labor relations were fairly tense. Wages were lower than those in the Gold Coast and Nigeria, and after one dispute in which a number of rubber trees were burned, Firestone set up its own security system.

Altogether the company was too powerful, and disputes between company and government increased in bitterness, until in 1952 the loan was repaid, an event the Liberians celebrated by erecting a monument whose dedication read: "This monument erected by the people of Liberia is dedicated to the great relief brought to the country by the Tubman administration in the retirement of the 1926 loan with its humiliating and strangulating effects on the economy of the nation." [6] Since then the situation has improved slightly, as a thriving mining industry has been developed with Swedish and American money. Although Firestone is still a major force in the economy, other interests are now as important and the government has rather more options open to it. Nevertheless, the country as a whole remains dependent on America, using United States dollar bills for its currency and U.S. Army fatigues for its soldiers. But at least it is no longer a satellite state of Firestone's.

Union Minière and the Congo

The ex-Belgian Congo (then known as Congo [Kinshasa], now known as Zaire) has undergone the most tragic experience of the colonial era. Vast (roughly the size of non-Russian Europe) and rich (it produces 80 percent of the world's industrial diamonds, plus tin, copper, cobalt), it has been the scene of some of the most terrible barbarism over the last seventy years, even taking into account the centuries when the slavers swept through the land, carrying off men, women, and children to the sugar and cotton fields of the New World.

It was the celebrated Henry Stanley who first opened up the country for Western exploitation. He became the agent of King Leopold II of Belgium and was responsible for the kind of dubious deals with local chiefs that we recounted in connection with Cecil Rhodes. When the great imperial grab for Africa started in the 1880's, there was general unwillingness to see the Congo fall into the hands of any of the major powers, so it was handed over to King Leopold as a personal gift, thus making him sole lawmaker and owner of a territory the size of Europe. Leopold was perhaps one of the most despicable of all colonialists. His administration in the Congo became an international scandal, so that even the French Foreign Legion, an army not noted for its squeamishness, despised the soldiers from the Belgian Congo as barbarians.

Some 2,000 white agents were sent to organize the rubber trade. Under their leadership, an armed headman was installed in each village. Reputable estimates suggest that between 5 and 8 million Congolese were killed in the course of twenty-three years. Roger Casement's investigations in 1904 showed that the Congolese were expected to produce twenty baskets of rubber from the jungle four times a month for no pay. If they did not die of exposure or fall prey to wild animals, they would eventually be killed or mutilated by the Belgians if they were late in fulfilling their quota. Their only escape was into the jungle.

Eventually even European opinion could no longer stomach

this state of affairs, and the Belgian government bought Leopold off in 1908. It continued to run the country, using most of Leopold's men, who curbed their worst excesses and moved from rubber (which was being hit by Malayan plantations that exploited the work force more rationally) into mining, particularly copper and diamonds. However, in 1906, just before he relinquished control, Leopold created a number of companies, one of which was called l'Union Minière du Haut–Katanga (henceforth Union Minière). At the time of independence in 1960, about 48 percent of this vast country was given to such companies for mining concessions, which they could, of course, exploit only in minute parts.

Independence in 1960 was disastrous. The Belgians had always followed a policy of direct rule from Brussels, so that there was no chance for local Congolese to acquire the necessary experience in responsible positions. It was only in 1957 that the first carefully controlled elections were permitted, and at the time of independence the number of Congolese University graduates could be counted on the fingers of one hand. At the best of times, it would have been surprising if the country had not fallen to pieces, but this was 1960, with the United States, Russia, and, to a lesser extent, China testing the new balance of power in the Third World in the era of "positive neutralism." Besides which, 60 percent of the world's cobalt came from the Congo, which made the country of positive strategic value in the nuclear race. It did not have a chance.

For a start, the capital city was a long way from the seat of industrial activity. Leopoldville was near the Atlantic Coast, while the bulk of the copper, diamond, and uranium mines were thousands of miles away in Central Africa, in the province called Katanga, which is close to what we now call Zambia. The chief industrial power in Katanga was the Union Minière, which controlled the bulk of this mineral treasure chest. But the company's ultimate owners were the Société Générale, a holding company that controls virtually everything worth owning in Belgium. In the dispute that was to come, we find that the Société Générale would be making policy in Belgium while events were developing on the other side of the globe.

The company began making political decisions concerning Congolese events around 1957, when the first elections were held. In Katanga, there were two main African parties. One of these, Conakat, had close ties with the white settlers and, even if it did not take orders from the whites, was expected to have a moderate attitude toward Belgian interests. The other party, Balubakat, was less desirable to Union Minière, since it represented the immigrant Baluba workers in Katanga. The first party, led by a minor (and unsuccessful) businessman, Moise Tshombe, was the obvious one to back, but the company eventually gave money to both—though it is assumed that more went to Conakat than Balubakat. Tshombe and his "safe" party duly won, and talk now turned to the question of a possible Katangese secession when independence came. Such a secession would be welcomed by the mining company, especially as Union Minière had very close links with the mining companies dominating the then Northern Rhodesia, which was closer to Katanga than Leopoldville. But the company did not dictate the secession policy, for which, from Tshombe's point of view, there were good tribal and self-serving excuses. Nevertheless, secession was made more likely by the company's presence in Katanga, and whatever the company's official position at independence (René Lemarchand suggests that at that point they did not favor secession), the fact that it paid taxes of some $40 million a year to Katanga rather than to the officially recognized central government in Leopoldville determined that the civil war lasted longer than it might have.

At the outset, company headquarters was cautious about its official stance, but the role of the local Belgian employees in Katanga was clear. They looked to Leopoldville and saw what were to them a bunch of dangerously left-wing, unstable leaders like Patrice Lumumba; they saw mutinies, tribal and racial killings, and therefore committed themselves to maintaining the independence of Katanga. Thus, when Tshombe raised an army of 12,000 men, led by white mercenaries, U Thant alleged that company officials had openly allowed the manufacture of armored cars and bombs, while putting many of the mercenaries on the company payroll as a form of camouflage. There fol-

lowed an extremely complicated period when all the great
powers got involved, and a United Nations army was sent in to
crush the Katangese revolt (Dag Hammarskjold, the United
Nations Secretary-General, was killed in an air crash while on
a mission to Katanga). At one stage, Tshombe was persuaded
to accept the failure of the Katanga secession and to become
prime minister of the whole Congo, but he was deposed, and
in 1965 General Joseph-Désiré Mobutu seized the presidency.

Since then, a tortuous relationship between the Congolese
government and the Belgian interests in Union Minière has been
worked out. In 1966 the old Union Minière company quite
hamfistedly antagonized the Mobutu regime by refusing to consult with it before announcing rises in the price of copper (the
copper companies in Chile and Zambia consulted their local
governments). In the row that followed, the management
showed an arrogance that destroyed all chance of a compromise.
The Congolese tried a form of nationalization, but Union
Minière was able to stop any sales abroad, so that the government was forced to revert to a more moderate position. Finally,
a deal was struck with Société Générale des Minerais, another
part of the giant Société Générale holding company, whereby it
would produce, process, and sell copper for Gecomin, a state-
controlled body that now had all the old Union Minière concessions. So although the Congolese government was really dealing
with the same Union Minière interests, the hated Union Minière name would no longer be seen and the position of the
Belgians would be contractual, rather than the previous "state
within a state." Since then, Mobutu has been trying to introduce a wide number of nationalities to break the Belgian
stranglehold on the economy. He and his cabinet have resolutely
blocked any attempts by Union Minière to return to the Congo
—as in 1970, when the company announced it was studying a
new mining venture, which was quickly scotched, and the deal
went to a consortium, which involved Standard Oil of New
Jersey (United States), Anglo-American (South African),
Mitsui (Japanese), and a French group.

There have been one or two attempts to defend Union Minière, notably by Crawford Young in a massively researched

book on the whole Congo crisis. He points out that the company has been held responsible for the actions of its employees and that different parts of the company were pulling in different directions. He also makes the point that some of the less intelligent colonial companies were simply bewildered by the speed of events, having little experience in survival techniques during periods of severe political unrest. Anthony Sampson makes the point that at one time the Société Générale in Belgium was resisting pressure from both the United Nations and the Belgian government to pay its taxes to the central Congolese government rather than secessionist Katanga. In their refusal to bow to such pressures, the ultimate Belgian controllers of Union Minière undoubtedly prolonged this particular incident in Congolese history, and the resulting bloodshed and international tension are very much their responsibility.[7]

Biafra and Shell–BP

It would be heartening to think of Union Minière as the last of the dinosaurs, those colonial companies that plowed ahead with self-seeking policies, regardless of anyone who got in their way, and with not the slightest thought that they might provoke counterproductive retaliation from the local nationals they were exploiting. To some extent, the Biafran crisis suggests this might be the case,[8] for the oil companies involved took roles that were very much more passive than Union Minière's in Katanga. In fact, the two crises have much in common. Both involved attempted secessions by local leaders of mineral-rich parts of newly independent African states, and both involved a great deal of bloodshed. If anything, the Biafran crisis was the more horrifying, with conservative estimates in 1971 suggesting just under a million civilian deaths.

The war was definitely triggered by actions forced on Shell and British Petroleum concerning their joint production subsidiary in Nigeria. Moreover, the relative positions of Shell–BP and the French firm ERAP depended very heavily on which side won the war. If the secession succeeded, ERAP would have benefited at Shell–BP's expense. If the central federal government won (as it did), ERAP would be in trouble (as it is). However, this case cannot really be substantiated. The main player, Shell–BP, showed little enthusiasm for an independent role, choosing to follow the British government line, despite the fact that this might lead to the destruction of Shell–BP property or even the loss of the lives of Shell–BP employees.

The Biafran war is not in fact dissimilar to the West Pakistan/Bangladesh crisis, with a newly founded oil industry superimposed on an already fraught situation. Like Pakistan, Nigeria was a nation more in theory than in practice. Ruled by the British as a single entity, Nigeria in fact contains 150 to 200 different tribes, of whom three are particularly important—the Moslem Hausas in the North, the Yorubas in the West, and the Ibos in the East. The British left a system that allowed a fairly weak federal government, with three relatively strong regional governments, to represent the three main tribes. The whole system was fated to collapse.

After independence in 1960, the federal government was in the hands of the Northerners, who demonstrated a fair degree of corruption, in particular by fiddling the 1962–3 census so that in the 1964 general election the power of the North was maintained. In this atmosphere, regional antipathies abounded. The Northerners used a political trial to extinguish the opposition party in the West, and in January 1966 this triggered a coup, when five middle-grade officers in the Nigerian Army assassinated the Northern political leaders. This was almost entirely a pro-federation coup, but it was interpreted by the North as an attempt by the Ibos in the East to destroy the North as a political force. The army started to break up into tribal factions, and in October 1966 the Northern personnel of the Nigerian Army organized a pogrom in which 30,000 to 50,000 Ibos living in Northern towns were killed. Those who survived fled to the safety of their tribal homelands in the East, and the country was now polarized into three mutually antagonistic regions. The gravest tension was between the federal government in the North and the Eastern Ibos.

Important oil discoveries had been made, and at that time,

the bulk of the production was located in the East. From having no oil industry at all in 1960, Nigeria was already among the top ten oil-producing countries, and Shell–BP was producing over three quarters of the yield, from a field that was Shell's most promising new source of crude oil for years. A number of other companies were also active (Tenneco, Mobil, Phillips, Gulf, AGIP), but with the exception of SAFRAP, a subsidiary of the French oil company ERAP, none of them was active in the East.

By the beginning of 1967, the East was starting to push for a looser federation, in which the regions would have much more power, but this soon came down to the question of how the oil revenues should be shared. After all, the federal government in the North felt it would be unfair that the Ibos should benefit from the historical accident that oil was found on Eastern territory. The Ibos of course felt that the oil was their one major trump card in their push for greater freedom. Shell–BP was caught in the middle, with both sides hoping to receive the next royalty payments. Shell–BP would clearly have preferred to pay the Easterners directly. The Ibos have traditionally been the commercial power in Nigeria, and they were generally more satisfactory partners than the less commercially minded Northerners. More specifically, there were four hundred company employees in Eastern territory in offices and at the company's main Nigerian refinery at Port Harcourt. Finally, there are some legal precedents from China in 1949 that allow commercial interests to make their peace with *de facto* rulers, even if the parent government of the firms has no dealings with the new regime. This brought the company into conflict with the local British officials, who came down heavily on the side of the federal government.

As summer approached, the company found it hard to stall any further. Minor payments were no problem, like the cost of tankers visiting the terminal at Bonny in the East—they simply called at Lagos first and paid harbor dues there as well. Gulf Oil made its payments to the federal government, but then its production facilities were not in Eastern hands. Shell–BP, however, was not in such an easy position. By the beginning of July, it was becoming clear that the company would make a payment to the Eastern government. If this happened the federal government said it would invade the East. On July 2 it believed that the payment had been made and a blockade of the Eastern states was begun. Within a couple of days it was made clear that the company had written to Colonel Odumegwu Ojukwu, the Eastern leader, offering him a down payment of $700,000, with the full payment of $20 million to follow. This was roughly what the East would have received under the normal formula adopted by the federal authorities, but Ojukwu found the token payment insulting. By this time General Yakubu Gowon, on the federal side, had given orders to his troops. They invaded the Eastern territories, which were henceforth to be known as Biafra.

Once the war had started, Shell–BP still had to be careful. It soon became clear that oil could not be exported from Biafran territory (the federal government quickly captured the ocean terminal). However, the Biafrans still held Stanley Gray, the British manager of Shell–BP's Nigerian operations, and the company could not switch to full backing of the federal government as long as he was a hostage. However, a definite commitment to the federal side was necessary, since there was considerable resentment toward the company and talk of expropriation was in the air. Delegations were even sent to Moscow by the federal side to sound out the Russians about the possibility of technical assistance. Gray had to be extricated from Enugu, the Biafran capital. A day or two after his arrest, a group managing director of Royal Dutch–Shell, Frank McFadzean, turned up in the federal capital of Lagos. Several days later he left Lagos by chartered plane, crossed the Niger by boat into Biafra, and then went by road to Enugu. He had no guarantee of his safety. The story then becomes murky. The next press reports announced that Stanley Gray had been released and was driving to Lagos with McFadzean, who turned up a day later at Heathrow Airport, London, telling pressmen that his trip to Enugu had been "wasted" and that Mr. Gray had secured his own release. Gray had allegedly arranged an interview with Colonel Ojukwu and had talked his way out. "If you knew Mr. Gray," said McFadzean, "you would understand how this was possible . . . no ransom was paid at all." The next day, Shell International said that even if they had wanted to make such a payment, it would have been extremely difficult, a statement that needs taking with a pinch of salt.

Whether the Biafran Swiss bank account did actually receive a donation is of little importance now, but what the incident does show is the specific constraints that affect a firm. The more geographically spread its activities, the more likely it is to find itself with interests on both sides of a dispute. It will take steps to look after its managers, but at the same time, such people can easily be used as hostages. It may well be that in some disputes it just cannot win and will take the line of least resistance, committing itself as little as possible until the winner emerges. However, after this incident Shell–BP joined the federal ranks, and in December the published Nigerian figures showed the central bank's reserves had jumped by just under $20 million within two weeks. The company was now backing the winning side.

In the meantime, the French had nailed their colors to the Biafran mast. Through French firms like ERAP and Michelin, they were already represented in the Eastern territories, with about 3 percent of French oil supplies coming from Nigeria in 1966. When the crunch came for Shell–BP, SAFRAP paid its royalties direct to the Biafran authorities (July 1967) as part of a general French government policy of support to the secessionists. It is not clear whether SAFRAP was following its own policy, but the French government gambled on a Biafran victory as part of a general attempt to make inroads into British influence in Africa, in which case the government-owned firm would merely have followed official policy. Whatever the true motives of the French government, the company has suffered. For a full year and a quarter after the war ended in January 1970, the company was officially banned. It was only in April 1971 that the Nigerian government allowed it back, but on the condition that the government take an immediate 35 percent interest in SAFRAP, which would later rise to 50 percent. This was the first time that Nigeria had taken such a stake in a foreign-owned company.

Compared with the experience in Katanga, the role of the various companies was relatively passive. They were in an impossible position, and despite some tactical mistakes, the non-French companies like Shell–BP did not seek to play an active role in the conflict. They did not try to act as king makers, and they did not engage in dubious activities like financing white mercenaries. This was, in fact, a very different situation from the Union Minière in the Congo, which showed itself to be a company arrogantly convinced of the rightness of its cause. In Biafra, the companies seemed more concerned with looking after the lives of their employees and, secondarily, the safety of the plants, than with playing any significant political role. Shell–BP may have precipitated the war, but the situation in July 1970 was such that *any* action would have had the same result.[9]

Vietnam, the CIA, and Other Exotica

So far we have concentrated on the impact multinationals can have on Third World host governments, and it is now time to look at their impact on the foreign policy of their parent countries, like the United States. A lot of good muckraking research has gone into the United States foreign-policy-making machinery, showing how an interlocking elite of businessmen, militarists, and politicians formulates and controls policy. But the power of this establishment to protect its interests outside the boundaries of the United States has proved quite ineffectual.

The crudest of these conspiracy theories will argue that because large multinationals are in one part of the world, anything that benefits them (be it a coup or a generally beneficial United States government policy) was caused by them. And yet, as I've been arguing in the previous pages, clear-cut cases are hard to find. The 1954 Guatemala coup was certainly not carried out by United Fruit, and there is good cause to surmise that the United States foreign-policy establishment under John Foster Dulles would have stooped to subversion against any Latin American government of the time that showed signs of going too far toward the Soviet orbit. More recently, attention has been focused on firms like Gulf Oil in Bolivia, where a careful study by Laurence Whitehead shows that the company and the United States embassy specifically threatened the government with suspension of all economic cooperation if there was any attempt to deny newly found deposits of natural gas to the company. However, there were other forces at work in Bolivian politics. It was not, for instance, a man from Gulf who attended all cabinet meetings but a representative from the International Monetary Fund, who had a veto even if he had no vote. As the years go by, an increasing number of parties are interested in unfortunate states like Bolivia. The relatively right-wing coup of August 1971 would once have been taken as simple evidence of United States involvement, and Gulf Oil would regain the position lost when it was nationalized in 1969. As it happened, the Chileans and Cubans stressed the roles played by Brazil and Argentina, two neighboring countries with as much interest in Bolivia as the United States. Certainly, the fate of Gulf's former Bolivian interests is very much in doubt. Argentina and Brazil have no reason to save them.

Perhaps the ultimate conspiracy theory was based on the discovery of oil interests in the Vietnam crisis. After the 1967 Suez closure, the industry embarked on a massive search for less politically sensitive sources of crude oil. After discoveries in Indonesia, Southeast Asia emerged as a good potential source, especially given its proximity to the thirsty Japanese market. During 1969 and 1970 a private geophysical company, reportedly working for a consortium of ten United States companies, made some interesting seismic discoveries off the South Vietnamese coast. In December 1970 the local government passed the necessary legislation regulating offshore exploration, and the oil companies started sniffing about in earnest. The radicals got hold of the story, while Presidential adviser Henry Kissinger blandly told questioners, "Ridiculous. There is no oil in Vietnam." [10] Immediately people wanted to know what influence the oil companies had had on United States policy toward Vietnam, whether the United States government was giving the oil companies advance information about its current policies, or whether the war might be prolonged for the profits of the oil industry. This is one case where the surprise of State Department officials when questioned seems absolutely genuine. At the beginning of the Vietnamese crisis in the 1940's and 1950's, no one imagined that offshore drilling (then a new technique) would make Vietnam a vital source of oil in another twenty years' time. A reading of the Pentagon Papers reveals no instances of policy-makers being worried about the oil industry (for that matter, there is virtually no evidence that anyone was thinking in strictly commercial terms, or that companies played any specific role in the formation of this policy, though top company personnel may well have been part of the establishment that formulated it). In fact, about the only major multinational with any significant stake in South Vietnam was Michelin, with some rubber plantations (what happened to them?). *Business Week* claims that the State Department was now telling oil companies that the future of Vietnam was "inscrutable" and that the normal channel for the insurance of foreign investment risks, the government-sponsored Overseas Private Investment Corporation, was unlikely to get involved.

A conspiracy theory does not really work in this case, though this will not stop a number of radicals from arguing that the Vietnamese war was fought to preserve capitalist, specifically oil, interests, despite the lack of hard evidence. But this situation is interesting because it shows a growing interest in the political activities of firms and has led to more skeptical questioning of their motives.

A more complex argument draws on work stimulated by sociologists like C. Wright Mills, whose work on the "power elite" described how intertwined and incestuous the American political, economic, and military establishment really is. William G. Domhoff probes deeply into the membership of key bodies like the Council for Foreign Relations, which has played an active role in formulating policies that have only much later been presented to and approved by the U.S. Congress. He cites the impressive lists of companies subscribing to its "corporation service"; he shows how the council is tied in with the big foundations like Rockefeller, Ford, and Carnegie; he demonstrates the high social background of its directors; he cites names and quotes statistics, until the mind reels. The objection to this approach is that the cases are too selective and are often open to more than one interpretation. If the business community is defined simply as a homogeneous, coldly calculating body, does it then follow that there is one "business" position on free trade or aid that business representatives will automatically ram through the policy-making machine? In fact, the business community has been increasingly split, as over the protectionist issue in 1971. Not only have the internationalists been losing, despite the fact that they have the more impressive list of establishment names, but the preservation of American jobs has been put higher than a placid acceptance of the shibboleths of the free-trade movement. As Charles Kindleberger asks in *Power and Money,* if these companies are so powerful, why is the United States still backing Israel, when it would make the oil companies' lives so much easier just to ditch her? Similarly with South Africa: why have companies with economic stakes in South Africa been so unsuccessful in getting the price of gold raised? Or why have they been so slow in pressuring the United States government to act decisively against the steady deterioration of the American economy in the 1960's? Why have they been so unsuccessful in getting the Hickenlooper amendment[11] activated when their possessions have been expropriated around the world?

Companies that have tried to influence government policies in directions that would help their profits have met with a conspicuous lack of success. There have been exceptions, like the lifting of the embargo on chrome imports from Rhodesia in 1971, but this was a full six years after the imposition of sanctions. If business interests were that powerful, sanctions would never have been imposed over a non-economic issue such as the rights of the majority of Africans in Rhodesia to determine their own destiny. However, even if the days of the gunboat and the sympathetic coup are over, big business can exert its influence in more subtle ways.

There is a fascinating book by Miles Copeland called *The Game of Nations,* one of the few "warts-and-all" memoirs of an ex-intelligence man that deals with business interests. He was on the fringes of the CIA, working in official and semi-official positions around the American diplomatic corps in the Middle East during the late 1940's and early 1950's. He became one of the chief experts on Nasser's reactions to specific problems and, in the course of this study, developed friendly relations with Nasser and some of his supporting Ministers. He was one of a group of officials who felt that the important thing in the Middle East was to have governments that would survive and gradually create a middle class, which would eventually introduce some form of meaningful democracy. In the short run, these officials accepted that governments in a position to achieve this happy end might well make decisions against American interests. Even before King Farouk was overthrown, they had an understanding with the army officers most likely to take over about what kind of working relationship they would like between a new regime and the United States government. Once Nasser emerged as the real power in the army coup, the relationship developed, only to be poisoned by the bureaucracy of the State Department, which would not give Nasser some minor equipment needed for morale-boosting purposes by his army. When he turned to Communist sources, the paranoid anti-Communism of Washington came into play and the downward spiral of mutual distrust began.

Copeland points out how badly organized the oil companies were in the Middle East at this time. It was only as the 1950's progressed that the foreign business community in Beirut began to play an independent role. At first there were no major problems with Nasser, and the international oil companies had little influence even over the 1956 Suez crisis. What pushed them into open hostility to Nasser was his attempt to overthrow the various reactionary regimes in the Middle East by assassination and the stimulation of pro-Nasser mobs. This resort to naked violence scared the companies stiff, and they were one of the first groups to call for the Marines when the situation in Lebanon became critical in 1958. Despite the fact that some oil employees in the field remained objective, the oil lobbies in Washington got busy, hounding and denouncing "pro-Nasser" officers in the State Department, so that eventually the more moderate elements were neutralized. However, the ability to persuade the State Department to take a hostile line toward someone like Nasser is a far cry from making life impossible for him. Nasser merely turned to the East for further help and kept his hold on Egypt through judicious and injudicious foreign adventures. If anything, American hostility may well have made his position more secure. With the exception of the 1953 pro-shah coup in Iran, which was organized by a CIA adventurer, the companies have been unsuccessful in playing local politics in the Middle East.

Leverage

Companies today are not meddling in any significant way with the domestic politics of particular countries. There is also little evidence that they are persuading intermediary bodies like the CIA to do the job for them. However, their negative power is still quite formidable. Since Teresa Hayter's exposé about the conditions laid down by aid-giving bodies like the World Bank, the term "leverage" is quite common. It describes the influence the donor body tries to exert on the receiving government through more or less open threats. Ultimately, the issue resolves itself to a bargain—"We will give you aid or invest in your country provided you follow certain practices." A multinational by itself rarely has much power in this sort of dispute, since it is only when the total investments of private firms are added together that they become very significant. However, where private investment is being treated badly, the firms can often persuade the aid bodies to stop giving assistance. For instance, Peru's and Chile's militancy has been met by savage cuts in the aid channeled to them by the Inter-American Development Bank. For instance, Chile got 9.9 percent of the bank's loans from 1961 to 1970; in 1970 it received a mere .63 percent. The same thing happened to Bolivia after its nationalization of Gulf Oil's assets. Peru's dispute with the International Petroleum Company led to a United States veto on an IADB housing loan granted in 1969. During 1971 the feud continued, and the United States Export–Import bank refused Chile's request for a $21 million loan to buy three Boeing 707 airliners. Apparently the State Department wanted to take a soft line, but it was overruled by the White House, which was being influenced by business lobbies. A further area for leverage is in the fixing of quotas on various products that affect the Third World. Thus, in the debate on the 1971 Sugar Bill, which fixed sugar quotas for imports, a clause was included, aimed specifically at Peru, stating that the President would be able to withhold $20 a ton from countries that have confiscated assets owned by United States citizens or corporations.

This kind of pressure is nothing new. In the early 1960's Peru's sugar quota was doubled as a reward for being the first Latin American country to break off relations with Cuba. In 1960 Khrushchev allegedly told Nasser during a dispute, "Think of the spare parts, Gamal," a threat that is even more specific. Threats like this are infuriating to Third World governments, who think they have a genuine case against the firms involved, but I doubt if these financial pressures are damaging to countries as relatively well developed as those in Latin America. It would be more serious if the hostility of one country's firms could close off every source of aid, but there is no evidence that the World Bank, for instance, is being unduly influenced by disputes between governments and firms.

Anyway, this is a matter for further investigation. Aid flows are probably the most useful weapon in trying to get a member of the Third World to follow "reasonable" policies, and there is definite evidence that where the interests of United States investors are directly affected, American aid flows are being reduced, if not cut off. For instance, in the United States–Andean Pact disputes, it would be interesting to know the exact role of the Council of the Americas, the chief lobby for American business in this area. It would also be worth knowing the extent to which American business interests can influence bodies that are officially international, like the World Bank. If such influence can be shown, how is it channeled?

The power of the multinationals is easily overrated. They can have significant power over the Third World only through the aid machinery, and most determined governments can live with this. It was the gunboats and the coups that were dangerous. Control of aid is a mere irritant.

Notes

1. Kindleberger does a readable demolition job on the cruder theories in his *Power and Money*.

2. I've relied heavily on Lockhart and Woodhouse's *Rhodes* for this and subsequent details about Rhodes. For a more general account of the British empire see Cross, *The Fall of the British Empire*. West, *Brazza of the Congo*, gives many details of the techniques used by people like Stanley to get concessions from the Congolese tribes. Kay, *The Political Economy of Colonialism in Ghana* covers the philosophy of the British colonial authorities in Ghana. Amin, *L'Afrique de l'Ouest bloquée*, covers the same era from a French viewpoint.

3. Cross, *The Fall of the British Empire*.

4. For general analyses of economic imperialism in Latin America, see Gerassi, *The Great Fear*; Gordon, *The Political Economy of Latin America*; Herring, *A History of Latin America*. For the Vanderbilt story, see Hoyt, *The Vanderbilts*. United Fruit is attacked in Kepner and Soothill's *The Banana Empire*, defended in May and Plazo's *United Fruit Company*. See also Frank, *Capitalism and Underdevelopment in Latin America*; Diaz Alejandro, "Direct Foreign Investment in Latin America."

5. Part of an extraordinary letter written in 1920 by a United Fruit manager to the company lawyer concerning Honduras. A much fuller version can be read in Gerassi, *The Great Fear*, and should be read by all students of the bizarre.

6. Taylor, *Firestone Operations in Liberia*, p. 57. See also Beckford, *Plantations and Poverty*, for a wider discussion of the role of plantation companies like Tate & Lyle, Unilever, Brooke Bond, and Harrisons & Crosfield.

7. General sources used: Gérard-Libois, "L'Affaire de l'Union Minière du Haut-Katanga"; Lefevre, *Uncertain Mandate*; Legum, *Congo Disaster*; Lemarchand, "The Limits of Self-Determination"; Nkrumah, *Challenge of the Congo*; Young, *Congo*; Sampson, *The New Europeans*.

8. This was written before ITT's activities in Chile were exposed.

It showed that some companies still want to play God, but it is significant that they found very little response from other American companies in Chile or from the higher echelons of the American government.

9. I have used Barnes, *Africa in Eclipse,* heavily in describing events up to the war's outbreak. Events involving the companies are based mostly on contemporary press reports.

10. *Ramparts,* May 1971.

11. This amendment states that the United States administration must cut off all aid to countries expropriating American property without giving adequate compensation.

Further Reading

Most of the important books have been mentioned in the notes above. For an introduction to the problems of Asia see Panikkar, *Asia and Western Dominance*; Pugach, "Standard Oil and Petroleum Development in Early Republican China." The Caribbean is covered by De Kadt, *Patterns of Foreign Influence in the Caribbean.* A useful radical reading is Petras and Zeitlin, eds., *Latin America: Reform or Revolution?*

3 : : *Economic Domination*

THE chief arguments against the multinationals stem from the fact that they are larger and more profitable than their local competitors and that they are concentrated in the Third World's growth industries. These factors could well lead to their perpetual domination of the future economies of these countries. However, even in the short term, the multinationals are abusing their dominant positions by devices that benefit the company first, their parent economy second (i.e. the United States and Europe), and only then their host economy in the Third World.

To the strict economist it may not matter a jot who actually owns a particular plant; a German capitalist enterprise, an American one, or a Brazilian one is motivated in much the same way, and its economic behavior should be similar. However, to argue this as an economist is to ignore the very powerful nationalist feelings that are aroused whenever a local firm falls to a foreign one. After all, Europeans were all stirred when Jean-Jacques Servan-Schreiber first brought out *The American Challenge,* which argued that Europe was menaced by American investors. The response he got came from citizens in mature economies where United States investment came to well under 10 percent of the economies in most cases. However, when we are dealing with reactions in the Third World, we should remember that it is not uncommon to find economies in which between a quarter and a half of their modern industry is controlled or influenced by firms that will appear far larger than people in Europe imagine. It is sheer hypocrisy for European industrialists who are frightened of the Americans, or American industrialists apprehensive of the Japanese, to argue that the Latin Americans are being totally unreasonable when they act against the multinationals. The discrepancy between the economic power of the Third World and the developed countries is so great that it would be unnatural if the multinationals were accepted without question.

In 1969 United States companies alone accounted for 12 percent of Latin American total production and one third of all exports, employed two million Latin Americans, and provided one fifth of all tax revenues (*Fortune,* October 1969/ *Time,* July 11, 1969). In key areas, this concentration has been increasing, despite the growing caution of multinational investors. For instance, in 1957 United States-controlled companies accounted for 12 percent of manufactured exports from Latin America; from 1957 to 1966 41 percent of such exports were generated by United States-controlled subsidiaries.[1]

There is every reason to expect this concentration to increase if governments do not intercede. There is clear evidence that the multinationals are particularly strong in consumer durable and capital goods industries, which are precisely those that will grow fastest. The Latin American economist Celso Furtado cites work done in Mexico in 1962 to show that of the one hundred major companies operating there, fifty-six were either totally owned by foreigners (thirty-nine cases) or had a substantial foreign shareholding (seventeen). However, these fifty-six companies accounted for 77 percent of the sales invoiced, and even if we looked at the four hundred largest companies, foreign-controlled companies still accounted for 70 percent of sales.[2] If one looks at other parts of the world, to countries that are only just starting on the path of development, one finds, for example, Swaziland, where the report of the first Census of Industrial Production (which looked at all units employing more than ten people) showed that in 1967 the 50 percent of the units that were Swazi-owned produced a mere 13 percent of the total output; eighteen of the fifty-one units studied were South African-owned, producing 39 percent of the gross output; while the six units owned by countries outside South Africa produced 49 percent of the gross output.[3]

The evidence is patchy, but it looks as though the late starters like Swaziland are going to be more dominated by foreign investment than the countries of Latin America. Furtado could see this happening with the smaller Latin American countries, like Peru, Venezuela, and Colombia, which had only just started attracting investment in the manufacturing sector. If one looks at Africa, for instance, the picture is even clearer. While the indigenous entrepreneurs struggle to amass significant amounts of capital and managerial know-how, the multinationals swarm over the continent, establishing themselves in all the complex industries. If we take the car industry, the American, European, and Japanese companies are competing in every significant market for the right to assemble trucks, tractors, cars, or whatever they think the market can stand. No African entrepreneur has a chance at this time of entering this industry. It would be like asking a small farmer, or the owner of four or five "Ma and Pa" stores to develop, manufacture, and distribute cars from scratch. Even African governments show extreme caution about entering such industries. The hold of the multinationals over Africa will probably be far more comprehensive than the hold they have had over Latin America. Obviously one has to adjust for their different levels of development, but certainly when Latin America's evolution was comparable to present-day Africa's (some time in the nineteenth century), foreign investors were mostly concerned with some kinds of tropical agriculture (like bananas) or the extractive industries. Foreign entrepreneurs in those days had neither the knowledge nor the resources to grasp hold of an entire economy from its agriculture to its manufacturing industries. Today multinationals have that power. There is no reason to think that this trend toward multinational domination of key sectors of the economies will be stopped unless the relevant governments step in with extreme nationalistic policies. All the evidence points to the multinationals making relatively greater profits from their subsidiaries than their local competitors make. The statistics are patchy, but major studies of individual economies confirm this. Michael Kidron shows that in India, between 1957 and 1961, foreign-controlled firms were earning some 20 percent more than Indian firms.[4] He points out that the Indian firms were probably more uninhibitedly crooked in evading taxes, but he also cites evidence suggesting that the multinationals have their ways of understating profits too, through manipulation of transfer prices. As further support, he observes that there are few cases of foreign subsidiaries calling for higher tariff protection, though this is a common cry from local Indian entrepreneurs. There were even cases, as in the aluminum industry, where local firms clamored for higher protection, while the foreign subsidiaries asked for lower. This would suggest either that the local Indians have a very high opinion of what is a fair rate of return, or that the local competition is more insecure than the foreign. When Firestone could manage a 64 percent return on investment between 1947 and 1953, it is easy to see why local competitors might be worried. Most other evidence is more circumstantial, showing that United States and British firms tend to get higher rates of return in the Third World than in their home economies. For instance, United States firms in Africa in 1960–8 earned 19.2 percent on their investment; 15.9 percent in the Middle East, Far East, and Oceania, against only 12.6 percent on investments in Europe; and 8.9 percent on those in Canada.[5] Unless the local competition is getting these returns as well (which is doubtful), the multinationals must increase their hold, unless they are sending all their profits back home and not reinvesting.

Why should the local competition be doing so badly? First, the multinationals come into a country with internationally known products, trademarks, and full patent protection, so that local entrepreneurs will find it easier to join with the foreigners than to try to develop their own products in competition. Moreover, the local consumers will often positively favor foreign goods over locally produced ones. Thus, Kidron tells the story of one Indian firm that had managed to develop ball bearings independent of outside help. It had completed the trials, had the machinery installed, and was all ready to go into full production when Tata's, its major Indian competitor, went into a ball-bearing project with SKF, the Swedish specialists in this industry. Immediately the viability of the first company's indigenous venture was cast in doubt. It was forced to enter into collaboration with another foreign firm, solely to use its trademark to impress the local consumers.

Complaints about the stifling of local enterprise have always been common. The British, in the name of the free-trade doctrine, destroyed India's textile industry, which at one time showed some potential. The freed slaves in the West Indies tried diversifying from sugar into animal and vegetable farms, but the British government legally forbade this. In particular, André Gunder Frank has traced this process at work in Chile and Brazil during the nineteenth century. Both countries then had thriving commercial and manufacturing sectors, but between 1868 and 1888, as foreign investors poured into Chile in the hunt for nitrates, the Chilean merchant fleet was reduced from 276 to 21 ships in a mere eight years, copper smelters went from 250 to 69, flour mills from 507 to 360. As he puts it: "Having been a producer of capital equipment in the nineteenth century, Chile now imports 90 percent of its investment in plant and equipment. Provided by nature with ample coal, petroleum and hydraulic resources, Chile imports fuels. Having been a major exporter of wheat and livestock products in the past, Chile is now heavily dependent on food imports from the metropolis [the United States]." [6]

In Chile the financially strong foreigners uprooted and destroyed the fragile first shoots of local entrepreneurship. The same process is repeated today whenever an infant industry has a slump. The local firms with poor financial backing go bankrupt, and the relatively rich multinationals are able to acquire the remnants. This has happened with one of the few genuinely new industries of the last decade or so, Peruvian fish meal, where drops in world fish-meal prices in 1962–3 and 1967 led to the largest operators in Peru (mostly North American) increasing their power by buying out their bankrupt Peruvian competitors. A similar situation has occurred in Brazil, where since 1966 a tightening of credit led to the collapse of Brazilian entrepreneurs manufacturing drugs, textiles, plastics, and electronics to the benefit of their foreign competitors, who, with their international strength, were able to survive what was to them a minor slowdown. The multinationals caught cold, while their Brazilian counterparts died of pneumonia! [7]

United Africa Company and
United Fruit—Kinds of Dominance

The kind of economic dominance to be described will have little
in common with any European or American model, or even with
the kind that United Fruit used to exert over Central America.
It may well be of a degree we in the developed countries have
never experienced. We saw with United Fruit how the company
was nicknamed the Octopus as a result of the number of activities in which it was involved: shipping, bananas, railways,
stores, etc. But by today's standards, the company did not
diversify widely. Its main role was genuinely entrepreneurial
in the classical, Schumpeterian sense—it was developing an un-
exploited industry and its markets; it was taking risks and pushing into the unknown, just like Carnegie, Ford, and Rockefeller,
who were pioneering their respective industries in the United
States. Competitors fell by the wayside by guessing wrong on
markets and technologies.

Today in the Third World the risks are totally different. A
company that is well established (whether multinational or an
indigenous operation) is able to study the development of large
numbers of economies, confident of the type of industry that
is needed at each stage of development. Guesswork is no longer
necessary, as it was in the early days of the automobile industry.
Today's entrepreneur in the Third World is an adapter who
is operating with a degree of hindsight and knowledge that
would have made the good old classical inventor-cum-entre-
preneur green with envy. Success depends partly on skill in
putting together deals both with the local political establishment
and with the foreign companies, partly in running an efficient
assembly or manufacturing operation once the deal has been
made. The risks are relatively minor compared to the old days,
and provided the companies are careful, the first ones in the
field can find themselves in a position of near-monopoly throughout an economy.

The United Africa Company, a subsidiary of Unilever, first
went to Nigeria for the palm oil that was important for Uni-

lever's margarine business in Europe. In addition it soon became Nigeria's largest importer; it needed to fill its ships up as they otherwise would return from Europe empty. At the end of the 1939–45 war, it was by far the largest company operating in Nigeria—in fact, even in the 1960's it was four times larger than its nearest rival.

Gradually competition grew in the import-trading field as the market expanded and became more attractive, so the company started to concentrate on those markets in which there was least competition, generally those requiring considerable capital and technical servicing skills. It tended to drift into import-substituting manufacturing, which involved relatively large risks and would tend to keep out potential competitors altogether. In its traditional mercantile role, it diversified into department stores (Kingsway), earth-moving and civil-engineering machinery, air conditioning and other electrical goods, office equipment, motor vehicles, etc.

Up to the mid-1950's this policy had not been standardized. The company had gone into beer production in 1949 to preempt the competition, but that was about all its manufacturing investment. However, around 1957, with Nigerian independence expected, a deliberate policy of redeployment was worked out. It began withdrawing from its traditional produce trade (the palm-oil business), which did not promise further growth, and set up its first assembly plants for trucks and bicycles. Thus between 1956 and 1964, although its gross investment stayed much the same, fluctuating between £2.0 and 2.8 million ($5.6 and $7.8 million) its industrial investment trebled at the expense of investment in transport and plantations, which were gradually transferred to Nigerians.

Its industrialization policy was a classic example of import substitution. Of its twenty-eight industrial investments up to 1965, only one (a plastics factory) was not directly connected with its existing marketing activities. It was rare for the company management to go into a project entirely by themselves. What normally happened was that either they approached their traditional suppliers to come into a joint venture (lager, yarn, printed textiles, etc.), or else the foreign manufacturer took the initiative, approaching the company for its local knowledge, commercial management, and distribution facilities (sewing thread, cement, radio assembly, etc.). Either way, the usual form was a joint venture between the United Africa Company and a foreign manufacturer.

By the late 1960's, then, the company was involved with major investments of over £1 million ($2.8 million) in printed textiles, cotton yarn, sugar and its by-products, stout, and cement. In smaller ventures, it was involved in vehicle batteries, cigarettes, fiber-board packaging, foam rubber, radio assembly, reconstituted milk, beds and mattresses, ice cream, pigs and meat products, sewing thread, building contractors, truck and bicycle assembly, plastic products, timber, plywood, and furniture. In other words, Nigerian industrialization really meant the industrialization of the United Africa Company, since many of these plants are the only ones making the particular products; where there is competition, it comes from one or two competitors at the most.

Now the United Africa Company case is illuminating because it shows in a very pure form some of the dynamics at work in the Third World. It does not have a reputation of aggressive management, and the parent company, Unilever, seems to have decided merely to maintain its investment in West Africa, not to divert any new capital there. It has followed an intelligent policy and has ended up dominating the modern sector of the Nigerian economy to a degree to which no ten or even twenty United States firms dominate the mature American economy. It is, moreover, impossible to compare this form of industrialization with what occurred at similar levels of development in the United States or Europe. This is industrialization carried out by the "intermediary," an individual or firm that adapts existing technology and products to the market in his own economy via licensing or agency agreements, or by joint ventures. If the intermediary is well established, negotiations should go smoothly—provided the political situation remains stable. In fact, as we shall see in the next chapter, a government's attitudes can quickly change direction, and it is no surprise to find Nigeria in the forefront of West African countries that are following policies of economic nationalism. The company has already been forced out of retail trade, and the pressures on the rest of its activities will undoubtedly become more severe.[8]

"Tie-in" Clauses (Import and Export Restrictions)

Subsidiaries of multinationals are not allowed any freedom in buying materials and components, or in choosing export markets. The Third World economy may thus be harmed by being forced to use expensive inputs and may be unable to take advantage of promising markets, which the multinationals' headquarters may decree should be supplied by some other part of the company.

Kidron's study of the Indian economy led him to conclude that in the past the existence of sole-supplier agreements (the Third World operation can buy only from one specified source) was so general that it did not even need substantiation. He cites evidence from a 1955 investigation of the dyestuff industry to show that sole-supplier agreements with the American firm Cyanamid and the Swiss firm CIBA led to the Indian-based firm Atul Products Ltd. paying up to double the market price for its raw materials and intermediates. A more recent study in Colombia confirms this general picture. Constantine Vaitsos shows that, out of thirty-five contracts in the chemical and pharmaceutical industries, where his investigators could get relative information (later in this chapter we will see how thorough this study was), only two contracts explicitly permitted the free use of raw materials from whatever source of supply the companies chose. In the immediate post-Nkrumah era in Ghana the new government threatened to repudiate the agreement between the State Distilleries Corporation and the British alcoholic beverage company Duncan, Gilbey & Matheson, which was supplying its concentrates and essences at inflated prices. Michael Tanzer's study of the oil industry describes the battle the Indian government had, to try to get the oil multinationals to use inexpensive Russian crude in their Indian refineries. The companies insisted on using their own relatively expensive supplies.

The companies argue that such restrictions are necessary if their global activities are to be well integrated, and obviously there are a number of industries where the idea of buying from any source whatever makes little sense. A Fiat assembly plant would make little sense if it started buying components from Ford. However, this argument should not be pushed too far. The American abrasives firm Carborundum automatically allows its subsidiaries, associated companies, and licensees anywhere in the world to become its distributors in their areas of all the products made by Carborundum anywhere in the world. Thus, its dealers in Colombia can offer grinding wheels from the United States, Germany, Mexico, and Brazil. They are still tied to Carborundum products, but the right of the local managers to choose between various sources rather than having their sources dictated to them is an important one, given the evidence that multinationals tend to overcharge (or at least manipulate) where there is a tied market.

Similar controls are found over exports. Vaitsos found that seventy contracts in the pharmaceutical industry in Colombia forbade exports, against seventeen permissions; in chemicals, the score was eleven to seven; in textiles eleven to one. Again, Kidron's study on India confirms this. He found such conditions almost universal, despite the fact that the foreign company might still be able to sell its own products in India in competition with the local company. In some cases the Indian producer would be allowed to sell in India only through the foreign company's marketing organization, and where exports were allowed, they were normally confined to narrow regional markets like Pakistan, Burma, Ceylon, Nepal, or Afghanistan, which the foreign companies could not be bothered with themselves.

The companies argue that they increasingly build an export capability into their subsidiaries and that the host country benefits from this, even if it has no say over which markets are thus supplied. There is some evidence from Vaitsos that wholly owned subsidiaries in Colombia were given greater freedom to export than joint ventures or indigenous firms, suggesting that the multinationals are frightened of setting up new competitors for themselves and that the export restrictions are in part a simple self-protective device. Some authors go further and point to the relatively high activity of the multi-nationals in the export trade of the Third World. Thus, José de Cubas argues that between 1957 and 1966 United States subsidiaries increased their exports in manufactured goods from Latin America by 704 percent, while all other firms (Latin American and other foreign owners) increased theirs by only 51 percent. In a later section we will consider the positive role multinationals have in stimulating exports, but to rely solely on such figures is to miss the point. The Third World believes, rightly or wrongly, that the parent company will keep the most profitable export markets for itself, and the existence of specific negative provisions in contracts between the multinationals and their local affiliates can only confirm this suspicion. It is not enough to show that exports are in fact rising, since everyone in this field has had it drummed into his head that the total proportion of world trade handled by the Third World is con-tinually declining.

It is really a question of how visible the decision-making process is. If the decision as to export markets is made in the mists at the top of the multinationals' corporate headquarters, no one is ever going to believe that the Third World is not getting its usual raw deal. Even if companies cannot go as far as the Carborundum example, which might on occasion lead to a zealous exporter setting up a competing distribution system in some markets (this would probably be stopped), they can at least ensure that the local affiliates have a genuine chance to bid for the right of supplying given export markets, and that it should be clear that the ultimate decisions are indeed made on economic rather than political or nationalistic grounds. It may well be that if such bidding systems were introduced (and some of the larger multinationals like IBM have versions of them), the average politician would still not believe that these decisions were not weighted against his country. However, at least some of the local managers and partners will be convinced, and that will be worth some goodwill in maintaining morale.

This problem of export allocation is one that is going to grow as the multinationals spread their manufacturing activities and as governments increasingly emphasize the need for export creation. Some conflicts will be inevitable, but the wise firm should ensure that as far as possible its decision-making process should be defensible if challenged by involved governments.

Multinationals as a Drain on National Resources

Multinational investments are an expensive bargain for the Third World if one merely looks at the inward and outward flows of foreign exchange. This is a serious drawback at a time when the majority of these countries are struggling with massive foreign debts, which are probably the main check on development in the Third World.

It is impossible to overstress the importance of this debt problem. The situation is now so bad that by the mid-1970's there is a real chance that large parts of the Third World will be paying back to the developed economies *more* than they will be currently receiving in aid. In 1965–7, 87 percent of all aid to Latin America was needed to cover debt repayments; for Africa the figure was 73 percent, East Asia 52 percent, and South Asia and the Middle East 40 percent. Countries like Indonesia and Ghana got themselves so badly embroiled that they have had to get their debts rescheduled, and there has already been a time between 1963 and 1967 when Brazil, Argentina, and Uruguay, with almost half the Latin American population, had a net outflow of resources totaling $2.5 billion. "One might say that for them, this was a Marshall Plan in reverse." [9]

Most "aid" comes in the form of investment or loans from companies, individuals, and government and international bodies. Very little of this aid is an outright gift. Normally interest is charged. The pattern at the moment is that the Third World cannot generate enough extra internal growth to do more than pay back part of the interest owing. Certainly, it is unable in most cases to pay all the interest and to start repaying the original loan in order to reduce the interest obligations. However, each year brings further aid and attendant obligations, so that in certain circumstances the overall debt starts to spiral. The government comes to rely on new aid to repay old interest obligations, thus diverting it from its purpose in helping the economy grow until it becomes self-supporting.

Obviously, a number of solutions have been put forward to overcome this kind of problem, the customary approach being to lower the rates of interest charged, even if donors cannot be persuaded to make straight grants (i.e. with no interest). However, it is clear that they will work only slowly, if at all, so that the Third World will remain extremely worried by its external debts, at least in the short-to-medium term.

This perpetual shortage of foreign exchange can be psychologically debilitating and can lead to severe bottlenecks. One study in Pakistan showed that at any one time only one third of its industrial plant was actually in use, mainly through lack of foreign exchange to buy the necessary spare parts from abroad.[10] Egypt had the same problem after the 1967 war with Israel, when factories were being closed down for want of parts that sometimes cost no more than a few thousand dollars.[11] Four out of the seven jets owned by United Arab Airlines were grounded for the same reason, despite its record as a hard-currency earner. Governments find themselves forced to ration the foreign exchange available, as in Turkey's 1969–70 devaluation crisis in which local industrialists had to wait thirty-seven weeks for essential foreign exchange, while other importers had to wait over a year. In this kind of atmosphere it is not surprising that governments are hostile to any bodies that seek to squander their scarce foreign-exchange resources.

The first complaint about multinationals is that they do not necessarily bring in much foreign exchange in their original investments. Unless they are prevented, it is normally extremely easy for the multinationals to borrow from local banks and investors. Kidron cites a whole string of foreign companies in India that marketed issues at 50–100 percent above par, thus having to pay relatively low dividends to the Indian investors. Second, the investment may be in the form of machinery. Thus, Peter Kilby cites the case of the United States textile firm Indian Head Mills, which promoted a $5.7 million textile venture in Nigeria, toward which it contributed $170,000 in cash and forty-year-old machinery valued at $1.7 million, in return for 70 percent of the equity. It also provided good management and the venture has been successful, but this approach can obviously be open to grave abuse, since the machinery can be grossly overvalued. There will always be the suspicion that the company is merely dumping a lot of rubbishy equipment for which there is no market back home. Third, there seems to be a tendency for subsidiaries to be set up abroad with extremely high gearing (i.e. the company will control a small block of shares, while the dominant part of the capital will be in fixed-interest debt; once the profits start coming in, the equity holdings become extremely rewarding). A picture therefore emerges of multinationals whose "investments" become somewhat unconvincing the closer one looks at them.

Despite this, the multinationals have no inhibitions about shipping the profits back smartly, using up that foreign exchange that they may not have contributed in the first place. Moreover, unlike a straight loan, for which the rate of interest is fixed and a date for repayment of the whole loan is set, a multinational's investment is an open-ended commitment. The companies have the right to repatriate profits as long as they like, and should their enterprises be profitable, there is no upper limit to the dividends they declare. It is thus possible to find claims like that of a Ceylon minister who noted that one foreign investment of Rs 400,000 had five years later resulted in repatriation of dividends totaling Rs 1,050,000. Again, the oil industry is generally attacked for high rates of profit remission. Michael Tanzer cites a study of this industry in the Middle East showing that from 1900 to 1960 the companies paid governments $9.9 billion, made profits of $16.3 billion, and reinvested only $1.7 billion. The rest went back to company headquarters for investment elsewhere. The Organization of American States produced figures suggesting that United States oil companies in Latin America were reinvesting only about 5 percent of their profits there during the 1960's; the total for manufacturing firms was 58.4 percent in 1960–4, and 52.3 percent in 1965–7.[12]

Stated profits, however, are only part of the picture, and there are those who claim that the multinationals drain out a far higher proportion of foreign exchange than the bare profit figures would suggest. "Profits" merely reflect what is left over after meeting local costs and making payments to the parent multinational for management services, licenses, components, raw materials, and machinery—and these "within-the-company" deals can be almost as expensive as the remission of profits. For instance, in 1968 India's payments for dividends, profits, and interest came to $86.4 million; for royalties, technical know-how, technical and professional services from abroad, $50 million; for management fees and other incidental charges, $2.4 million.

One major study has been done on these phenomena in Colombia. Constantine Vaitsos, with the cooperation of a number of Colombian officials, looked at the policies followed by foreign companies in the pharmaceutical, rubber, chemical, and electronics industries in Colombia. They obtained price quotations from manufacturers and distributors in at least six European nations and, on a few occasions, in the United States. Specialists in the various industries then excluded products where quality differences justified important price variations. They compared the prices quoted to them as prospective buyers in Europe with what the multinationals were charging their subsidiaries and affiliates in Colombia. After taking into account shipping and insurance costs, the differences were pretty startling. They found that seventeen pharmaceutical firms were overpricing (after suitable weighting of the sample) by 165 percent; eleven electronic firms overpriced by 54 percent; three rubber firms by 40 percent. This meant, for instance, that the pharmaceutical companies in the sample overcharged the Colombian economy by $3 million, and if this is extended to firms and products not in the sample, the whole pharmaceutical industry may have cost the Colombian balance of payments some

$20 million in 1968, which is perhaps more than the total known annual explicit payments made abroad for industrial technology by the whole Colombian economy.

This was not the only irregularity discovered. Although the inquiry was not specifically investigating machinery imports, it found cases of a multinational selling machinery 30 percent cheaper to a Colombian competitor than to its own subsidiary. There was also a paper firm that imported used machinery, which it valued at $1,200,000; the Colombians asked for quotations for this machinery when new in the international market, and the highest price was $800,000. Vaitsos concludes that if Colombia could have reduced prices of intermediate goods and capital goods by an average of 20 percent, in 1968, it would have "saved" the foreign exchange equivalent of more than 50 percent of all its exports outside of coffee and petroleum. He also uses the concept "effective return," which is the sum of the subsidiary's royalty payments, reported profits, and intermediate product overpricing. He concludes that for his sample of the pharmaceutical industry, reported profits made up 3.4 percent of effective returns, royalties 14 percent, and overpricing 82.6 percent.

This is a reputable, systematic study that cannot be dismissed, even if detailed criticisms may whittle away at some of the absolute figures. Moreover, it is confirmed by other incidental evidence. Kidron cites Indian evidence from the 1950's claiming that the tire producers in India (Dunlop, Firestone, and Goodyear) had consistently undervalued their profits by the use of transfer pricing devices. James Shulman cites a case in Mexico where, as local manufacturing was demanded in the auto industry, a parent multinational merely attached the markup previously connected with forbidden components to those imports that were still permissible, thus maintaining its overall income from this investment. Jack Baranson[13] also cites the small returns multinationals may well accept on their initial investment in the auto industry, for which they are compensated by profitable returns on technical services and the sale of specialized equipment and spare parts.

At the moment, it is impossible to gauge the universal relevance of such findings. Charles Cooper and Francisco Serco-vitch cite a study in progress of the Indian scientific-instruments industry to suggest that transfer pricing is not a problem there. But in general we need a number of detailed case studies like that of Vaitsos's and until these are forthcoming, we can only remark that these "hidden" payments are a factor that exists but to an extent we can only guess at. However, the defenders of the multinationals can take no satisfaction in the fact that the first major study of this phenomenon should reveal such dubious behavior.

There are those who claim one should not be too hard on the multinationals caught out in this way. Certainly they evade paying taxes in the host country, though eventually they will have to declare those profits somewhere and will thus be taxed. However, their defenders argue, if they declared their full profits in the Third World, they would show up the inefficiency of the local competition. If they were forced to declare their full profits, they would be under pressure to reduce them, which could lead to lower prices, which would put the local entrepreneurs out of business first. This is interpreted as the fault of the governments, which do not know enough about specific industries to bargain properly with them. Vaitsos points out that the amount of ignorance a government has about a particular industry will vary by continent and by industry. For instance, it is no accident that it was in the research-intensive pharmaceutical industry that these practices were most marked—governments in the developed economies have experienced difficulties with it, and the Third World will not escape its share. To handle such problems, there should be one government unit whose prime job is to investigate the contract terms between multinationals and their local affiliates. This is a highly specialized job, and if the bargain is just between the local entrepreneur and the foreign company with no central check, it can be fairly assumed that in the early days of industrial development, very few local entrepreneurs (or managers in nationalized bodies) will have the world experience to evaluate a bargain. The less experienced a country is with international investors, the more essential such a unit would be. However, once its nationals grew accustomed to playing off multinationals against each other, the unit would become redundant. The Vaitsos evidence suggests that it could serve only an initial, short-term function.

Machinery Merchants and Export Credits[14]

I once interviewed a manager in a well-established firm operating in West Africa. "Please," he begged, "make a distinction between the reputable firms out there like us and some of the sharks who are floating around." When one looks at the early days of West African independence, one sees what he meant.

Ghana, under Kwame Nkrumah, its first president, entered independence in 1957 with the utmost confidence. Independence meant final control of the economy, and control of the economy meant rapid industrialization. Nothing could go wrong. Then the salesmen moved in. Some of the stories that were eventually disclosed were tragic. The State Fishing Corporation invested $40,000 per employee in new boats, etc. ($12,000 was typical of a United States fishing fleet at that time), failed to train the local crews, and did no research into the industry in question. Ten Soviet-built trawlers were never used, and a United States consultant could only suggest later that they be filled with concrete and used as a breakwater. Twenty-one million dollars was spent on silos that were unsuitable for storing the bagged cocoa beans when ready for shipment. In the later days of his regime, Nkrumah signed contracts worth $175 million with a little-known European firm, Otto Bertran, to put up a vastly ambitious series of plants in the agribusiness field. After his fall, these contracts were quietly dropped. Farther up the coast in Nigeria, German, Italian, and Israeli machinery merchants notched up some $74 million worth of sales for mostly uneconomic projects. Thus, one firm, Coutinho Caro of Hamburg, won turnkey factory projects worth $50 million—two glass factories, a textile factory, a cement factory, a clinker-grinding plant, a cocoa-processing plant, and a palm-kernel-processing plant. And yet, in December 1966,[15] not a single turnkey project in Nigeria was earning a profit. What went wrong?

There was overselling on the part of the firms, which tended to be machinery merchants rather than machinery manufacturers, who would probably have been more careful of their reputations. Moreover, the merchants sometimes put together plants with process equipment from different manufacturers that was not well-matched in terms of capacity or rate of through-put. This particular form of overselling was made easier by the existence of export credits from the developed countries, which meant that countries like Ghana and Nigeria had to put down only a small proportion of the total cost, although repayment had to be fast and the rates of interest charged were high. The important thing was the low initial payment, and these countries got themselves into severe debt problems through being unable to repay these short-term loans as fast as they were committed.

Finally, there was the problem of corruption. Many of the deals were made possible by almost automatic bribes to the relevant officials. After Nkrumah's fall, a number of commis-sions were set up to investigate these charges, one of which claimed that the German firm Henschel had paid $56,000 for a contract for rolling stock, that ZIM of Israel paid $840,000 on a $14 million shipping contract, that $225,000 was paid on behalf of the British Aircraft Corporation, that the local firm A. G. Leventis Ltd. had paid $170,000 to get permission to buy buses from Germany for the Transport Ministry. The firms de-nied these charges, and no further action was taken. But there is little doubt that in general extensive bribery did take place, and this helps explain why so many poorly judged investments were made.

But the chief lesson to be learned from this post-independence era has been the danger of relying too heavily on export credits. From 1959 to 1965 Ghana increased its export debt from $2.8 million to $700 million. The main creditor nations were Britain and West Germany, though just over $100 million was owed to Communist countries as well. After Nkrumah's fall, the World Bank and International Monetary Fund were called in to pick up the pieces, but only on condition that the new government renounce this kind of finance in future. However, this form of "aid" will be difficult to stamp out. Governments often approve of it, since the recipient country has to buy from their firms, thus creating "tied" exports. By the end of the 1960's, it made up about one eighth of total "aid" flows, with Austria, Belgium, Denmark, and Norway making over half their contributions in this form, plus Italy (49 percent) and Japan (40 percent).

The objections are, first, that it leaves the Third World little choice. Its governments will invest in projects, not necessarily because they are the most suitable but because certain firms can offer the most tempting credit facilities. Second, it hinders the use of independent advice. Third, it is expensive for countries who are trying desperately to reduce the interest on the loans they receive and to extend the repayment periods. Then, it benefits only areas or countries that are already at least partially developed, for the most deprived areas know in advance that they cannot justify buying the capital-intensive technology. Nevertheless, private export credits are becoming more popular, almost doubling in annual volume from 1966–71, and now comprising 30 percent of all forms of private "aid," compared with only 15 percent in the early 1960's. This is, perhaps, the most controversial form of help that is offered to the Third World. However, it could be argued that it should not be counted as aid at all, since it is ruthlessly used to benefit the immediate interests of the donor and ignores the needs of countries for which there are no suitable products from the multinationals.[16]

Technological Colonialism?

One of the most persistent complaints in the Third World is that it is condemned to be "a hewer of wood and a drawer of water," while the developed nations monopolize all forms of advanced technology. The complaint is not unreasonable, especially considering the difficulties in getting the developed countries to liberalize imports of manufactured and semi-manufactured goods from the Third World. The multinationals are inevitably accused of being party to this process, and although it is unfair to single them out, they have certainly not played a constructive role in bringing the most suitable technologies to the Third World.

There is a permanent dispute between firms and governments

on the role of patents. The firms see the patent system as a
device to ensure that their research is ultimately rewarded in
royalty and license payments. It is an integral part of the research process. Without it, much research would be impossible
through the commercial system. However, to the Third World,
the process is infuriating. Governments see a commonly used
product or process in the developed world that could be of
use in the Third World, but when they approach the firms
responsible they find the latter will allow the use of the products
only on payment of royalties which may well be beyond the
reach of the Third World economies. The governments feel that
such technology should be transferred free of charge to the Third
World, while the companies legitimately point out that they are
not in business for charity. It is disturbing to see how, in India,
about nine tenths of patent registrations are by foreign companies, and some of these registrations are made for purely
defensive reasons, so that local entrepreneurs will not try to
move into these areas (about one quarter of such patents are
never exploited).[17]

These disputes are almost always most bitter in the pharmaceutical industry. Even within Europe, customers in countries
like Britain look enviously at Italy (which has no patent protection), where drug prices are considerably lower. It is not
surprising that in India the patents bill that was discussed in
1970 protected pharmaceutical patents for only seven years at
the outside (for other patents it was to be fourteen years). If
this whittling away of patent protection spreads, the little research done by commercial firms with the specific needs of the
Third World in mind will be severely restricted. There is no
reason why patent-protected processes should not be part of
the general aid system, but compensation would normally have
to come from somewhere, since firms are commercial bodies.
The fact that a company refuses to let go of products without
payment is no more to be condemned than a developed world
that in general refuses to give significantly to the Third World.

The multinationals are also part of the process whereby the
developed economies systematically produce synthetic substitutes for the precious primary products around which so many

of the Third World's economies are based. Probably about $1 billion per annum is now spent on research into synthetic materials like plastics, fibers, and rubbers; this is almost equivalent to the entire expenditure on research of all kinds in the Third World. Thus, in 1950 natural rubber made up 67.1 percent of world production of natural synthetic and reclaimed rubber, plus stockpile releases; by 1964 this was down to 40.3 percent.[18] A "tin can," which was once sheet steel dipped into molten tin, is now electrolytically coated with tin (giving a much thinner covering), with plastic linings inside.[19] In industry after industry the picture is the same. The few products of the Third World face growing competition from synthetic products, which to some extent explains why the proportion of world trade between the Third World and the developed economies has been falling.

The main charge against the multinationals, however, is that most of them follow an "extension" strategy—that is, they merely sell the Third World products that have been developed for the mature economies and that can be sold to the Third World as a bonus. A second charge is that when they set up plants in the Third World, they use technologies totally unsuited to local needs.

Firms make products that they can sell at a profit to the greatest number of people. The biggest markets are inevitably in the rich, developed economies, and unless circumstances change drastically, it is difficult to see many companies making significant amounts of money from providing for the specific needs of the Third World. So it is not altogether surprising that the multinationals tend to sell products developed for richer markets. In the publicity handouts and company reports of the world's leading multinationals, there is more space devoted to their contributions to, say, the United States space program, or to the pollution-control market, than to products developed for the Third World. When the last is mentioned, it is for products like refrigerator fronts of Formica-brand laminate (American Cyanamid), car radios (Bosch in Brazil), or the lighting and traffic-light systems and illuminated fountains for eighteen miles of road in the oil-rich Trucial States (Philips). None of these is crucial to the development of the countries concerned, and though we shall see in a later chapter that some firms are trying to concentrate harder on the real development needs of the Third World, in practice it is the car industries, the arms firms, the consumer-goods firms that make the largest profits.

Probably the most serious charge is that the multinationals unconsciously tend to Westernize the thinking of the local, urbanized ruling classes in societies where attention should be turned more toward the rural, uneducated poor.

In East Africa there is a term *Wa-Benzi,* the Tanzanian name for the African elite, which rides about in Mercedes-Benz luxury cars while the peasants and the unemployed starve. This is an elite that is psychologically attuned to the consumer society of the Western world and that has opted for the soft life. It is an elite that buys its clothes, alcohol, soft drinks, radios, motorcycles, and cars from the United States, Europe, or Japan, while peasants in the fields are forced to rely on animal or human labor instead of simple, two-wheel tractors, which would lighten their burdens. The *Wa-Benzi* still cling to educational systems that are carbon copies of those in the developed economies, when the desperate need is for researchers and technologists who can take local raw materials and discover ways of utilizing them for the benefit of local society. Above all, this is an elite that is more concerned with running airlines than with improving the health of slum dwellers. It is a brutal fact that, thanks to the financial interest of President Ferdinand E. Marcos, the Philippines, which already has one international airline, is due to acquire two more (with TWA and Pan Am link ups). Similarly, in Thailand the genuinely efficient Thai International (technical assistance from SAS) is about to be joined on the international airways by Air Siam—a move for which there is no economic justification when airlines all around the world are losing money. If the 1950's can be characterized by the universal demand for steel plants and the 1960's for a car industry, the 1970's will be remembered for the growth of an airline industry, whatever the cost.

As John Kenneth Galbraith has argued, where you rely solely on the workings of the market economy, you will get distortions in social priorities ("private affluence and public squalor"), and in the absence of any positive decisions, the developed world has largely left dealings with the Third World in the hands of the multinationals, which are avowedly commercial organizations. It is unrealistic to expect these firms to behave in a non-commercial manner, but one can expect them at least to be aware of the impact of their actions. The aircraft salesman should be conscious that he is draining scarce resources from a country; the soft-drink firms should be concerned that their tradenames lure the inadequately nourished from local drinks that are often more nutritious; the car firms should acknowledge that by displaying their wares before urbanized elites, they are making it less likely that they will concede the redistribution of wealth and power, which would put the firms' prizes out of their reach. Many of the states we are dealing with are "soft" ones (Gunnar Myrdal's term) in which the poor, the oppressed, and the miserable have few, if any, channels to make their case felt. We may not be able to change the system, but at least we should be aware of our impact upon it.

Multinationals and
Alternative Development Models

If we sum up the arguments of the last two chapters, two main attacks on the multinationals stand out. The first argues that the firms contributed very little to the Third World by the standards of today (a point which has to be conceded) and also that they stifled the spontaneous growth of these economies by killing off potential industries and competition (Frank's arguments are sometimes used to support this charge). The second is that development today can take place more efficiently without using the multinationals. Let us examine these arguments more analytically.

"Development" is a tricky concept often used as a synonym for "economic growth," though there is now a tendency to play down strict attention to pure "growthmanship." However, the most impeccable schemes of social and economic reform can hardly be counted as "development" if there is not at least some accompanying economic growth. Therefore, in examining the two basic arguments we will take into account not only the efficiency with which finance, management, and technology continue to run the economic machines but also the side effects on the society in question.

My first model is "spontaneous growth." Even if we concede that the multinationals could have been more generous, we are still left with the question of what would have happened if they had not invested at all. The implied argument, in books like those of André Gunder Frank, is that the Third World would have spontaneously developed on its own. This assumes that the industrial revolutions of Britain, Europe, and America would eventually have been paralleled everywhere. Admittedly, Chile, Brazil, and India in the nineteenth century had some promising entrepreneurs, but to have benefited fully from the industrializing Northern economies these countries would have had to have mobilized large sums of capital for investment, sums that in practice came from the firms that invested in them. Either this capital could have come from internal savings (a slow process in the best of times), or else the countries could have borrowed independently from Europe and America, which they did, often with disastrous results. The local entrepreneur would then have had to find his world markets, a process that would have been difficult when communications were so bad. As it is, the firms brought capital that was essential in those days when aid was unknown and international loans were extremely risky. They also brought knowledge of world markets, so that the production of unsaleable goods was reduced. The extreme vertical integration of these firms (railways, plantations, ships, processing plants, etc.) was highly adaptive in the early days, encouraging fast and accurate responses to changes in commercial conditions. So although I concede that local entrepreneurs were swamped, I cannot accept that spontaneously produced entrepreneurs would have developed Argentina's economy so fast that by 1900 her gross national product per head was more than that of Italy (Argentina's steady decline since then is due partly to Commonwealth preferences, which excluded beef from her main market, Britain, and partly to unfortunate

government policies, which have overstressed industrialization).
Similarly, despite the worst excesses of United Fruit, the banana
countries of Central America still have a standard of living
well above that of most other countries in the Third World.
Could local entrepreneurs have really developed the industry
so quickly?

The second model is the "blank check" or "multinational"
model, which assumes that the best model for development is
to allow the multinationals the maximum freedom to invest as
they choose. They can bring a package of financial, managerial,
and technical experience that purely local bodies (be they
governments or Third World entrepreneurs) find hard to match.
The most convincing argument concentrates on the transfer of
technology from one location to another, which is particularly
complicated if the receiving organization has had no previous
experience in that technology. Whereas a multinational can call
on expertise from all over the world to develop a project, a
local operator who comes to a technology for the first time will
have to make all the mistakes the multinational has already
made and still not have a modicum of the older company's
experience. It can, of course, be demonstrated in their defense
that the multinationals have brought in foreign currency, helped
in import substitution, and developed exports; but this ignores
the fact that there are other, equally viable methods, and here
we come to the third model, the "selective approach."

The multinational brings a package of skills, but each element
of this package can be isolated:

Foreign Exchange   This no longer has to come through
multinationals. There are aid programs, and bodies like the
World Bank (though historically this body has been reluctant
to lend money for projects that the oil industry could tackle);
there is even the Euro-dollar market, which countries like Ice-
land, Mexico, Ireland, Argentina, and Hungary have been able
to tap. The cost of such loans against the multinational investment is difficult to calculate. Some rates available from the
World Bank, etc., are far lower than anything a commercial
company could accept as a satisfactory rate of return, and above

all, they are fixed-interest loans, meaning that there is an upper limit to what can be paid out in interest (though if the project is unviable, interest will still be due, while dividends will be passed).

Technology The Japanese have based their growth on an extensive use of licensing from abroad. They admittedly began with a well-educated managerial elite and with a very intelligent central government, but as the second development decade progresses, a similar mix of informed central planning and good education is being found in a significant number of to-day's Third World countries. A further technique is the "turn-key project," in which an outside contractor is brought in to build a plant which, on completion, is handed over to the local operator. In the past, railway and tramway systems could be built like this; today, a wide variety of technologies is available, for instance the USSR's purchase of a complete car plant from Fiat at Togliattigrad. The only drawback is whether the country has the manpower to run the plant once it is commissioned.

Management In some cases, individual key workers can be hired on contract, but more common is a "management contract," in which the day-to-day operation of a plant will be given to a firm that is then paid a flat fee or some percentage of profits or turnover. There are dangers here in that the payment systems may reward the contracting firm when the whole project is making a loss (as can happen if they are paid according to turnover), but on the whole, the system would seem to offer some of the managerial benefits of attachment to a multinational without losing total control or being milked of profits if the project is successful.

Marketing Skills Internal markets should not pose a problem, but finding export markets is not so easy. This activity can also be contracted out for a fee, or else state trading organizations can be developed to play the sort of role that the Japanese trading companies have played in the history of Japan—concentrating the knowledge of world markets into a few bodies, which then act as the exporting agent for most of indigenous industry. This knowledge of world markets is one of the most difficult multinational skills to replace, but the Japanese model is instructive. Decisions as to which markets to attack, and with what type of product, have always been made near the top of the country's industrial machine and not left to the individual exporter.

No accurate conclusion can be reached on the benefits of one approach over the other. The multinational model is still fairly convincing. There is little doubt that most multinationals will use the resources available in a technically efficient way. The counterargument relies on the question of cost and impact on the host society. In terms of foreign exchange, the selective approach could well be cheap, but this depends on the ability of the individual governments to put together a suitable package of foreign exchange, technology, management, and marketing skills. If the project runs late and is technically inefficient, the higher cost of the multinationals' investments will not matter. But as technologies get simpler and markets more local, the "selective" approach will pay bigger dividends. Even if this approach is marginally more expensive, a sound case can be made that the social side effects of self-sufficiency are likely to be less disruptive than heavy reliance on foreign multinationals. The investment process is a package and it is misleading to isolate one element. A desirable technology may justify terms that are disadvantageous to the balance of payments. Any attack or defense of multinational investment can take place only by comparing models. It is not enough merely to state that a specific multinational has introduced a desirable technology and brought in foreign capital. It is vital to examine alternative ways by which the same operation could have been achieved. Then some of the hidden costs of relying on multinational investment will become visible, as will the value judgments behind the various strategies considered. Acceptance of multinational investment may provide growth for countries like Taiwan, Brazil, South Korea, or Iran, but it will also create degrees of inequality, which the governments of Cuba, Tanzania, and China are trying to avoid. The argument cannot take place in a vacuum, because, in practice, multinationals are not going to have the freedom their defenders would like. Economic nationalism, which is built around variants of the "selective" and "spontaneous growth" models, is here to stay. The role of the multinationals will of necessity be limited.

Notes

1. Vernon, "Foreign Investors' Motivations," citing Council for Latin America, *Effects of United States and Other Foreign Investment in Latin America.*

2. Furtado, *Economic Development,* p. 174, summarizing Cecena, *Los Monopolios en México.*

3. Murray and Stoneman, "Private Overseas Investment," describes Swaziland's plight.

4. Kidron, *Foreign Investments in India.*

5. De Cubas, "It Pays to Speak Out."

6. Frank, *Latin America,* p. 102.

7. For further reading on investment in Latin America, try the factual Business International, *Nationalism in Latin America,* and Roper, *Investment in Latin America;* also Diaz Alejandro, "Direct Foreign Investment."

8. This section has relied heavily on Kilby, *Industrialization in an Open Economy,* which, with Kidron, *Foreign Investments in India,* is one of the two best studies of the relationship of specific Third World economies with foreign business interests. But see also recent books by Markensten, *Foreign Investment and Development: Swedish Companies in India,* and Nehrt, *Political Climate for Foreign Investment* (deals with ex-French North Africa). For further details of UAC's activities, read Wilson, *The History of Unilever.*

9. Avramovic, "Latin American External Debt," is very sound and detailed on Latin America's dilemma. For a more general picture, see Pearson Commission, *Partners in Development.*

10. Hans Singer, personal communication.

11. Copeland, *The Game of Nations.*

12. Avramovic, "Latin American External Debt."

13. Baranson's work on the auto industry and industrial technologies in general is well researched and documented. It is particularly worth further attention. Nader and Zahlen, eds., *Science and*

Technology in Developing Countries, is also worth looking at. For an analysis of one of the more inappropriate technologies, see Stockholm International Peace Research Institute, *The Arms Trade with the Third World.*

14. These are also known as suppliers' credits.

15. Kilby, *Industrialization in an Open Economy.*

16. Barnes, *Africa in Eclipse*; Moussa, *The Underprivileged Nations*; Van Dyke, "Who is Aiding Whom?" were all used in this section.

17. Kidron, *Foreign Investments in India.*

18. Sussex Group, *Science, Technology and Underdevelopment.*

19. Aymans, "Technology and Natural Resources."

Further Reading

Ady, ed., *Private Foreign Investment and the Developing World,* came out after this book's text was finished—it is worth reading. See also the interesting Evans, "National Autonomy and Economic Development." Useful readings are Livingstone, ed., *Economic Policy for Development,* and Seers and Joy, eds., *Development in a Divided World.*

4 : : *Economic Nationalism*

It is, of course, always galling (apart from political considerations) in any country to see an enterprise doing well without local people being interested. It is contrary to human nature, however well a concern like that may be directed, or however much it may have the interest of the people at heart, not to feel there will be a kind of jealous feeling against such a company.

Sir Henry Deterding[1]

. . . An investment in the creation of a middle class, financed by resources extracted from the mass of the population by nationalistic policies, may be the essential preliminary to the construction of a viable national state. This problem, however, belongs in the sphere of history, sociology and political science rather than economics.[2]

ECONOMICS have little or nothing to do with economic nationalism. Multinationals are pilloried because they are large, obtrusive, capitalist, and alien in an era that stresses central planning and the creation of national identities. Conventional left-wing political ideologies are not important. Many a leading economic nationalist is an anti-Marxist operator who realizes that competition from multinationals hits him where it hurts—in his anonymous Swiss bank account. There is a definite case to be made that few Third World leaders can follow policies giving multinationals a free rein and still survive. The perfect investment climate may well be a politically unstable one that must at some stage collapse. Nor will economic nationalism vanish in the night. It is a movement with a surprisingly long history, growing intellectual support, and institutions to contain and channel it. It now has a momentum of its own. The shrewd manager will accept this fact and come to terms with the changed environment. Those who persist in denying the facts of life will be driven out of business.

It is a mistake to think that economic nationalism is something new; in Latin America, at least, it has roots that reach back to the beginning of this century and sometimes into the last century. In Chile there was José Balmaceda's attempt in 1886 to break the English monopoly of the nitrate industry. In Uruguay in 1910 Jose Batlle y Ordóñez and his associates launched a program of mild state socialism. In the 1920's a number of countries refused to allow their oil sector to fall into the hands of the oil majors. From the outset Chile and Uruguay had state ownership of oil, while Argentina (1922), Peru (1934), Bolivia (1936), Colombia (1948), Brazil (1953), Cuba (1959), and Venezuela (1960) have created state enterprises with greater or less control over the industry. At the same time, pressures slowly built up against foreigners involved in the energy, transport, and communications sectors, and by the 1960's Mexico and Chile had taken control in all these sectors, while countries like Argentina controlled the railways and steadily extended their control over energy.

Individuals like Juan Perón of Argentina and Getúlio Vargas of Brazil in the late 1940's and early 1950's followed extreme nationalist policies. The elderly Vargas, in fact, committed suicide in 1954 in the vicious aftermath of his creation of the state-controlled oil corporation Petrobras. He left a suicide note (possibly forged), which listed the range of complaints Brazilian nationalists had against the "international economic and financial groups." Bolivia had in 1953 one of the few genuine revolutions seen in this century (Mexico and Cuba are the only other Latin American examples), though its probity was gradually whittled away. And then there was the confrontation between Mexico and the oil companies in 1938, the great pioneering clash of the economic nationalists and the multinationals. The nationalists won.[3]

The 1938 Mexican Oil Crisis

Oil exploration in Mexico started in the early 1900's and was led by a United States oil promoter, Edward L. Doheny (later of the Teapot Dome scandal), and an English civil engineer, Weetman D. Pearson (later Lord Cowdray). Despite the revolution, oil exploration and production forged ahead until, by 1921, a quarter of the world's output came from Mexico. Pearson sold his shares in the Mexican Eagle Petroleum Company to Royal Dutch in 1918, and Standard Oil of New Jersey controlled the American interests. The living was easy under the pre-revolutionary Diaz regime, with taxes in 1912 a quarter of those imposed in the United States, and with the Mexican owners of oil-producing land charging rents that went as low as 150 pesos for land producing 75 million barrels a year. The revolution was a minor nuisance, with the occasional armed band of Mexicans demanding "taxes," but there was no serious trouble. In the 1920's the companies had a mutually lucrative arrangement with the new strong man, Plutarco Calles, who overlooked the companies' violations of the constitution in return for gifts, like a large hacienda near Mexico City, which came from the United States ambassador. However, tensions arose as Venezuelan production overtook Mexico's, as the companies stopped drilling for new fields, as world prices fell, and as Mexican production fell (in 1932–3 output was half that of 1927, less than one fifth the levels of the early 1920's). Then Calles made the mistake of picking a genuinely honest president, who also happened to be a populist, Lázaro Cárdenas; he took office in 1934.

The dispute that followed involved three fascinating characters. There was Cárdenas, an unlettered soldier, picked because he would be easy to control, but who took on a populist life of his own, turning into one of those rare Mexican presidents who actually believe that the revolution is meaningless if the people of Mexico do not benefit. There was President Franklin D. Roosevelt and his "good neighbor" policy, by which he declared that no state had the right to intervene in the internal or external affairs of another. By actually living up to his stated policy,

Roosevelt hindered the attempts of the oil companies to fight back after the 1938 expropriation. Finally, there was a truly extraordinary United States ambassador, Josephus Daniels, who was that even rarer creature—an ambassador who wholeheartedly sided with the host government against the industrial interests of his own nation. Seventy years old, unable to speak Spanish, with the distinctly unpromising record of having been Secretary of the Navy in 1914 when the Marines went into Veracruz (126 Mexicans killed, 195 wounded), he sensed the domestic pressures on Cárdenas and gave strong moral support to Franklin Roosevelt in his battle with the hawkish State Department.

By 1937 Cárdenas had expropriated and redistributed some of the larger estates and had nationalized the unprofitable Mexican National Railways. In the oil industry, labor troubles culminated in a strike, which led to a conciliation board that sided with the workers. The companies withdrew their cash reserves, thus threatening the peso. Cárdenas threatened to nationalize the industry. The American company decided to call his bluff, confident of the backing of the State Department. On March 13, 1938, Cárdenas announced their expropriation and promised compensation. Daniels wrote to the United States Secretary of State, Cordell Hull: "Between you and me, I wonder at the ineptness of the representatives of the oil companies who are their spokesmen here. Some of them are so dumb that if they had to start a business of their own it would be foredoomed to failure. Initiative and tact are not in their vocabulary—or if so they conceal it." [4] Jersey's (i.e. Standard Oil's) high officials were certain there would be a revolution within thirty days, demanded immediate compensation, and used their service stations to warn United States tourists of the dangers of travel in Mexico. The British took a totally uncompromising line, and broke off diplomatic relations with Mexico as a result. Meanwhile, Roosevelt warned a Jersey attorney that there would be no revolution in Mexico.

The oil companies used what was to become a favorite ploy. Their oil fleets refused to handle Mexican oil; United States manufacturers were dissuaded from selling capital goods to the

oil industry even when prepaid in cash. They put in wildly inflated estimates of the value of the expropriated property. The
U.S. Department of the Interior's geological experts valued Mexican reserves close to the Mexican calculations, but far removed
from the oil companies'. The experts valued United States property at $13,538,052, while the oil companies were claiming $450
million (to cover future earnings as well as assets). The Treasury
went over Jersey's tax records and found that the value of its
Mexican properties came close to the estimates of the geological
surveyors. Finally, with the Second World War in progress, the
United States needed bases in Mexico and peace was forced on
the reluctant companies. A joint United States–Mexican survey
team went in to sort out the valuation problem. The American
experts found large quantities of old corroded equipment. "We
were pretty embarrassed at times," recalls one of the American
appraisers. "We insisted that Standard Oil had invested over
$400 million on their properties, only to have the Mexicans
bring out the books of the oil company which plainly showed
they had put in much, much less." Peace was finally made, and
the oil remained in Mexican hands.[5]

By all the laws of these affairs, Mexico's victory was well
ahead of its time. It was lucky with the key Americans facing
it, who were much more sympathetic to the Mexican cause than
might have been expected. Also, the 1939–45 war came at a
time when an impasse had been reached. It is quite possible that
without such propitious circumstances the Mexicans would have
had to settle for some form of return by the companies. Certainly, the Iranians in 1953 had to concede defeat after their
1951 nationalization of Anglo–Iranian's facilities. Here the combination of an industry boycott and a CIA-affiliated coup led to
the downfall of Dr. Mohammed Mossadegh, who had led the
onslaught on the company (now British Petroleum). Mossadegh
was a man who came too early. The power situation in the oil
industry would change, but in the 1950's the oil companies still
could not be trifled with.

Given the foreign companies' loss of interest in Mexican production, the complex relationship between labor unions and
Mexican presidents, and Cárdenas's personality, nationalization

was inevitable, so that a straight comparison of PEMEX (Petroleos Mexicanos) and what the foreign companies might have achieved is not strictly relevant. Exports suffered, and it was not until 1946 that the output of 1937 (47 million barrels) was exceeded. Since then production has been chiefly concerned with meeting the demands of the expansion of the internal economy. In recent years exploration has been stepped up and important offshore finds have been made. PEMEX has diversified heavily into petrochemicals. On the whole, Mexicans seem happy with the activities of the company. Perhaps the foreign companies would have expanded faster, but would they ever have been confident enough of their position to expand with an emphasis on Mexican interests?

Japan—the Successful
Economic Nationalists

Throughout this era there were two major countries that specifically followed policies of economic self-sufficiency, the Soviet Union and Japan. The latter is perhaps the more interesting case, because its approach has been similar to that of some Third World countries. In strictly economic terms, Japan has been more successful than Russia. Indeed, success has been so spectacular that its own enterprises are now posing serious threats to those older multinationals who would have invested in Japan if they had had the chance. The U.S.S.R., on the other hand, chose (and was partly forced) to follow a more stringent policy, whereby all significant technical and economic links with the non-socialist world were severed. Japan for roughly a century has been following a more selective line of taking what is best from the Western world, without allowing the latter's firms to invest in any major way in Japanese enterprises. It has been a very successful modified "hands off" policy. Is Japan a special case, or is it a genuinely acceptable model for today's developing nations?

The origins of Japanese xenophobia stretch back into the sixteenth century, when European traders and missionaries like Francis Xavier first reached Japan. The missionaries posed a serious internal threat to the newly formed Tokugawa Shogunate (established 1603), and finally, after a series of bloody uprisings, all foreigners were banned from Japan, with the exception of a few Dutch traders who were allowed to live on a small island linked to Nagasaki. From 1641 to 1853–4 all forms of trade or contact with foreigners were forbidden, to the extent that no seagoing vessels could be built. Finally, in 1868 the Shogun was overthrown and replaced by a young pro-Western emperor, Meiji. An epoch began in which the Japanese surrendered themselves to Western technology and culture—at the height of this craze some of them were dressing even their children in top hats and black morning suits. But while the new regime sent its citizens around the world to look at the most modern technology, and while it accepted (indeed welcomed) a number of Western technical advisers, foreign countries were not permitted any significant rights. The imperialists who carved up China were a powerful warning that enthusiasm for Western technology could lead to political and economic concessions to the Western powers, who, given the opportunity, would have dismembered Japan too.

Suspicion of the motives of the West naturally extended into dealings with inward investment by Western firms. From the start the emphasis was on developing indigenous industries, and well before the 1939–45 war the Japanese were conscious of the costs involved in foreign debts and kept a rigid central control on foreign borrowings. The Industrial Bank of Japan and the Yokohama Specie Bank were able to attract foreign money at better rates than individual firms, and this exchange was then loaned out to the domestic firms; thus they were kept under close supervision. Although there was some direct investment in the early days of the century, Japanese industry relied overwhelmingly on technical agreements with foreign firms like General Electric, Westinghouse Electric, Siemens, and the Canada Aluminum Company. This reliance on foreign licenses was not just a passive affair, for Japanese industry has consistently spent about four times what it has paid in royalties on research and development, which has been mostly adaptive. The success of the Japanese effort can be traced to a number of factors. First of all it has been led for the last century by an extremely intelligent elite with well-formulated priorities. In particular, the impact made by the reforming zeal of the emperor was important. Many of today's Third World countries start with only part of Japan's advantages. They do not possess long-established national identities, which give their elites unquestioned authority. The nearest modern equivalent of a consciously modernizing traditional leader like Emperor Meiji is the Shah of Iran with his "White Revolution." On the other hand, most of today's Third World elites want to modernize, however weak their overall authority, so on balance, although these leaders start out in a weaker position, they are moving in the same direction.

The second factor helping the Japanese was a good educational system, which soon allowed the foreign experts to be replaced by capable Japanese. Again, although educational bottlenecks are a major factor inhibiting the development of the Third World, primary and secondary schooling is expanding and universities are springing up, so that eventually it may be possible to emulate Japan.

Japan's pattern of governmental guidance with the cooperation of a few key industrial decision-makers can be easily imitated. In fact the model of the Zaibatsu, those four vast prewar business empires, Mitsubishi, Mitsui, Sumitomo, and Yasuda, may well be more significant than the sprawling industrial structures that resulted from the more decentralized American and European economies. They were a key factor in Japan's success, working closely with the government and channeling the bulk of the country's exports through giant trading companies that they also controlled. The system was quickly responsive to central decisions. The Zaibatsu knew that the government would bail them out if they ever got into financial trouble through following government policies, and the government and its chief economic ministry, the Ministry of Internal Trade and Industry (MITI), have been able to provide good analyses of the most promising technologies and world markets, which the Zaibatsu and their postwar successors have then attacked. Already in some parts of the world we can see similar alliances being made between governments and firms. Greece, for instance, has been persuading

its shipping magnates like Niarchos and Onassis to involve themselves with Greek industrialization. In fact, since the model
seems so likely to be emulated, we can foresee the problems
that arise when a very few decision-makers effectively control a
rapidly growing economy—and here we must note that many
countries in the Third World are growing at rates that are as
fast as, if not faster than, the Japanese record in the first half
of this century. The prewar Zaibatsu came to play a political
role in their own right, and even the Americans after the Second
World War were not able to break them up.

The Third World can learn from the basic principles of the
Japanese success, which were to keep tight central control on
foreign borrowing and to concentrate the exporting role among
specialist foreign traders. Most countries today are creating development banks, or at least taking control of the commercial
banking system so that central planners can have tighter control
over the spending of foreign exchange. On the export side, countries like India have created state trading bodies, while one of
the strongest arguments for the multinationals is that their worldwide knowledge of markets can be used for the benefit of Third
World enterprises.

There are problems in the Japanese approach. Eventually the
economy will have to be liberalized for foreign investment, and
the more completely the economy has been protected from foreign investment, the nastier the shock of liberalization will be.
Also, Japan is now running into difficulties with foreign companies who are reluctant to license technological know-how to
such formidable competitors. The switch from adaptive to innovative research is currently being made in Japan, and there is
no automatic guarantee that it will be able to continue to grow
through self-generated high-technology products. But these are
minor problems connected with a process that has experienced
a high growth rate for so long.

One factor, however, makes the Japanese model rather misleading. It has always had a large population (now around 100
million), and there will be problems for smaller countries with
populations of 15 million and under. Internal demand may never
be enough to support the spontaneous growth of certain indus-

tries, which is why Third World commentators have stressed the importance of regional economic links like common markets. By their nature, there will always be problems in adjusting the various national interests, but with this one major provision, the model seems a perfectly feasible one for much of the Third World.[6]

Decline of Ignorance

The multinationals can keep their hold on the Third World only as long as the latter is ignorant, divided, and lacking a hostile ideology. The trends are working against the multinationals. Vaitsos made the point, in his study on the machinations he uncovered in Colombia, that sheer ignorance was one of the factors that allowed the companies so much opportunity to maneuver. One of the strongest company bargaining points is superior knowledge of a specific technology, market, or management skill. But governments are more knowledgeable than they were in the past. Ministerial educational qualifications are higher and experience is broader. Thus, a Peruvian minister for industry will be trained at M.I.T., or Libyan civil servants dealing with oil matters will have worked eight years in the finance department of Shell of Libya.

A whole range of advisers is slowly evolving to counter the highly skilled advisory groups who work for the companies. For instance, the oil industry has spawned a number of experienced anti-company consultants based in Lebanon. The chief figure here is Dr. Nicolas Sarkis, a Beirut-based consultant, director of the French-language bi-monthly, *Le Pétrole et le Gaz Arabes*. He was consulted by the Libyans in their 1970 oil negotiations, and in the autumn of 1970 his Arab Center for Petroleum Studies, the Association of Arab Economists, and the Algerian state oil company Sonatrach organized a four-day seminar on "Petroleum and Its Role in Economic Development in the Arab Countries" that drew an impressive array of papers from Arab sources. Similarly, Lebanon called on the former general secretary of OPEC when negotiating with the United States consortium, the Iraq Petroleum Company, in 1970.

Genuine local entrepreneurs can play a valuable role in advising governments. Thus a Cypriot businessman in Zambia, Andrew Sardanis, played a key part in Zambia's drive for economic independence. A friend of President Kenneth Kaunda even before independence, he was put in charge of the nationalization and development of Zambia's industry and mining. He was widely respected, even by the copper companies he was helping to curtail. It was a classic case of setting a capitalist to catch a capitalist. Local industrialists, however untrustworthy, will always be happy to help cut down the activities of the multinationals and, if used carefully, can give governments valuable practical knowledge of how to deal with foreign companies.

State-controlled industrial bodies also provide useful practical commercial experience, even if the cost is high. It is difficult, for instance, to discuss the Libyan oil negotiations without considering the role of the Algerian state-owned oil company Sonatrach, which is not only experimenting with ways of working with foreign collaborators but has been helping the Libyans with advice and training. State bodies like India's Hindustan Machine Tools Ltd. and the Brazilian state oil company Petrobras are successful enough to convince their governments that such companies can be run efficiently, despite some failures in India. At the very least, governments refer to such bodies for commercial advice when bargaining with multinationals. In extreme cases, they can be used to convince the multinationals that threats of expropriation should be taken seriously. Either way, it is easier to call the multinationals' bluff.

Finally, there are the advisers from the developed world or from the international institutions. The World Bank, on one epoch-making occasion, actually refused a loan to the government of Gabon unless far tougher terms were imposed on the French forestry companies and the iron-ore consortium that would benefit most from the railways the loan would finance. The bank also insisted that the construction of the railway be open to international tender. Apart from being a notable example of "leverage," these provisions also suggest that governments can benefit by calling on the advice of people in the various international aid bodies who have a good overview of the whole development process in different parts of the world. A number of them will have experience in the bargaining strategies of the multinationals and will know what tactics to employ.

There are also the academics from the developed economies. Some will be ideologically hostile to the multinationals and will not neglect the opportunity to put the boot in. Later in this chapter we shall examine the influence of some highly respected academics on the Latin American scene. There are academics who have made objective studies of various industries (particularly oil) who find themselves being called upon to advise governments. There are also academic consultants, like Harvard's Development Advisory Group, who are invited to countries as senior advisers and civil servants. This particular organization has gone into Pakistan, Indonesia, Liberia, and Jamaica and seems to be doing a reasonably uncontroversial job. Indonesia, since the fall of Sukarno, has also had the benefit of advisers colloquially known as the "Berkeley Mafia." The more respectable groups are not likely to advise their hosts to hang every local multinational manager from the nearest lamppost, but for certain countries like Liberia, which need advice on how to profit from their resident multinationals, such groups provide a vital service.[7]

The Rise of Ideology

There is no single ideology that unites the economic nationalists, but there are several issues that, even if not closely related, help to explain the policies of some quite disparate governments.

One ideological impetus comes from the anti-imperialist, anti-capitalist, and relatively pro-Soviet atmosphere of most independence movements in the 1940's, 1950's, and 1960's. The Soviet Union was the prime model of an anti-imperialist state. From it the ideology of "planning" came into being; independence meant an economic plan that would place strong emphasis on the state-owned sector. It also meant heavy industrialization in imitation of the way the Soviet economy had been developed.

The early charismatic leaders of the Third World like Nasser, Sukarno, Nehru, Nkrumah (and to some extent Tito) were all cast in a similar mold, and where they showed signs of accommodating Western interests, heavy-handed pressures from Western governments and the World Bank (then very much a pro-American agency) made sure that their immediate post-independence ideologies were maintained. They developed a number of variants on "socialist" ideology ("African socialism," etc.) that made an attempt at strong central planning and some nationalization of key industries.

The number of Third World leaders who now call themselves socialists has rendered the term almost meaningless. An eminent industrialist like India's J. R. D. Tata, when addressing the Bombay Rotary Club, called on his "socialist" friends both within and without the government "to look beyond our shores and see for themselves the magnificent achievements of twentieth-century socialism in country after country around the globe." The *reductio ad absurdum* came when President Somoza announced that Nicaragua, a country not noted for progressive government, was in fact socialistic. With comrades like this, genuine Third World socialists like Martinique's and Algeria's Frantz Fanon might have been tempted to go over to the other side.

Raul Prebisch

The Soviet-oriented, quasi-socialist school is, however, only one aspect of economic nationalism. Equally important have been the activities of a man who has provided the theoretical justification for most of the Latin American economic nationalists who have so upset the United States business community in particular—Dr. Raul Prebisch. He is a man with an underground reputation. Not widely known in the English-speaking world, his influence on events in the Third World has arguably been as significant as the earlier role of John Maynard Keynes in the developed economies. He holds non-Marxist theoretical positions, using economic arguments that are often challenged by other professional economists. But he has contributed a theoretical framework to a generation of Latin American government officials and created the institutions needed by the Third World in its drive for economic independence.

Born in Argentina in 1901, he became Professor of Political Economy at the University of Buenos Aires at the age of twenty-four. After holding some minor government posts, he organized and became the secretary-general of the Argentine Central Bank (1935–43). After the coup that installed President Perón, his popularity waned, and in 1948 he was exiled from Argentina. He then wrote a critical paper on the ills of the region that was accepted by the United Nations and, after some hesitation, Prebisch took the position of executive secretary of the newly formed UN Economic Commission for Latin America.

By this time he had developed what is often called the "Prebisch thesis," which argues that the Third World will remain poor as long as the terms of trade work against it. While the Third World relies solely on the export of raw materials and staple commodities, it is doomed because the export prices of such goods have been steadily falling over the years, while the prices of manufactured goods, the preserve of the developed world, have been rising. Aid and technical assistance are only palliatives as long as Latin America is not industrialized and as long as the ruling elites maintain inegalitarian societies. So, while running ECLA, Prebisch stressed the need for planning for development, for equality of education, adequate housing, and health programs, land reform and the modernization of agriculture, industrialization, reformed taxation systems, and intra-Latin-American cooperation and integration. Today, this may sound orthodox and reformist, but in the Latin American context of the early 1950's the ideas were revolutionary.

Under his leadership, ECLA became a tight-knit, fast-working research unit that pestered countries into producing statistics and putting their chaotic budgetary and administrative systems in order. It would organize meetings of experts, who would then go back home and persuade governments to take action. Many of these "Cepalinos" (CEPAL are the Spanish initials for ECLA) went back to hold office in their own countries, and by the mid-1960's there were at least two thousand ECLA-trained economists, engineers, and civil servants working throughout Latin America, inspired by Prebisch's message that development in Latin America can come only if the Latin Americans work for it. However, his emphasis on import-substituting industrialization has probably led Latin America into relative neglect of the agricultural sector, and some economists claim that his views on the terms of trade are simply wrong. But he was the prime mover behind the Latin American Free Trade Association, without which the more militant Andean Pact could not have gotten off the ground—and he turned ECLA into a UN body of rare effectiveness.

With the 1960's designated as the "development decade," it became clear that a world conference on the role of trade and development was needed. U Thant sent Prebisch as his personal representative to an assembly of developing nations organized by President Nasser, where Prebisch made a considerable personal impact on the Arabs, Asians, and Africans, indicating that he would be the most suitable person to head the United Nations Conference on Trade and Development, which was to be held in 1964. Taking official control in 1963, he welded UNCTAD into a permanent body that the Third World could use in its assault on the miserliness of the developed nations. As someone once put it to me, the new body had become "Prebisch, Prebisch, and Prebisch." The 1964 conference did not achieve very much, but by 1968 schemes for generalized preferences by which the developed nations would accept manufactured and semi-manufactured products from the Third World without tariffs were finally accepted in principle, leading to the European Economic Community's adoption of such a scheme.

Finally, in 1969 Prebisch retired from his UNCTAD posts and settled in Chile to continue as director general of an economic and social planning institute that he had helped run all through his United Nations career.

It is dangerous to place too much emphasis on the impact of one man. There were for instance the "structuralists" like Anibal Pinto, Osvaldo Sunkel, and Celso Furtado, who argued along Prebisch's lines. But he developed most of the original ideas and created the positions of influence through which the ideas could be put into practice. It is hard to think of any major development in the Latin American and Third World scene over the last twenty years in which he was not involved. The creation of bodies like UNCTAD, LAFTA, the Inter-American Development Bank, and the increasing sophistication and self-confidence of Latin American planners, the move toward schemes of preferential tariffs for the Third World were perhaps inevitable, but Prebisch was the instigator and should receive the credit.[8]

The Growth of Third World Institutions

Every trade unionist knows that he is only as strong as the union behind him. The analogy holds true for the Third World, and the necessary institutions are slowly and hesitantly being created.

At the outset there were informal ad hoc conferences and meetings between Third World leaders that were concerned primarily with the development of political independence. Thus, the various Pan-African congresses brought together many of the African leaders who were to lead the independence move-ment in Africa. The 1955 Bandung conference brought together the leaders of the newly independent Afro-Asian countries, and the delegates strove to develop the concept of "positive neutral-ism," which was to be an ideological "third way," independent of the American and Russian superpowers.

Gradually, however, specific economic needs brought groups of the Third World together in attempts to act as pressure groups on the developed world. The resulting organizations have been outright failures or only partial successes, but their importance to the international business community is that any break-throughs against companies are quickly made known and will be used against companies in other continents or industries. On the other hand, a government that makes a deal that is favorable to the multinationals will be under considerable moral pressure to be tougher (as happened with the Libyans in the early 1960's).

The only group that has met with any success is OPEC in the oil field. This body, formed in 1960 as a result of price cuts by the oil companies, now has eleven members (Nigeria, the eleventh, joined in July 1970). It was not easy to be effective in the 1960's, with oil production running ahead of world markets; OPEC's job was to ensure that the oil companies did not try to cut payments to the producing governments any further. It was successful, and by 1965 it had won the right to hear of price changes in advance. By 1970, the basic situation had changed and the breakthroughs of Iran and Libya were generalized through to the other members. The 1971 negotiations, in which the Gulf States in OPEC bargained together against the oil companies as a group, were a major break from the historical pattern of individual deals between countries and firms. Even so, there are limitations in OPEC that the present tight oil market has tended to gloss over. The formation of OAPEC (Organization of Arab Petroleum–Exporting Countries—Saudi Arabia, Kuwait, and Libya to start with) in 1968 reflected the role played by non-Arab oil-exporting countries like Iran in undercutting the attempted boycott by the Arab countries against the United States and Britain in the aftermath of the 1967 Arab–Israeli war. Again in 1968 and 1969 the "solidarity" of OPEC was tested when Iran played on its role as the oil companies' favorite by winning annual monetary increases from the companies that were larger than those won elsewhere. There was a real possibility that the companies might start restricting output from some of the other countries in favor of Iranian production, for which they were paying these advance royalties. However, the continuing boom in the industry and Iran's location on the wrong side of the blocked Suez Canal meant that the problem did not actually arise. Another example that shows the limitations of OPEC "solidarity" is the attempt between its various members to plan oil output. Although this has been discussed in the past, it has never gotten any further than talk.

OPEC's importance lies in the rapid transmission of break-throughs in negotiations between countries and companies. It is now extremely difficult for the oil majors to play off one country against another. As soon as a deal was made granting certain countries 55 percent of producing profits, all the other members of OPEC automatically put in demands that they, too, should get 55 percent of their local profits and it was impossible for the companies to avoid conceding the point. Currently, as we saw in Chapter 1, OPEC is getting around to discussing forms of participation in the industry, and again, once the companies' position is breached in any part of the world, all the rest of the OPEC countries will demand similar terms. Above all, the existence of OPEC is thwarting the dream of all oil majors, which is to find oil in some part of the world where governments are willing to undercut the OPEC countries. It could be that the European governments controlling the North Sea discoveries, or the American government controlling Alaska, will indeed be overkind to the companies, but new producers like Nigeria have seen the benefits of joining OPEC and have demanded similar terms. So, although OPEC has its soft spots, it remains the one major organization in which members of the Third World are really starting to act as a trade union. In fact, the reaction of the advanced economies in deliberately deciding to increase their safety stock of oil against a possible refusal to produce oil by OPEC countries is exactly the same as that of the employer who builds up his supplies and inventories in anticipation of a possible strike.[9]

The copper-producing countries have tried to follow OPEC's lead with less obvious chance of success. Their organization, CIPEC, was formed in 1967 with a Paris secretariat. The four main copper-producing countries, Chile, Peru, Congo (Kinshasa), and Zambia, are its members. However, unlike oil, copper will be in oversupply until 1975 at least, so the role of CIPEC is basically to find an answer to fluctuating and possibly falling world prices. It has been looking at various schemes like the creation of buffer stocks or the introduction of support buying, but late in 1971 it had not come up with any convincing solutions.

For the moment, then, its role is mostly as a talking shop, but we should note that many of the major developments in this industry came through informal relationships that existed before CIPEC's formation, and they should act as a warning to any businessman who notes merely the weakness of these bodies. They may not be able to control production or prices, but they can certainly transmit the latest developments in economic nationalism. The key factor in this industry was that Kaunda and Frei had met each other before they become presidents of Zambia and Chile respectively. Both devout Christians, moderates, and "humanists," they kept in touch, and top-level Chileans visited Zambia, while in 1966 Kaunda visited Santiago. During this time Frei had inaugurated his policy of "Chileanization," and he and his officials were horrified when they looked at the copper legislation that Kaunda had inherited with independence. In June 1967 in Lusaka a conference was held at which CIPEC was formed, and in 1969 Zambia moved against Roan Selection Trust (major shareholder American Metal Climax) and the South African-owned Anglo-American Corporation, demanding 51 percent ownership in their Zambian activities—a demand based heavily on the Frei "Chileanization" formula.

This is an interesting example of personal relationships helping to spread economic nationalism—the creation of CIPEC was almost an afterthought. It is also a case where Latin American experience was spread to another continent, Africa, and the Zambian nationalizations were important within the African continent since, apart from the Congo (Kinshasa) conflict with Union Minière, it was the first time that a black African nation had really tackled a major multinational company head-on. So Zambia gave practical support to the Tanzanian policy of economic nationalism, and countries like Uganda followed with nationalizations of their own.

Fittingly, this burst of economic nationalism was then transferred back to Latin America into a new industry—aluminum. Forbes Burnham, Guyana's prime minister, has never been known for his militancy or radicalism. In fact, on occasions it has been clear that United States and British interests have

helped him win elections against his Indian and Marxist op-
ponent, Cheddi Jagan. In September 1970 he paid a sentimental
visit to Africa, touring countries like Zambia and Uganda.
Burnham was impressed with their nationalizations of foreign
interests, went back home to Guyana, and, under strong domestic pressures, took a 66 percent stake in Demerara Bauxite
(part of the Alcan empire), which was the chief extractive industry in his country. After some abortive negotiations, this
became a full-scale expropriation of the firm. Now this action is
due to have a further "ripple" effect, since Jamaica, an even
more important bauxite producer, has decided not to follow
Guyana's lead; however, the mere fact that someone else has
nationalized a bauxite firm means that the issue is now part of
the Jamaican political scene, and the Jamaican government has
to prove that its alternative approach is in fact benefiting the
country.

The significance of these cases is that Third World leaders are
no longer working in a vacuum. Even without the existence of
formal organizations, personal contacts are enough to spread
some forms of economic nationalism. With the existence of
formal organizations, communication of new ideas will be even
faster and more accurate.

Knowledge itself is not enough. The power of any organization depends ultimately on the sanctions it can bring to bear
on any particular issue, and here the Third World is weak. The
"terms of trade" thesis makes the point that the majority of the
Third World products are ones for which prices have been
relatively static or falling, or for which overproduction and price
fluctuations have been the major problem. In this kind of situation, the power of the Third World is limited, and attempts to
get concessions from the developed economies have been very
disappointing. In a number of commodities cutthroat competition between producing Third World countries is a real problem.

At one time Brazil was the major source of coffee. As African
countries entered the industry, prices plummeted and Brazil
tried to stabilize the market by agreements with competitors,
so that prices were maintained at a level that gave the producers
some profit. So in 1962 the International Coffee Agreement

was created, with sixty-two countries, growers or consumers involved. This is a highly unstable structure, with the Africans trying to get their production quotas increased at the expense of the Latin Americans, and the American soluble coffee processors trying to stop the producing countries like Brazil from doing the processing at source. The only constraint on the consumer countries is the knowledge of the ill will that would be created if they simply bought at cheapest world prices and allowed the producing countries to destroy each other's industries. However, that would mean that coffee could be bought cheaper, and so the producing countries have no real economic leverage at all. They are like workers unable to strike because the enterprise is uneconomic and will just be closed down. The only answer is cooperation—and that is difficult.

Finally, there are the macro political bodies like UNCTAD and the various common markets like LAFTA (Latin America), CACM (Central America), CARIFTA (Caribbean), Andean Pact (Chile, Peru, etc.), the East African Common Market. All these bodies are still pitifully weak—some on the verge of disintegration—but the majority are at least managing to survive. UNCTAD's role as the Third World voice within the United Nations framework has had limited success with generalized preferences for manufactured and semi-manufactured products from the Third World. But there are obvious limitations stemming from the ultimate lack of Third World sanctions. For instance, if the U.S. Senate's plan in 1971 to cut off all aid had not been defeated, there was nothing the Third World could do except state its claim as powerfully and clearly as possible through such bodies as UNCTAD. All the Third World can do is to make itself as attractive as possible without compromising its overall independence. This is why the common markets, for all their weaknesses, are a promising strategy. By putting a number of small markets together, they make a single market, which, with luck, will be large enough to attract plants and firms that would have been uninterested in any of the small original ones. Once the firms are hooked, the governments can start bargaining.

Decline of Business "Solidarity"

Every trade unionist knows the "blackleg" or "scab" who refuses to fall in with his fellow workers and undercuts their more
militant line. Even the multinationals are now faced with this
problem. In the old days it was normally possible for a company in dispute with a particular government to ensure that its
competitors did not try to muscle in while the dispute was on.
Thus, Standard Oil and Shell were able to keep competitors
out of Mexico after the 1938 expropriation; Anglo-Iranian was
similarly able to prevent Mossadegh's Iran from selling any of
the expropriated Anglo-Iranian oil in the 1950's. Similarly, in
critical contract negotiations, the major firms would normally
have more or less explicit understandings about what concessions
would or would not be considered unsporting. Today this solidarity is crumbling. Partly this is because the old Anglo-Saxon
domination of world industry is diminishing as competitors from
newly established economies arrive on the scene. Crucial breakthroughs in the oil industry came when the Japanese and Italians
concentrated on entering the industry. In 1957 the Arabian
Oil Company, a Japanese firm, turned up in the Middle East,
making a bargain with Saudi Arabia and, the following year,
with Kuwait. To gain these concessions, it agreed to pay an
unheard-of 57 percent of its profits in tax and then agreed to
let the governments concerned purchase at par 10 percent of
its shares after discovery of oil in commercial quantities. At the
same time, the Italian company ENI, under the aggressive
leadership of Enrico Mattei, was making, through its subsidiary
AGIP, a similar deal in Iran. What is more, ENI went aggres-
sively after concessions in North Africa and Nigeria, and
started to pioneer a policy of active cooperation with developing countries in which they would build refineries with the joint
participation of local governments. Spanish interests have become active in Kuwait, and as we saw in Nigeria, the French
through ERAP have been following aggressive policies of their
own. On the fringes of these battles lurk the Communist oil
interests: India, Ceylon, and Cuba have all at some stage tried

to play them off against the oil majors but with no startling successes. Today, the threat comes more strongly from state firms like Petrobras, the National Iranian Oil Company, and the Algerian Sonatrach. The more governments become involved in the industry through such bodies, the greater pressure there is on the established majors.

This kind of blacklegging shows no signs of dying in the oil industry, where, for instance, the Italians and the French played "lone wolf" roles in the 1971 oil negotiations, while the rest of the industry negotiated jointly. In particular, both the Russians and the Italians moved into Iraq, despite major threats from the American-owned IPC, and signed agreements to develop parts of the concessions that had been in dispute between IPC and Iraq since 1961.

In other industries, the search for blacklegs is more difficult. In fact, one can almost say that industries like copper and bauxite are roughly at the stage today that the oil industry was after the collapse of the Iranian expropriations. The indications are that major blacklegs will soon be found, but at the moment they are not willing to come forward. For instance, it has been alleged that when Zambia was thinking about ways of controlling its copper firms, it almost reached agreement with some Scandinavian firms, who would have taken over some of the management roles of the existing copper firms. At the last moment, however, these companies withdrew—probably because of pressures from the established companies. Chile and Peru are still looking for such help with their expropriated copper industries. Chile has found a couple of smallish companies that are willing to market copper in Europe in place of Anaconda's sales outlets and in August 1971 was organizing the search for further reserves through finance from the United Nations Development Program, with technical assistance from the Rumanian government, while UNIDO (United Nations Industrial Development Organization) was to help set up a center for mineral and metallurgical research. Peru in 1971 was also searching hard for new partners in its copper mines, with a lot of tentative promises but few cases where the parties were willing to sign on the dotted line. There were Japanese and European consortia on the sidelines, but they seemed to be waiting until they knew more about Peru's plans for the treatment of foreign investors. Again, with Guyana's bauxite expropriation, there were Yugoslavs ready to handle the management, with a couple of European companies willing to take half the produce. This was enough to strengthen Guyana's resolve against Alcan, though no one can predict how well this arrangement will work.

Properly used, this breakdown of the solidarity of the multinationals due to the arrival of new, unrestrained competitors is one of the strongest cards the Third World has to play. In some industries like copper, the search for blacklegs may be difficult, especially as the Soviet bloc seems relatively weak in basic mining technology. Thus, while Chile has been looking for technical help from new sources, the USSR has itself been approaching companies that might be interested in helping exploit the Siberian copper reserves. In other industries like oil and the more "mature" manufacturing processes, the search is easier. Kenneth Kaunda in Zambia could not find a blackleg in the copper industry, but he has had experience in playing off British firms in general against Italian newcomers. He realized that the established British companies were inefficient, so he encouraged the entrance of Italian competition in things like building cement plants, training and supplying the Zambian Air Force. He also started talks with the Italians about entering oil distribution and the setting up of a car-assembly plant, in which the government would hold 70 percent of the equity. All reports suggest that the British interests started to take Zambia seriously again. This strategy of playing the multinationals off against each other is an absolutely essential precaution that governments must take wherever possible. Reliance on a single multinational or multinationals from one country is dangerous. New plants should be erected after some form of competitive bidding, and established operations should be challenged by new competition whenever they show signs of ignoring the interests of the country concerned. It is not always easy to get multinationals to compete with each other, but it should be attempted, and the evidence is that it will become easier to achieve.[10]

Which Industries Are Vulnerable?

In some industries the multinationals cannot win. Whatever they do, their actions will be misrepresented. Extractive industries are a case in point. A country's natural resources are destroyed for the dubious benefit of people in a foreign land. If Welsh nationalists in Great Britain are enraged because water from Welsh reservoirs supplies English cities like Birmingham, then what must be the reactions of Chileans or Australians to foreign-owned extractive organizations? Land is an emotive issue, and a number of countries have legislation limiting the right of foreigners to own property. This is becoming a major issue as tourist industries expand, since the land in question is often the most attractive in the country. Transportation systems are vulnerable, particularly the railroads, but increasingly air and shipping lines are also under attack. The airlines are mostly used as symbols of national unity and sophistication, but the shipping industry is often seen as one way in which the developed economies keep the Third World under control. This is a particularly touchy subject, since the dominant shipping conferences are such obviously restrictive devices and since the United States specifies that the goods bought with her aid must be carried half the time in United States ships whose high costs thus significantly dilute the value of the aid in the first place. Financial institutions like banks are vulnerable. Even South Africa is considering a report that recommends that they follow the Australian example of forbidding non-residents to establish banks and preventing companies with more than 10 percent foreign interest from registering in South Africa.

In the early stages of development there are various industries that are seen to be "keys" to national identity and to central planning. As the economies develop, more and more attention is turned to the more technologically advanced sectors. Thus, besides electrical power, insurance, banking, railways

164674

and telecommunications, Mexico has closed the oil and heavy petrochemical sectors to any foreign investment; from 1968 they also demanded majority Mexican holdings in mining, light petrochemicals, road transport, fishing, shipping, and soft-drink bottling. Since Mexico is probably one of the most sophisticated economic nationalists, this is about as good a list of priorities as we can get.

But over and above the vulnerability of certain industries, there are degrees of concentration or foreign "visibility" that will make specific firms more or less vulnerable. Kidron's study of India allowed him to conclude that there was a definite rule that governed state intervention in industries. The state would move in whenever foreign investors appeared to have unchallenged control of an important industry, whether the threat came from a single firm (matches, soap, tin plate, aluminum, transformers, some drugs, industrial gases, and shipping) or a group of firms acting in concert (oil, tires, electrical equipment). There were no general rules about the type of intervention the state might resort to, but even if "the method and timing have varied, the fact of intervention has not." [11]

Size can present a problem. However minor a particular investment is, it will bear the name of the parent multinational and will acquire a significance often not deserved. On the other hand, governments are now starting to move into industries that are not oligopolistic enough and are thus driving out multinationals that have already established themselves. Industries can become overfragmented because of the "miniature replica" effect, which is what happens when all the major companies in an industry flood into a country on a "follow-my-leader" principle. At its sanest, this means that an American industry with five main firms will lead to all five of these companies establishing themselves in Canada once one of them decides to make the move. In the Third World, the situation can get out of hand with the Americans, Europeans, and Japanese all setting up in an economy that can barely support two of them. In 1964 Chile had twenty-two companies manufacturing 7,800 vehicles, at a cost four times that of cars imported directly from abroad. The economic planners have, therefore, started deliberately to cut down on the number of firms involved in certain industries. Mexico for some time has been squeezing out auto companies that have been unwilling to accept given requirements of local components and, increasingly, given export targets. Peru has subsequently decided to cut back the number of car firms from fourteen in 1970 to six in all, with Chrysler the first company to agree on terms for remaining.

What Are the
Economic Nationalists Asking For?

Financial Demands The first set of demands tries to limit the cost of the permitted investments. These will include controls on borrowing within the host country, so that the multinational is forced to bring in foreign exchange when it invests. On occasions government and firm will bargain over the level of profits allowed where the government controls price. In 1971, British Leyland Motors Corporation was negotiating with the Israeli government over the future of BLMC's Israeli subsidiary. The company wanted price rises giving them a profit of 6 percent on turnover (25 percent on investment), while the government was willing to give them only half of this. This is a major problem because firms and governments often have a totally different idea of what a "fair" profit is. Firms on the whole will aim at returns around 15 percent on the capital they invest, while leading Third World statesmen will sometimes consider a 4 percent return "fair." For that rate of return, investors would more profitably put their money into a neighborhood bank where they can get higher rates of interest. Basically this boils down to how much the two sides need each other, but however accommodating a firm may be, it is still a capitalist institution that cannot function on such low rates of return.

Whatever the profits, the question of remitting them soon arises. It is very tempting for the local government to insist that they all remain in the country. There is no doubt that controls of some sort are needed if foreign exchange is to be conserved. The Andean Pact agreed to limit profit remittances to 14 percent of the capital invested. This is not too onerous a demand, though some industries like mining and oil are accustomed to far higher remissions. In extractive industries there is normally a distinct limit to investment in any one raw material, and after a certain amount of exploration, it becomes clear that new reserves are relatively unprofitable, and so the companies withdraw sufficient profit to develop new areas or countries. This policy has led to some classic "enclaves," like the oil industry in Venezuela, where, apart from the immediate infrastructure needed for the oil industry, the country has not really benefited in other industries or parts of the country. One or two oil countries like Algeria are now starting to demand some form of compulsory reinvestment in the countries in which the profits are made. This policy overlooks the fact that Algerian oil would be unsalable unless the companies invested in refineries and distribution systems elsewhere in the world. Nevertheless, companies can expect growing pressure, and it may mean that some of them have to consider diversification into new industries, since there are limits to the expansion of their traditional activities in any one country.

Demands for Greater Impact on Local Economy   A basic drive all around the world is to replace imports with locally made products. This is not specifically a policy of economic nationalism, since often local entrepreneurs and foreign multinationals are simultaneously affected by such import-substitution methods, although they can be used to discriminate against the foreign firms. Typically, firms are given a deadline by which they are expected to be selling only products with a given proportion of local "value added." This is normally an expensive policy to follow, since a narrow market means a small turnover and therefore loss of production economies of scale. It also means the development of local suppliers who will often be relatively inefficient. In Mexico, which is well developed for a Third World country, import substitution led to costs that were on average 80 percent higher than those in industrialized countries. In some cases, costs could be 200 percent greater. Multinationals will sometimes protest these pressures, especially when they are forced to cut back on plants in other parts of the world that used to supply the goods or components in question. The conflicts reach their peak in the extractive industries, where the drive for higher value added leads to demands for processing plants in the host country rather than elsewhere in the world. A typical case is that of Ghana and Valco (owned 90 percent by Kaiser Aluminum and 10 percent by Reynolds Metals). During Nkrumah's regime Valco started to build the Tema aluminum smelter for $130 million. The location was attractive because of the cheap electricity that would come from the gigantic Volta dam, and under the original terms, it could use imported aluminum, which it could carry in its own ships free of customs duties and exchange control. At the same time, Ghana has 350 million tons of unexploited bauxite, the raw material for aluminum, and the pressure is now on Valco to help develop these reserves (the Japanese are involved in exploration, too) and to use this bauxite in the Tema smelter. In other industries, the pressures are the same. The copper countries want the copper to be smelted before leaving their shores; the banana economies want the fruit boxed and to some extent processed before leaving their countries; coffee countries like Brazil are fighting to have a greater proportion of soluble coffee made in their countries instead of in the consuming countries. The firms have economic arguments against some of these proposals. Soluble coffee may well be made from a mix of coffee beans from a number of different countries. A soluble coffee plant in one country would only partly use the local beans, and the logistical problems of coordinating the flow of different beans from country to country might well be more complicated than the present system. The oil companies use similar arguments against locating refineries in the producing countries.

Finally, there are increasing demands for export, and firms are allowed in only if they guarantee a given proportion of exports. Mexico has a version of this that ties the company's rights to foreign exchange to its export performance. This is a neat way of tackling the problem, but whatever form they take, export requirements have taken over from demands for import substitution as the most glamorous demand upon the foreign multinationals.[12]

Xenophobic Controls   Earlier in the chapter we discussed how certain industries might be barred to foreigners, but xenophobia can reveal itself in less extreme ways. There may be tax discrimination against the foreign multinational (even West Germany in the autumn of 1971 was planning a tax system that discriminated against profits remitted abroad). There may also be barriers against foreign takeovers of domestic firms, though whatever the legal situation there will always be local hostility to such acquisitions, and trade-union responses or bureaucratic delays may make such deals considerably less attractive than they first seemed. As a last resort, there are outright onslaughts, such as nationalization or expropriation.

The Battle for Ownership and Control   Many governments are pushing hard on policies whereby local citizens replace the expatriate (i.e. foreign) managers who have traditionally run the multinational subsidiaries. This type of control obviously gives the host government more confidence that the firm is being run for the benefit of the local community but it is also a policy that is easier to decree than to carry out. For instance, the great mining companies like Union Minière and those in Zambia traditionally used up to five thousand foreign managers and technicians, and the Zambians and the Congolese have had to tread warily in replacing them. In the 1967 crisis between the Congo and Union Minière, President Mobutu's determination to bring in non-Belgian interests foundered because the 2,400 European workers in Union Minière's Congolese operations were all ready to leave; a face-saving compromise between the government and the Belgian parent company was worked out, since the government knew it would be unable to replace these foreigners with local personnel.

But the battle is more for greater control as shown in .equity holdings. Thus governments in countries like Zambia, Chile (under Frei), and Uganda all carried out part-nationalizations, whereby the governments would be given shares in the local operations in anticipation of payments that would come from the company's future profits. Increasingly, also, firms are allowed to come into the country only if they join in a partnership with local investors. The Andean Pact, for instance, requires new investments to be at least 51 percent controlled by local owners. Every so often, in some key industries like oil, the demands go further and call for shares in the parent company itself. We saw how in the case of Alcan Norwegian representatives now sit on the parent board as the result of a deal made with the Norwegian government. Most companies dislike these requirements but are forced to accept them. They argue that in order to plan globally they must have total control over their subsidiaries. It may be true that subsidiaries owned totally by the multinationals tend to export more than partly owned ones, but already, within the better-run multinationals, there are organizational devices that allow the various subsidiaries to put forward bids for new plants or products within the firm's overall activities. It is understood that the final decisions by the parent company are compromises between the demands of the subsidiaries, the ideas of the center, and the *Realpolitik* of the multinational world, whereby subsidiaries cannot be treated too differently without either destroying managerial morale or raising nationalist responses among local politicians and trade unions. Allowing jointly owned subsidiaries a fair share of the action would require that these procedures be formalized and outsiders allowed into the firm's decision-making process, thus offending the multinationals' preference for secrecy. Already government officials in Britain have been allowed to sit down with the managements of firms like Ford to discuss the companies' future plans as they affect Britain and to argue for better treatment of British interests. Already trade unions have been granted some ad hoc rights to discuss the European plans of a company the size of Philips. So, if the right to consult on companies' global plans has already been granted to some powerful customers, one cannot argue that it is impossible to bring local partners into the overall planning process. Certainly it will mean a loss in the power of the centralized decision-makers, but if companies are being forced to accept local partners around the world, then common sense dictates that the managers learn how to get on with the outsiders, even if it means giving them a say in the overall planning process.

The social implications of this drive for local participation in multinational ventures are fascinating. We saw, for instance, that the United Africa Company had acted as an intermediary between the foreign companies and the Nigerian economy. Local entrepreneurs play the same role elsewhere with strong government encouragement (sometimes government and local entrepreneurs may be the same people). This means that three or four key firms or individuals may have deals with all the major multinational companies. Thus, when the UN's Food and Agricultural Organization (FAO) wanted to put H. J. Heinz Ltd. in touch with a partner in Turkey, it chose Vehbi Koc, whose companies import or manufacture under license Ford cars, Fiat tractors and trucks, Burroughs accounting machines. He also bottles and distributes Coca-Cola, owns the most important hotel after the Hilton, and has been asked to head Turkey's new export campaign. One of the few historical studies of a Third World entrepreneur shows how important the foreign license has been. Thomas Cochran and Ruben Reina have written a history of the Italian-born Argentine entrepreneur, Torcuato di Tella, who created SIAM, which by the late 1940's was the largest general machinery manufacturer in Latin America. Starting by producing dough-making machinery to his own design, he manufactured and assembled gasoline pumps (license with Wayne Pump Company of the United States), water softeners (Permutit), water pumps (some General Electric components), refrigerators (Kelvinator and then Westinghouse), scooters (Innocenti), washing machines (Hoover Ltd.), and cars (British Motor Company). As the biographers comment: ". . . Di Tella was [always] looking for new patented products or processes which SIAM could first distribute and eventually manufacture." This philosophy sums up the bulk of the Third World entrepreneurs, and in fact one calls them "entrepreneurs" with some hesitation. After all, what they contribute are not new products but powers of "fixing"—of obtaining licenses and favorable interpretation of regulations and procedures from local officialdom, mediating with local financial institutions, etc. On the whole, the local partner is likely to take responsibility for purchasing, sales, publicity, and labor relations, while the foreign partner concentrates on technical operations, day-to-day management, foreign suppliers, and finance.

The whole process breeds corruption. There was the "Omani question," which bedeviled Arab politics from 1955, when the Imam of Oman rose in revolt against the Sultan of Muscat and Oman in the Persian Gulf. For long years different countries recognized one or the other of the two parties and the dispute dragged on. Eventually the Arab League brought the two sides together, and the Imam announced that he would agree to the terms the league suggested, provided one of two demands was met: "My first condition is that I get the agency for 'Pepsi-Cola' and my second, if that is impossible, is that I get the Shell agency for distribution of oil products." [13] Disaster and stalemate! The sultan's uncle had the Pepsi concession and the sultan's adviser owned the Shell agency. Neither of these worthies would budge.

Frantz Fanon saw these developments right from the start. "The national bourgeoisie," he said, "steps into the shoes of the former European settlement; doctors, barristers, traders, commercial travellers, general agents and transport agents . . . From now on, it will insist that all the big foreign companies should pass through its hands, whether these companies wish to keep on their connections with the country or open it up. The national middle-class discovers its historic mission: that of intermediary." [14]

The Fade-out Formula

Among major nuisances facing the multinationals are the American academics who produce findings or ideas that are immediately used by Third World leaders to curtain the companies' activities. The most important idea is that firms wishing to invest in the Third World should sign a contract that sets down the terms under which the company would eventually sell or give back a given proportion of its investment to local investors. Normally a period of ten to twenty years is mentioned, and the intention is that the Third World should get the full benefits of multinational investment with its efficient combination of money, technology, and management in one package, with minimized costs. In many ways the idea is neat. Its authors point out that during the two world wars and during the Great Depression many British and German investors transferred assets into the hands of local nationals. It is suggested that the whole process could be facilitated through an International Divestment Corporation, which would buy up the subsidiaries about to be "faded out" until local buyers could be found. If foreign private investment is relatively expensive, then forcing it to sell out at some stage would put an end to repatriated profits.

This formula has been evolved almost solely through the writings of academics, though Raul Prebisch has also backed it. Harvard's Professor Albert O. Hirschman is normally given most of the credit, though other academics like Paul Rosenstein-Rodan (University of Texas) and Paul Streeten (Oxford) have played their role in publicizing the concept. Business interests hate the idea, and the Council of the Americas has branded it as "unworkable and unrealistic." "Foreign investors," it claims, "do not invest to go out of business." The businessman's natural contempt for the academics is strengthened by other academic attacks on the idea. Jack Behrman of the University of North Carolina, another leading authority on multinationals, has done a hatchet job on it, while Virgil Salera (1970) wrote that "foreign investors in Latin America face enough uncertainties . . . without the gratuitous and synthetic kind that stem from half-baked American academic analysis." In the meantime, earnest young Latin American nationalists, anti-American to the core, defend the formula: "But look, the idea must be good. It came from Harvard." Moreover, they have actually adopted a version of it in the Andean Pact, so it must be taken seriously.[15]

The major criticism is that it is unrealistic. Firms can expect guaranteed returns in other parts of the world, so why invest in places that will eventually expect you to hand your subsidiaries over to them? The formula's opponents argue this theme a little too loudly. Certainly, if just one country adopts such a policy, companies will turn to friendlier neighbors. This is precisely why the Andean Pact's decision that all foreign companies in their countries will have between fifteen and twenty years to pass 51 percent control to local hands is so important. Five countries have acted in unison to prevent black-mail. Second, it can be argued that multinationals are already making some very generous deals: Fiat has helped Russia build a car industry, which will be totally under Russian control and is producing vehicles that are being exported back into Western Europe. American firms have licensed their know-how to Japanese firms, thus breeding competitors. In both cases, short-run profits outweighed the dangers of creating new competition. At least with the fade-out formula, firms would have fifteen years or so of complete control before handing over the project. It would be rare for any company to plan an investment in a politically sensitive area without being certain of recouping its investment within five years at the maximum. However, it is too soon to tell what will happen with the Andean Pact proposals, especially as Chile's dispute with the copper companies means that the atmosphere is particularly charged with ill will.

Another criticism suggests that the formula is a thorough waste of money. Behrman points out that Perón bought out the British owners of the Argentine railways for nearly $1 billion in foreign exchange. Valuable exchange could have been better spent, for if the railways were being badly run, the government could have used legislative action to improve their performance. It is paradoxical to argue that the best way to cut the cost of foreign private investment is to be committed to the payment of large sums of foreign exchange at some future date. Profit remissions are spread evenly from year to year, while buying out foreign interests would involve years in which the country's foreign-exchange reserves would be sorely tried.

But the whole scheme is too rigid. Some formulas envisage setting out in the original agreement exactly how much the final settlement should be, but even if the terms are less specific, the question is why should a firm do anything but exploit its investment as hard as it can over the last five years or so before the end? It is possible to devise schemes like the one Venezuela uses in the oil industry, whereby the firms put money into a central fund, and if at the end of the concession period it is adjudged that the assets in question are in bad condition, the sum will not be returned.

The formula glosses over too many unpalatable realities. If the proposed terms are too good, the companies will make hay; if they are bad, the companies will simply not invest. But despite these the fade-out principle has its points. Chiefly it recognizes that the balance of power between government and company will change, but it makes the mistake of assuming that one can see how any investment will look in another decade, and it also assumes that only one model will suit the different kinds of power situations that can be found at any one time. In some parts of the world and in some industries, a fade-out principle would genuinely kill off all investor interest, but for Latin America as a whole, this threat is probably excessive.[16] In other industries, like oil, the investment opportunities are so attractive that the companies already accept the principle that they will own concessions on land for a limited number of years, at the end of which the concessions may be granted to other companies. In fact, what matters is getting both sides to accept that circumstances will change and that terms that are reasonable today may well be unsatisfactory to one party or the other in the future. The fade-out enthusiasts could probably learn from contracts in the extractive industries, for instance that between De Beers and Angola, in which the company is given land concessions that will be progressively reduced, until by 1977 the company will control only the area of actual operating mines. It is also accepted that the whole deal can be renegotiated after fifteen years, and every ten years after that.

What matters is not a strict formula but an understanding by both sides that situations change and that contracts may, therefore, be sensibly renegotiated every so often. Firms that go into the Third World thinking that the terms of a contract are indefinite are asking for trouble, just as companies that assume that a contract with a trade union is permanent are deluding themselves. Times change, and contracts should reflect that fact. Ten or fifteen years from now economic nationalism will not have disappeared and will probably be considerably stronger. The multinationals must learn how to live with this truth, however unpleasant it may be.

Notes

1. Nicholas Faith, *Sunday Times,* August 22, 1971. Deterding was chairman of Shell some fifty years ago.

2. Johnson, "A Theoretical Model of Economic Nationalism."

3. Frank, *Latin America*; Furtado, *Economic Development of Latin America*; Gerassi, *The Great Fear*; Rippy, *British Investments in Latin America*; Vernon, "The Role of US Enterprise Abroad"; González Aguayo, *La Nacionalización de Bienes Extranjeros en América Latina*; Petras, LaPorte, "U.S. Response to Economic Nationalism in Chile."

4. Cronon, *Josephus Daniels in Mexico.*

5. This account mainly comes from Cronon, *Josephus Daniels in Mexico.* But see also Daniels, *Shirt-sleeve Diplomat*; Furtado, *Economic Development of Latin America*; Spender, *Weetman Pearson.* See also Denny, *America Conquers Britain,* which has some lively accounts of the oil companies' active role in the Revolution.

6. Based mainly on Barr, *Foreign Devils*; Kahn, *The Emerging Japanese Superstate*; Okita and Miki, "Treatment of Foreign Capital"; Oldham, "Characteristics of the Process of Transfer of Technology"; Tsurumi, "Myths That Mislead US Managers in Japan."

7. Drucker, *The Age of Discontinuity.*

8. See Prebisch, *Change and Development,* for a typical example of his latter-day views. Otherwise this account rests on Business International, *The United Nations and the Business World*; Datis-Panero, "Import Substitution"; Frank, *Latin America*; Krieger, "Inflation and Growth"; Salera, "Prebisch's Change and Development."

9. Good sound accounts of oil's political background can be found in Hartshorn, *Oil Companies and Governments*; Penrose, *The Large International Firm*; Tanzer, *Political Economy of Oil.* Rouhani, *A History of OPEC,* charts the rise of a counterbalance to the companies.

10. In part based on Kindleberger, *American Business Abroad*; Penrose, *The Large International Firm.*

11. Kidron, *Foreign Investments in India,* p. 223.

12. Gordon, *Political Economy of Latin America.*

13. *Guardian,* September 4, 1971.

14. Fanon, *The Wretched of the Earth,* p. 305. General sources are Arrighi, "International Corporations, Labour Aristocracies"; Cochran and Reina, *Capitalism in Argentine Culture*; Kidron, *Foreign Investments in India.*

15. Hirschman, *How to Divest in Latin America*; Meeker, "Fade-out Joint Venture"; Ferrer, "Peru: The General as Revolutionary"; Salera, "Liquidate US Direct Investments?"

16. Meeker, "Fade-out Joint Venture."

5 : : *Company Responses*

THERE is no watertight case to be made against the multinationals who want to play it tough with governments, but there is a certain amount of circumstantial evidence to suggest they are cutting their own throats. The Canadian (once Czechoslovak) shoe firm Bata was expropriated in Tanzania after refusing to negotiate with the government; when a similar situation arose in Uganda, it had learned its lesson and negotiated a 60 percent share for the government. There is some evidence that the harsher treatment meted out to the copper firms in Chile reflects the more intransigent stance of the companies there; whereas in Zambia Chartered Consolidated offered the government a share in its operations soon after independence in 1964, while Anaconda refused to play along with President Frei. In the Congo, Union Minière suffered in 1966 through not observing the common courtesies the other copper companies around the world granted their host governments. There are also grounds for suggesting that the hard-line approach of the Council of the Americas and ITT has worked against the interest of all American multinationals in Latin America. Finally, an analysis of an abortive attempt by Bechtel to set up a fertilizer project in India suggests that a combination of overambitious demands, attempts to push the Indian authorities too fast, and the company's association with the United States government at a bad time in United States–Indian relations led to resentment among the Indian negotiators, with ultimately harmful effects on the progress of the talks.[1]

The ultimate objection to a tough line is that it makes the companies "visible" in an environment where this is quite often extremely hazardous. Economic nationalists in governments and

trade-union leaders tend to become active once a firm is identified as a problem. The experience of the German operators
erecting the Rourkela steel plant in the early 1960's revealed
that public interest was so keen (because of the size of the
project, not because the companies were being tough) that a
minor breakdown, which in Germany would have been brought
under control by a shift foreman, would be reported the next
day in all the newspapers and would lead to questions in parliament.[2] There is even some evidence, from a study on joint
ventures in India and Pakistan, to suggest that the larger the
company involved, the lower the profits of the ventures in
which they are concerned. The reasons for this are open to interpretation, but it does look as though the company's size
arouses unwelcome attention on the part of the host governments. More attention is paid to the wage levels and the prices
charged than when the foreign partner is relatively unknown.[3]

Companies cannot help their size, but they can avoid drawing
unnecessary attention to themselves. At its crudest this can
mean doing business through dummy subsidiaries with misleading names. Thus, in South Africa Du Pont sells sizable amounts
of chemicals and man-made fibers, but takes pains to see that
none are sold under the Du Pont name. Similarly, United States
firms doing business in the Mexican border area thwart the attention of United States trade unions by not putting their names
over factories. In particular, dummy subsidiaries have been used
when trading with Taiwan and China, and with Israel and the
Arabs. Companies can also avoid building up their market
share in a given country beyond a point that will trigger nationalist resentment, diverting their resources to new markets.
This may seem bad business, but it not only avoids stirring up
trouble, it also helps spread the risk, especially when social
systems are more extreme than those of the developed economies.

It is decidedly inadvisable for a multinational to own a newspaper or any other form of communications medium. However
clear it is made that writers have complete editorial freedom,
their views will be taken as the company's views, and this can
prove awkward. The British company Lonrho, which specializes

in Africa, was once negotiating a deal with the Congolese government. At the same time they owned a leading Zambian newspaper, although the Zambian government chose the editors. When President Mobutu paid a state visit to Zambia, the newspaper headlined a story about Congolese bandits invading the country and Lonrho's hard-won accord with the Congolese authorities was wiped out overnight.

Ultimately, however, companies that take such a hard line that they cannot do business in the Third World are gambling that, if they ever do need to open up these markets, they will not be "locked out" as an unnecessary latecomer. Many managers who are currently concentrating solely on North America and Europe dismiss this as a necessary risk. Many of the companies involved in the Third World believe that they are carving out market positions that are unassailable by latecomers. Peter Kilby's study of foreign investors in Nigeria found that over a quarter of them acted on this assumption. Certainly some governments are starting to limit the number of firms they will allow into a given industrial sector. Also, governments raise the risk of entering a market late by shutting off all imports once local production can handle foreseeable needs. This means that latecomers will not be able to test the market with exports before setting up production facilities. Europe was never as competitive as today's growth markets, and the non-European companies who are really thriving are those like Singer, Ford, and General Motors which came in during the earlier part of this century (or even in the nineteenth century). It is the newcomers, striving to break into Europe over the last decade, who have been struggling.

There is, therefore, a good case for companies to bend with the wind of economic nationalism. As long as they decide that Third World markets are going to matter to them in the foreseeable future, they cannot afford to be so aggressive that they are either booted out of countries or fail even to gain entrance. What should they do to ensure a reasonable working relationship with Third World governments?

The first and essential step, which most firms follow automatically these days, is to get local personnel into the key company posts and have an observable policy of cutting down on the number of expatriate managers employed. How fast the company has to go depends on the country, but there is no rationale for resisting pressures in this direction. If anything, such a policy is good economics. Using a manager from the parent country is normally expensive. Not only must he be paid at parent-company rates but he will require special allowances, such as removal and housing costs, travel for wife and children, and so on. Furthermore, if he is any good, he will want to keep his posting to any Third World country fairly short; and the average expatriate manager may take about twelve to eighteen months before he starts earning his salary. For these reasons, it is cheaper and simpler to find or develop local managers to take their places. However, once this policy is embarked on, there will be pressures to keep it moving forward briskly. This entails promoting people to positions for which they are unprepared by the standards of the parent company, but it is worth persevering, since keeping local nationals out of the top jobs in the subsidiary is counterproductive. The best local managers will choose to go into business for themselves or join local firms that give them a chance to get to the top. Also, a half-and-half policy breeds its own tensions, with the local managers asking (quite reasonably) why they, too, should not be paid at the expatriate rates and have regular subsidized trips back to the country of the parent company.

Multinationals have nothing to fear from such a policy. Provided other firms are subject to the same pressures, they will not lose competitively, and they have the opportunity of attracting, holding, and training a good proportion of the better local managers. But they will often find it difficult to keep the managers they train, since the latter will have plenty of opportunities to practice the skills they have learned in other firms. This is inevitable, but pursuing such a policy is basically simple and advisable, even though it has not been universally adopted. United States manufacturing firms were still, in 1966, employing 1,200 non-national managers from a total of 15,600 managers in Latin America, and it would be fair to assume that these foreigners held most of the higher-level positions. Firms should work on the principle that the employment of non-national managers is dangerous and should be kept to a minimum.[4]

As we saw in the last chapter, pressure has been exerted on companies to accept local partners in their Third World subsidiaries. There are no overriding reasons why firms should be reluctant to get involved with such joint ventures. In fact, the majority of firms now accept them, even if they are felt to be a compromise. The major study by Harvard's J. W. C. Tomlinson of joint ventures in India and Pakistan shows that only one in seven firms involved in joint ventures in India and Pakistan would not take part in other such ventures in the Third World; another questionnaire study showed that over 85 percent of the United States firms that responded accepted joint ventures as a general policy, while over 70 percent accepted minority positions, even if they would have preferred majority control.[5] This confidence would seem to be well placed. A study of 170 United States companies that in 1964 had 25 percent or more of their manufacturing operations overseas showed that of the 1,100 joint ventures, only 314 changed their ownership patterns; in 182 cases they became wholly-owned subsidiaries of the United States firms; in forty-six cases the terms were changed to give the United States firms control; only in eighty-four cases did the United States firms get out; and in two cases the terms gave the local firm control.[6] This would suggest that in most cases the ventures run smoothly, and the fact that well over half the changes were to give the United States firms greater control would confirm the suspicions of a number of commentators that formal ownership patterns are unimportant. In most cases, the foreign companies control the crucial technical, managerial, and marketing skills, and the local partners, whatever their formal ownership position, are dependent on them. Despite this, there is still a body of managerial opinion that considers that a minority holding makes business impossible. In 1970 ITT spokesmen were still claiming that they had to have at least 51 percent, and in some cases 65 percent, to manage effectively. Many firms survive with less.

Tomlinson fully supports those who propose joint ventures as a reasonable strategy. He found them just as profitable as foreign branches or formal subsidiaries of the multinationals; companies whose partner is the government ("mixed" ventures is the correct term) were revealed to be satisfied with the arrangement, some of them observing that governments are often the only bodies with the time horizons, conception of the problems of scale, and overall view of the market compatible with those of the foreign investor. Tomlinson also discovered that the less the foreign company was concerned with formal ownership of the joint venture, the more profitable it was, suggesting that local partners respond to trust and responsibility like everyone else in business. The only note of caution was that the strict fifty-fifty deal was sometimes dangerous because both sides spent too much time worrying about maintaining equality, and this could be particularly dangerous when decisions had to be made on reinvestment or increased-investment plans.

Management Contracts, Turnkey
Construction, Consultancy, Etc.

Some multinationals will accept far less in the way of legal control; they settle for the roles of consultant, management contractor, or plant constructor—roles the majority of multinationals are not yet ready to consider. And yet in certain circumstances and for certain firms such deals can be profitable and strategically well advised.

A management contract is one in which the multinational agrees to perform a certain number of managerial tasks involved in running an enterprise, generally for a fixed period of time and for a fixed fee. In other words, it carries out managerial functions without having the overall control that goes with share ownership in the enterprise in question. Thus, hotels may be built with Rumanian money (an actual case), but the American company Holiday Inns provides the know-how, staff training, and linkage to the company's international booking system. The day-to-day management will be left in Rumanian hands, but the multinational has agreed to fulfill a certain number of roles that the Rumanians feel they cannot yet handle. In other agreements, the multinationals may choose the managers as well, but the basic principle remains that they are there as contractors and can be replaced on the termination of the contract. Payment can be as a flat fee or can be tied to turnover or profits. The firms can also receive quite a wide range of fringe benefits. There may be agreements that allow the company to supply raw materials and component parts, or to market the finished product through its international links—either way, there is scope for profit-making elsewhere in the company's system. The main disadvantage to the firm is that it commits one of its scarcest resources, management time, for a reward that is not secure. As long as the company can use this managerial expertise elsewhere in the world and still get some form of equity stake in the enterprise, it is unlikely that it will be interested in any form of management contract. But in certain Third World industries it is very difficult for firms to find such openings. Airlines are so much the prime symbols of national identity that however badly they may be doing it is extremely difficult for the foreign airline giants to buy in. Instead, the major airlines have made a number of deals around the world in which they supply planes, technical assistance, training, or marketing skills to Third World airlines. Pan Am was giving such assistance to the national airlines of Afghanistan, Iran, and (through the United States aid program) South Vietnam in 1969. The Dutch line, KLM and the Scandinavian, SAS, have similar deals with Garuda (Indonesia), PAL (Philippines), and Thai International. The Australian line, Quantas, will be giving aid to the Malaysian Corporation, which emerged from the breakup of the joint Malaysia–Singapore airline, MSA, in 1971. SAS agreed in 1971 to help the Russian Aeroflot to train its cabin crews.

The airlines' reward comes occasionally in the form of equity participation (Thai International is more correctly a joint venture, with 30 percent SAS involvement), but normally it comes through straight fees and exclusive rights to fly to certain countries. These deals can also lead to new prospects for profits as the airlines' hotel interests can become involved in these countries' tourist industries. At the same time, national sensibilities are taken into account, and it is possible to change foreign partners. Thus, Air Ceylon in 1962 switched its links with KLM to the British BOAC. It is not unknown for a national airline to fly planes leased from its foreign contractor with crews similarly supplied; the only "national" aspect of the airline is the symbol painted on the tail. Such independence is merely a charade, except that the contractors can be changed by the Third World governments. This may not be much, but it is an improvement from the pre-independence days, when the colonies had no say over which shipping lines were to serve them.[7]

A further dilution of multinational control over the Third World comes through the use of "turnkey projects," where the multinational merely constructs a factory that upon completion is ready for immediate operation by local entrepreneurs or government bodies. On some occasions the multinational may also run the operation on a management contract, but again the principle is that the firm's activity does not buy any right of control over the final operation. This principle is found chiefly in civil-engineering projects. Once a dam, road, or railway is built, the civil engineers responsible relinquish active involvement. In many process industries we find the same approach, particularly in the developed economies. Thus, chemical companies that make technological breakthroughs will often license these to firms that specialize in constructing and designing plants for the other chemical giants. Companies specializing in the construction of turnkey plants are becoming an important force in the Third World, and as we saw in the discussion of Ghana and Nigeria, they may not always be a beneficial influence. However, there are now very few industries that matter to the Third World in which it is impossible to buy the necessary plant on a turnkey basis. This has been made particularly clear by the breakthroughs of Russia and Eastern Europe in setting up complete automobile industries through such deals with companies like Fiat, since the auto industry had been very successful in keeping control of its activities.

These deals (Fiat with Russia and Poland; various American companies with Russia over the Kama River truck plant) illustrate two main points. First, the balance of power has swung away from the auto manufacturers. Everyone in the industry knows that products from the new Eastern European plants will find their way back into European markets. Thus, the Soviet Fiats are already on sale in limited numbers in Europe. Despite this, the companies were not able to build in any prohibitions about what export markets the Russians can sell to. Second, Fiat and Renault in particular are developing skills that are distinct from merely constructing autos. They can now initiate and coordinate the design and construction of auto plants of any complexity on a turnkey basis, and by expanding this side of the business, they will be able to survive even if the economic nationalists make it difficult for multinationals to own the auto plants that will be springing up in the Third World.

A slight variant of this approach is the "project coordinator," in which the multinational handles a project that is more complex than the building of a single plant. Thus Northrop, the United States aircraft manufacturer, found that its military dealings with Iran enabled a subsidiary to win a $5,250,000 contract to build a satellite communication station, a project that went so well that a multinational consortium led by Northrop won a $175 million contract to build a national communications system that will install telephone, telegraph, and television networks. Not only has this contract grown in size since originally planned but Northrop is now favorably placed to win other major new contracts that come up.

It is important also to consider the firms that have started to act as consultants to governments on technical projects. In India ICI, Merck, and Philips have acted as frequent technical consultants to the government. Some companies have formalized this role, like the British company Booker McConnell, which used to be a good colonial sugar firm. Although to some extent it has diversified out of the Third World, its agricultural and technical services division is still extremely active. At one extreme it supplies turnkey sugar factories and will take on the management contracts to run them; at the other it will do studies for aid agencies on the future of the sugar industries of countries like Ghana or Saint Kitts. One of its more ambitious studies is for the World Bank, collaborating with Tate & Lyle (another British sugar company) and the Economist Intelligence Unit to assess ways of building up the Indonesian sugar industry. This is an unusual case in that both Booker and Tate & Lyle own machinery manufacturing subsidiaries, and the World Bank is usually careful to ensure that its consultants do not have these links.

There is not a great deal of money to be made from such activities, though a firm like Booker may do ten or fifteen such studies in the course of a year. However, the company picks up a great deal of incidental knowledge about conditions in different countries and gets first option on any management contracts or turnkey projects that arise, besides gaining an insight into the whole United Nations aid establishment. Such relationships clearly do pay off, for example in the case of the Italian contractors Astaldi Estero, who were called in to do a feasibility study of a hydroelectric scheme in the Congo in the early 1960's. When the final contracts were assigned, they were awarded the first part of the project, worth $43.5 million, without any public tender. If contracts are awarded this loosely, being a consultant could be very profitable indeed.

Public Relations and "Good Works"

Ideally, every multinational wants to be seen as a corporate "good citizen," and to this end companies have always stressed the good they have been doing on the side. Thus, we hear of Standard Oil's (New Jersey) investment companies in Venezuela and Colombia, Shell's interest in rural community development programs, Aramco's work on trachoma in Saudi Arabia, or Kaiser Aluminum's Development Corporation in Jamaica.[8]

All these cases undoubtedly reflect the idealism of a few people within these corporate structures, and yet it is difficult to resist the comparison with Victorian mill owners' wives who used to wander around the slums during the Industrial Revolution handing out kitchen scraps and uplifting religious tracts. The abyss between potential charitable work and actual good deeds is vast, even if such projects do buy better relations with governments and trade unions. Hostile commentators believe that these are "conscience" activities that, however idealistic their original formulations, become grist for the public-relations mill.

To convince anyone that the private sector's motives are not dictated merely by expedience, some major new commitment by the idealists among the multinationals is needed. One such scheme came up in discussions within the United Nations system about the role of private investment when it was suggested that three regional graduate universities should be set up to permit local graduates to study all that is best in the physical and social sciences and in business education within their own continents. If this proposal ever gets off the ground, it might make sense for the companies with development programs to sponsor research through them.[9] Another idealistic solution might lie in the creation of a non-profit-making foundation, funded by private enterprise, to concentrate solely on the problems of the Third World. Already, bodies like the Rockefeller and Ford Foundations have done valuable work, but their activities are not a necessary offshoot of Ford's or Standard Oil's policies. A fund to which any multinational can contribute, which is clearly identified with the Third World, would be rather more convincing than the efforts of a few firms, where the dividing line between idealism and self-interest is not easily demonstrable.

But multinationals are commercial, not charitable, organizations, and their task is to convince the Third World of their commitment within their commercial framework. Probably the most realistic proposal is for the creation of regional subsidiaries corresponding to the main Third World areas, Latin America, Africa (minus South Africa), Asia, and Australasia. To some extent the vital groundwork has been the creation, by some large multinationals, of regional headquarters to coordinate activities in these parts of the world. The need is for this corporate structure to be formalized so that local investors can buy shares. Its formal policy should be relative self-sufficiency with guarantees that the bulk of profits will be plowed back into the region, even if not back into the individual countries in which the profits are made.

To the dedicated nationalist this would not be enough, since it is all too easy to show that dispersed local shareholdings would not lead to any significant control. To most others, however, the multinationals would be able to demonstrate that they were committed to the region, though this would not be fully convincing until it was clear that the parent multinational accepted the fact that its investment was locked into the region and that its right to divest should be used only in the very last resort. This would, in fact, be a compromise between the extreme economic nationalist who might argue that the multinational should reinvest all profits in the country in which they are made, and the view of the multinationals that they should have total freedom to move resources globally and that local interests may buy shares in the parent company if they want a say in the multinationals' managements. There are already some precedents for such a move, with firms like Chase Manhattan setting up subsidiaries dealing specifically with minority enterprise in the United States, and with the development of a few mutual funds that invest only in "socially responsible" projects. There might even be some investment interest from the developed world as well, accepting, of course, that there are risks attached to such investment.

Such a step would be only symbolic to start with. A lot of critics would remain convinced that the whole thing was a farce, but looking at the realities of the situation, it is the one major step that the committed multinationals could take that would symbolize their continued interest in the Third World. Not all of them would want to do so, but for those who accept that they will remain in this area, this is a step they should take as soon as possible.

Advice to New Investors

A number of firms are planning their first investment in the Third World. Their concern is not just with economic nationalism but with how they can do business there at all. It is difficult to give comprehensive recommendations because the crucial factors (investment incentives, supplies of trained labor, general industrial infrastructure) vary from country to country. However, there are some general conclusions, warnings, and advice that can be given.

The first point is to commit enough resources and personnel

in the early stages so that problems can be resolved quickly and intelligently. This involves, for instance, looking at the new investment so as to go beyond the conventional rate-of-return calculations and to understand the specific political and cultural problems the new environment may have. This may seem an unnecessary warning, but even in Sicily a number of American multinationals have managed to get themselves into awkward situations: Raytheon tried closing its plant during a local election campaign, only to have it occupied by the local inhabitants, with the Italian government scaring off potential buyers. If the less developed parts of Italy can pose problems, no one should underestimate the dangers in other parts of the world. Massey–Ferguson reorganized its complete management system to handle overseas plants in their "nursery" stage, and now around 15 percent of its corporate earnings come from the Third World, against the more usual 2–3 percent of other multinationals.[10] Similarly, Philips has set up a pilot plant in Utrecht, where simplified manufacturing techniques can be tried out and potential managers from the Third World can be trained.

The second point is to ensure that corporate headquarters is aware, from the start, of political and cultural factors that may at some stage lead to difficulties. Different cultures place different interpretations on contracts (the Japanese, according to Herman Kahn, tend to assume that a contract becomes renegotiable as soon as there is a change in the conditions under which it was formulated). In some societies layoffs or redundancies are virtually unheard of; this was where Raytheon got into trouble in Sicily. An Italian firm discovered the hard way how much emphasis the Orient puts on "face": when one of their Japanese managers was harshly rebuked by his superior, he threw himself under a train! Awareness of these factors may also entail accepting that conflicts with governments or work forces will in places tend to be extreme and violent; plants may be seized, managers roughed up or locked in their offices; in Equatorial Guinea one West German pump manufacturer's local manager's wife was kidnapped by the country's president until the company paid a ransom of $1,600,000, which was the sum in dispute between government and company. Also, certain kinds of businesses are impossible in some cultures; the meat-packing firm Armour tried getting around the "sacred cow" barrier by going into Goa, which has a Roman Catholic majority, but to no avail. The extremist Hindu Jana Sangh Party learned of the project, called for an investigation, and Armour quietly dropped its plans.

Firms may have to get used to dealing with hostile, unwieldy bureaucracies that have life-and-death powers over particular investments. To firms used to maligning government bureaucracies in the United States or Europe, the first meeting with some of the Third World varieties can be daunting, since they are often vastly oversized—a cumbersome method of reducing unemployment (particularly among university graduates). One of the problems Bechtel faced in its abortive bid in India was that the various government bureaucracies were at cross-purposes, often unaware of decisions taken elsewhere in the system. As a result, the consortium Bechtel headed never knew whose word to accept. The United States oil company Tenneco had a similar experience in 1968 when it put forward proposals to drill off shore in India's Gulf of Cambay. This time the decision got bogged down at cabinet level for over eight months, and even after twenty-two visits to India by company officials no decision was reached.[11]

Bureaucratic delays are often prolonged because neither bureaucrats nor the Third World politicians have adequate personal commercial experience.[12] In large parts of the world, under names like "dash" or *"mordida"* (the bite), bribery is the rule. This is understandable, given low levels of wages; it is not of course unknown in more developed economies and need not be inefficient, but it does pose some specific problems for multinationals. A flat and righteous decision never to bribe may make it impossible to do business in some countries. In Mexico one official had a trick of letting his subordinates give verbal go-aheads for projects, which once under way would suddenly grind to a halt when the official denied having given his authorization. Without a "payoff" for a permit, the companies' investments would be wasted. Much of this bribery is mere trifling routine to speed or slow a legal process (e.g. payments to immigration officials to get up from their siesta), but the question becomes more complex when payments are expected in order to win contracts.

Most multinationals have to work on the assumption that they may get caught on any major deal and that the backlash will be unpleasant, to say the least. Nkrumah's fall in Ghana led to a series of inquiries into bribery allegations that named a number of embarrassed Western firms. On occasion, multinationals have even "shopped" each other. In India, the Aviation Minister claimed that Boeing sent him a photocopy of a letter from a Douglas representative offering an Indian airlines official $15,000 (later reports said $75,000—the letter being a bit illegible at this point) for every new DC-9 jet bought. All too often, a firm will put in a successful tender at a given price, only to be told by some official or minister to raise the sum, the difference going into his pocket. Companies run the risk of being caught in the middle of an internal political feud, with one side throwing "corruption" allegations at the other. Pan Am even found itself an integral part of the coup attempted in 1971 against King Hassan II of Morocco, which was bloodily repressed. The general who led the coup was worried about corruption in Morocco's government, which he felt could lead to a left-wing uprising. On a trip to the United States, he discovered that Pan Am was being "milked" on behalf of the royal family for licenses to build a chain of hotels there. He came back furious, and when no serious action was taken against the guilty ministers, he launched his ill-fated coup. But the problem faced by multinationals is that if they accept that business in certain parts of the world is impossible without some form of side payment, how do they check that their local representative is not double-crossing them? With bribery no receipts are given, and stories abound that local businessmen are paid by company headquarters for nonexistent bribes. Multinationals are too exposed to risk major bribery attempts, but there will be occasions when normal business cannot be continued without a nefarious deal. Companies should draw up a policy to deal with such eventualities, but they should also take advice from local partners, etc. before deciding on too rigid a strategy.

In addition to the psychological shock caused by blatant corruption, multinational managers are often troubled by the low productivity found in much of the Third World. They find it hard to get used to working with a telephone system that barely exists, a labor force new to industry and therefore erratic, or untried suppliers producing components of very unreliable quality. A manager from Fiat once told me that one of his company's greatest competitive advantages over the American, British, and German competition in the Third World was the fact that an Italian manager has been brought up in an environment much closer to those found in Africa or Asia. In the past, very few firms have discovered the method of extracting the full advantages from the cheap but low-producing labor of the Third World. The general feeling seems to be that it is virtually impossible to raise productivity in such plants to the average United States or even European standard. One company even sent foremen from its United States plants to man a production line in Latin America and was still unable to reach 65 percent of United States productivity levels.[13]

Given these problems, a certain degree of caution is required. It may be necessary to adapt models, designs, production layouts, and methods to the quality and experience of the suppliers and labor force. If the firm becomes involved in a market in the accepted way, first through importing, then by the assembly of imported "knocked-down" components, there should be no serious problems. In the simple assembly period, the company will be gaining experience in ways of getting the best out of the labor force. Then, as higher proportions of locally made components are required, the search for the efficient or ready-to-learn supplier can begin. The problems are really unmanageable for a "first-time" multinational only if it is required by strict protectionist policies to move into domestic manufacture right from the start. Then the newcomer could find itself in real trouble.[14]

These newcomers should also realize that they must cope with political as well as commercial risks. Adaptability is vital, when one third of the world's political leaders change every year. It is remarkable nevertheless how little constitutional change and even *coups d'état* have affected attitudes toward private investment.

The multinational company would be ill advised to rely on the judgment of local managers or partners. As Benjamin Weiner of the political analysts' Probe International put it: "If you were the managing director of a British company and you wanted to know the chances of protectionist legislation in the United States, or Nixon's chances in the '72 election, would you ask the plant manager of your subsidiary in Tuscaloosa, Alabama?" [15] The larger the venture, the deeper this political analysis should be. The oil companies now have sections that are almost replicas of the State Departments or Foreign Affairs Ministries in governments. Du Pont at one stage was experimenting with a model that analyzed the fifteen or twenty key interest groups in each country and then assessed the relative power and influence each would have over the others in policy areas that affected private investment. Moreover, companies do act on the basis of such analyses, even if they are not as elaborate as the Du Pont experiment. Thus, Dow Chemical and Union Carbide followed different investment policies in Latin America in the late 1960's because Dow felt that Latin American integration would be a long-term process at best and accordingly erected small protected plants in each country, while Union Carbide built large-capacity plants that would supply external markets until they could be switched to supply the future integrated markets its advisers predicted.

Every firm should occasionally rethink its traditional strategies for bargaining with Third World governments and partners. It is very easy to be "ethnocentric" (i.e. to think in American or European terms), and tactics that suit negotiations in the developed economies may be totally unsuited to the Third World. An American company can get away with a major attack on the activities of United States government agencies, but it is a moot point if the same company, as a foreigner, can afford to have public disputes with agencies in, say, Latin America.

Finally, companies should be aware that, whatever the political complexion of a government, certain areas or cities may

become unsuitable for business. In Calcutta a history of tension
between the city and the central government of India has led
to a total breakdown of law and order. Firms with factories
there have been powerless as Marxist trade-union leaders have
responded to the pressures that stem from the apparently unsolvable social tensions in the Bengal region. Even state enterprises have been plagued with strikes, violence, occupation;
and private firms have started writing off their investments.
The Canadian firm Bata closed down its plant employing twelve
thousand workers because the situation had deteriorated so
badly. Fiat has encountered the same problem in Argentina,
where its plant in Córdoba has put the company in the middle
of the struggle between a revolutionary company union and the
military regime in Buenos Aires. In response to the company's
dismissal of seven labor delegates, 2,500 workers barricaded
themselves in the plant, held executives as hostages, and
threatened to burn down the plant unless the dismissed men
were reinstated. Ironically, Fiat had encouraged the formation
of the company union as an alternative to the local Perónist
union of auto workers; the company union turned out to be far
more revolutionary (a typical slogan was: "No coups, no elections—revolution!"). In mid-1971 Fiat was trying to transfer
its operations to the calmer environment of Buenos Aires.

Open conflict is fermenting in other parts of the world, like
the Caribbean, where Black Power movements have radicalized
the whole industrial-relations structure. Moreover, there are
grounds for thinking that these situations will become more
common, since the uncontrolled growth of Third World cities
and the subsequent high unemployment rates provide breeding
grounds for extreme political movements. Where Calcutta has
broken down under the strain, tomorrow's cities will do the
same. Even in more developed economies like Italy's, similar
forces are at work. The Italian boom has rested heavily on the
immigration of rural workers from the depressed South of Italy
into the teeming cities of the North, such as Milan, Turin, and
Bologna. Until the mid-1960's Fiat and Pirelli encouraged this
process, but as the new workers discovered that these cities
could not provide the basic social provisions, like cheap hous-

ing, they became more and more radical, until from 1969 Fiat and Pirelli were hit by waves of strikes and militant demands from the labor unions. In 1970 Fiat lost 34 million man-hours, and where it was once a company well placed to dominate the European auto market, it is now struggling to maintain its market share and even to remain profitable. In contrast, the electronics firm Olivetti is based in Ivrea, a small company-dominated town to the north of Turin. The company has long followed a paternalistic policy toward the town and its workers, and this has paid off with an almost unblemished strike record compared to their rivals' in the big cities. Housing projects and experiments in job enrichment are expensive, but within the Italian environment the policy has paid off handsomely. It is too early to generalize from this example, since few firms have consciously experimented with their plant location in such situations, but the Italian experience would suggest that firms should be wary of locations in large cities that experience a rapid influx of migrants from the countryside. The Olivetti approach may prove more rewarding for all concerned.

Lonrho—The Rewards from the African Vacuum

When independence came to Africa in the 1960's, most of the old colonial companies lost their nerve, deciding at best merely to maintain their investments at pre-independence levels or, at worst, to get out of the continent at all costs. The vacuum thus created was filled by a company called Lonrho, which showed that it is possible not only to do business with African governments but to make very respectable profits at the same time. The company achieved this success despite being originally based in both South Africa and Rhodesia at a time when this position should have wrecked its chances of dealing with black African governments—and yet it is with these very governments that it has been most successful.

In 1960 this British-owned company was small and unremarkable, concentrating on mining finance and cattle ranching in Rhodesia. At this point a British entrepreneur called "Tiny"

Rowland came on the scene, and it was his practical knowledge of black Africa that inspired the company's drive into Zambia, Malawi, Tanzania, and Kenya, and into new industries like auto distribution (by the late 1960's it claimed to be the largest auto distributor in Africa), textiles, trading, sugar, and hotels. As a result of this attempt to come to terms with the aspirations of the new African leaders, profits climbed spectacularly from a mere £158,000 ($440,000) in 1961 to £16 million ($39 million) in 1970.

Part of this spectacular growth was encouraged by the conglomerate strategy of frequent acquisitions, the critical factor being that it was operating in Africa and not the United States. Thus, the company's management paid close attention to its share value, which until 1968 performed spectacularly enough for them to acquire old colonial companies like Ashanti Goldfields Corporation in Ghana and John Holt & Co., which is strong in Nigeria. Unlike the American conglomerates, which have had a rough time in recent years, these acquisitions have not had difficulty staying profitable. They could be bought fairly cheaply, since the old owners were pessimistic in view of potential political dangers in post-independence Africa. Lonrho has not yet fallen into the trap of paying too high a price for its acquisitions on the grounds that it can, as a conglomerate, combine its subsidiaries so well that they perform better than they would individually. Lonrho owes its success to the fact that in Africa today, with the necessary political courage, it is possible to buy cheaply into new industries and firms in the absence of competitors.

The company has managed to clinch deals that satisfy the local regimes and has always worked hard at maintaining close relations with important political leaders. Above all, the company believes in the personal touch, and "Tiny" Rowland flies about Africa in a Mystère executive jet from one deal to another. When the company was busy acquiring Ashanti Goldfields, there was some doubt as to the Ghanaian government's response, so Rowland flew in to sort things out. The same personal approach has been applied to the Sudan, the Ivory Coast, and Zambia.

The company has worked hard to get along with influential African figures who might add to its bargaining power. It signed up as a director M. Gill Olympio, the son of the late president of Togo, also the former International Monetary Fund representative in West Africa. He was a vital link in a £14 million ($34 million) deal with the Ivory Coast government for a plantation-to-market sugar complex, for which Lonrho would call upon its experience with the industry in Swaziland, Mauritius, and Malawi. Olympio's importance extends even further, since his contacts with the former French colonies like the Ivory Coast give Lonrho the chance to break away from its dependence on the English-language African countries. An attempt to sign up a similarly influential figure, Zambia's Andrew Sardanis, proved to be short-lived. Once President Kaunda's closest adviser during his nationalization programs, Sardanis became for four months in 1971 joint managing director of a special Lonrho subsidiary set up to bring together black African activities. Well respected, he was an important figure in Lonrho's attempt to get involved with diamond marketing in Sierra Leone, but he left the company, apparently because he wanted to rationalize each industry on a continental scale and became disillusioned with the company's failure to plan in this direction.

Although these tactics are undoubtedly suitable for the highly personalized politics of Africa, they can backfire with a vengeance, as the company has also discovered. The diamond-marketing deal with Sierra Leone went sour when the company's further plans for the production of textiles from locally produced yarns were judged heavily overoptimistic in the light of three other investigations of the proposal that suggested that the physical climate made it unrealistic. Sierra Leone felt that the company could not be trusted.

The major setback, however, came in the Congo (Kinshasa). In 1968 Lonrho felt that it would be worthwhile investigating prospects there, especially as Union Minière was in disgrace and there a chance of securing the management contract for the state-controlled mining operations. They therefore made a deal with one of the country's most dominant Belgian entrepreneurs, Martin Thèves, whose success since 1959 rested heavily on his close contacts with the leading Congolese politicians. Lonrho quietly bought control of Cominière, which Thèves was willing to sell, and then went after the management contract of the Congolese mines. It failed in this, but to aid its attempt it embarked on a survey of possible routes for a Congolese railway, which was dear to President Mobutu's heart. In February 1970 it delivered the report and then sat back to see if it would get the contract to build the railway—a deal worth some $300 million. Unfortunately, the company became overconfident, giving an interview in the *Financial Times* that suggested that it felt it was only a matter of time. The Congolese government was affronted, and then the *Times of Zambia,* owned but not editorially controlled by Lonrho, insulted Mobutu. This was disastrous. The government announced that Lonrho would have nothing more to do with the rail project and that it would be barred from any further projects. Moreover, the Congolese advised the rest of Africa to look at their links with the company, stressing its connection with Rhodesia. This was not strictly fair, since the company had refused to open its pipeline into Rhodesia in compliance with UN sanctions and had formally insisted on the resignation of directors on the board of its Rhodesian subsidiary. But the damage was done. Any hope of further business from the Congo was gone. The company's future is difficult to predict. There are those who were not unhappy in 1971 to see that some of Lonrho's local managers in South Africa were charged with fraud. It has made some powerful enemies among the traditional mining companies in Africa through its attempts to break into diamond marketing (the monopoly of Harry Oppenheimer's De Beers), its Congolese activities, and its movement into platinum mining, which will pay dividends provided platinum is an essential ingredient in devices for cleaning up auto-engine exhaust. The company later announced the acquisition of Wankel, the developer of the rotary engine, which could still replace the conventional auto engine. There seemed to be some dissension among Lonrho's financial advisers over this, and a couple of directors in Britain resigned. Wankel would appear to be a questionable acquisition, since there is still considerable question as to whether the Wankel will ever be more than a minor factor with General Motors.

On the other hand, the company is still capable of managing new deals that look almost foolproof. Lonrho was one of the chief beneficiaries of the 1971 successful countercoup in the Sudan, when President Gafaar al-Nimeiry fought off a pro-Communist coup and successfully re-established himself with the help of countries like Egypt, Libya, and Britain. Before the coup and countercoup took place, "Tiny" Rowland had been building on his contacts with Khalil Osman, one of Sudan's leading entrepreneurs and economic adviser to the Nimeiry regime. In June 1971 a Lonrho team went to the Sudan to negotiate a $24 million trade deal with British government help. The coup came in July, and the British government seems to have played a part in delivering two of the new leaders into the hands of the Libyans, who handed them over to Nimeiry, on his reinstatement, for execution. In September the Sudanese government appointed Lonrho as sole agents for the state purchase of capital and semi-capital goods from the United Kingdom. Hostile reports suggest that Lonrho may share just under $2.5 million from this deal with its Sudanese collaborators. As long as it can continue to make deals like this, the company will not be unduly worried.

The lesson from Lonrho's experience is that a company that really works hard at keeping close contact with governments in the Third World can make a lot of money. In many ways the "Tiny" Rowland approach is similar to that of Wendell Phillips, who has broken into the oil industry after starting his career as an archaeologist. He struck up friendships with local sheiks, who then offered him oil concessions, which he could in turn sell off to the majors for a percentage of the royalties. But Phillips, too, has had his troubles. In 1971 his offshore concessions in Oman were canceled, despite a twenty-year friendship with Oman's rulers, and he was unable for some time to get a visa to return to argue his case. But despite these setbacks he was able to "parlay friendships" with the Aga Khan,

Calouste S. Gulbenkian (the original "Mr. Five Percent" of the oil industry), and a number of local rulers into a fortune of over $10 million.

Lonrho itself does not seem in any danger of running out of potential customers. Its breakthrough into French-speaking Africa through the Ivory Coast could be a vast source of revenue. Likewise, its Sudanese deal would suggest that it is extending its interests into the Arab world. During the Wankel negotiations the company claims it was offered a loan from Kuwait, and the general impression is that the company feels it should be able to tap the funds of the oil-producing countries, which are currently in something of a financial vacuum. Provided the Mystère jet does not crash with the two or three key company wheeler-dealers (and even insiders admit that this could wreck their growth prospects), there is no reason why the Lonrho pattern of profitable deals should not continue, if it does not saddle itself with too many dubious European ventures, which might make it as vulnerable as any conventional conglomerate.[16]

International Basic Economy Corporation— Company with a Conscience?

The wheeling-dealing but quite secretive Lonrho makes a fascinating contrast with IBEC (International Basic Economy Corporation), the well-publicized creation of Nelson Rockefeller's, which specifically tries to follow the double goal of not simply making profits but of making them by identifying and filling the basic needs of the Third World. To its defenders it is a company with a conscience; to its detractors it is a pathetic attempt by the Rockefellers to make recompense for their predatory past.

An early effort to demonstrate the social responsibility of private enterprise, IBEC was created in 1947 to show that a United States firm could help upgrade the Third World's basic economies by lowering food prices, building reliable housing, mobilizing savings, and fostering industrialization, while still being profitable enough to encourage private investors. Originally it concentrated on Venezuela and Brazil, with ventures in farming, fishing, food wholesaling, milk production, and agricultural technical services. These early years were disappointing and the company lost money. It was a question partly of spreading its resources too thinly and partly of tackling the wrong sectors first. Thus, it found that its food-wholesaling operations had no effect on the ultimate consumers, since the retailers did not pass on any savings. So IBEC found itself moving into food retailing and developed the high-volume, low-price marketing strategy of supermarkets in economies in which the high-cost "Ma and Pa" store was still dominant. These were successful in triggering competition, and it is an indicator of the company's sometimes muddled objectives that company spokesmen stress how quickly national competition appeared against it and how 98 percent of food sales in Venezuela are still in national hands. A predominantly profit-oriented company would want to smash the competition instead of boasting about how well the local competition has done.

From around 1956, IBEC built on successful activities, like supermarkets, hybrid seeds, and milk, and also branched out into new fields. While the supermarket chains were spread into Puerto Rico, Peru, Italy, and Argentina, the company was also infiltrating other areas—such as the establishment of mutual funds or "unit trusts" in countries like Brazil and Spain, where local capital markets had been unable to attract the large reservoirs of hidden savings. And here the Rockefeller links with banking (Chase Manhattan) were very useful. IBEC also moved into housing and has been active in Puerto Rico, Iraq, Iran, Chile, Peru, and Mexico, where it has provided homes that are cheap by the standards of the developed economies but that still appeal mainly to the middle- and upper-income groups in the Third World. Finally, among one or two acquisitions it made in the United States to provide itself with a stronger dollar-earning base has been the poultry-breeding company of Arbor Acres, which has facilitated an even deeper involvement with the Third World's agricultural sector.

But has it been successful? If measured in terms of profits, by Lonrho standards it has been pretty sluggish. The early losses were entirely excusable, since the company was genuinely pioneering and it is probable that other companies with an equally ambitious program would also have come unstuck. However, its track record in the 1960's has not been particularly good. From a net income of $3.7 million in 1961 (£1.3 million) it moved only to $4.2 million in 1968 (£1.8 million) but then picked up to $8.1 million (£3.4 million) in 1970. This is not an impressive record, and during the 1960's IBEC was decidedly slow in weeding out its loss-making activities, such as a Peruvian sugar operation.

Since 1965 it has followed more profit-oriented policies and has become more ruthless. What is noticeable is that during its sluggish era it found itself diversifying back into the United States for security, thus diluting its stated policy; and its expansion into Spain and Italy, although commercially sound, was a move into two economies that are to all intents and purposes developed. Although IBEC has always encouraged the development of local partners, non-Americans have still not arrived at the top of the corporate structure. In 1971 it had one non-American Harvard Business School graduate as a vice-director, with a number of other non-Americans one level lower. It also points to the fact that at its 1970 annual meeting of Latin American public-relations officials, all the proceedings were in Spanish, despite the fact that many of the participants were American.

IBEC asks to be judged on its ideals, and even if the record is not as impressive as it might have been, there has been a genuine effort to innovate. The development of the supermarket concept in Latin America, where existing stores like Sears Roebuck were comparatively luxurious, was a move of some importance for a continent wracked by inflation. The experiments with mutual funds have been not only innovative but useful attempts to solve a major problem of the Third World—the transference of savings from under mattresses and Swiss bank accounts into productive investment. It may well be that there are socialist solutions to this state of affairs, but in the meantime the only competition has come from people like Bernie Cornfeld and his IOS (Investors Overseas Services), whose notorious activities in Brazil merely took a lot of savings and put them into Wall Street—an area not noted for its contribution to the development of the Third World. IBEC was active early in housing and hybrid corns, but its investments have primarily been for the benefit of the upper- and upper-middle-income groups. Its impact, for instance, on the retailing experience of the mass of Latin Americans is restricted to the way in which the supermarket concept affects the workings of local shops and markets. Its housing programs can do nothing for slum dwellers or peasants who do not have the necessary capital to purchase a desirable home.

Lonrho, although more profitable, has been less innovative and certainly less idealistic. Few development economists would argue that being the largest distributor of autos to Africa constitutes a vital contribution to the everyday life of the continent. However, one must not downgrade Lonrho's activities. Its sheer exuberance makes it a company often willing to compete against established interests and, in mining in the Congo and sugar in the Ivory Coast, it has taken on some powerful concerns. Whatever their motives, blackleg companies are always useful, though in the non-competitive economies of Africa today it may well be that Lonrho gets away with deals and practices that governments in later years will want to improve on.

To summarize these two different approaches to the Third World: it could be said that IBEC could do with some of Lonrho's undoubted entrepreneurial drive, while Lonrho could well add social conscience to its undoubted entrepreneurial talents. In the long run, Lonrho's survival and growth in Africa could depend on such a development.[17]

Notes

1. Kapoor, "A Consortium That Never Was"; Kapoor, *International Business Negotiations.*
2. Sperling, *The Human Dimension of Technical Assistance,* is a very readable account that should be read by anyone employing large work forces in the Third World. Sirota and Greenwood, "Understand Your Overseas Workforce," will also intrigue personnel specialists.

3. Tomlinson, *A Model of the Joint Venture Process in International Business*. See also Friedmann and Beguin, *Joint International Business Ventures in Developing Countries*.

4. De Cubas, "It Pays to Speak Out"; Shearer, "Industrial Relations of American Corporations Abroad"; Tsurumi, "Myths That Mislead."

5. Meeker, "Fade-out Joint Venture."

6. Franko, "Joint Venture Divorce."

7. Gabriel, *The International Transfer of Corporate Skills;* Rolfe, *The International Corporation*; Streeten, "The Contribution of Private Overseas Investment."

8. Collado, "Economic Development through Private Enterprise," refers to Jersey; Chandler, "The Myth of Oil Power," to Shell.

9. UN: Ecosoc, *Panel on Foreign Investment in Developing Countries*.

10. Baranson, *Automotive Industries in Developing Countries*; Turner, *Invisible Empires*.

11. Kapoor, "A Consortium That Never Was."

12. Kapoor, "International Business–Government Negotiations in Developing Countries."

13. *Business International, Organizing for International Production*.

14. Baranson, *Manufacturing Problems in India*; and *Automotive Industries in Developing Countries,* are the two leading books dealing with these problems.

15. *Financial Times,* July 14, 1971.

16. There is no book on Lonrho, so I've relied heavily on press reports and company statements.

17. Broehl, "Venture in Venezuela"; "The Company with a Cause"; Meads, "The Task Force at Work"; Rockefeller, "Turn Public Problems to Private Account."

6 : : *Multinationals and Development Needs*

FIRMS with the strongest defense against critics are those that are positively trying to help solve the real development needs of the Third World, instead of blindly selling products that satisfy only the desires of rich Europeans and Americans. For many multinationals this would mean revolutionizing their thinking, and it is clear that only a few companies are taking the challenge seriously.

In the early days of development planning, theory stressed the need for rapid industrialization. This was felt to be the main lesson of the early industrial revolutions and of the Soviet Union's rapid progress after the revolution. But slowly the emphasis of development thinking has changed. Industrialization can only scratch at the surface of the problems of countries that are still predominantly rural and even outside the money economy. There are also problems with the population explosion, rapid urbanization, and heavy unemployment, which are on a scale rarely experienced in previous industrial revolutions. Today the planners are willing to look at new models, like those of Cuba, Tanzania, and China, which stress the development of the rural sector even at the expense of conventional industrial projects. The problem is more often seen as the need to create workable, decent societies in lands that will still be poor, by comparable standards of material wealth, for the foreseeable future.[1]

Population and the "DDT Generation"

According to the growth rates of the Third World, the UN's "development decades" have been successful. There is clear evidence that the total economy of the average Third World

country has been growing considerably faster than the older industrialized nations did in the early days of their industrial revolutions or at any subsequent point. Thus from 1950 to 1968, the
total product of the Latin American continent grew by 5 percent
per annum. In the pre-1914 era only the United States came
close to this, with 4.2 percent per annum in 1870–1913, with
countries like Britain (2.2 percent), France (1.6 percent), and
Germany (2.9 percent) much lower down. Even from 1950–8
the average growth of the British, French, West German, Italian,
American, Belgian, and Swedish economies was 4.6 percent, still
below the Latin American average.

However, when the total growth of these economies is translated into growth per head of population, the situation is tragi-
cally reversed and the undoubtedly impressive achievements of
Third World economic planners (even allowing some statistical
exuberance) are cruelly undone. Population increase in Latin
America means that from 1950–68 per-capita growth was reduced to 2 percent per annum, which was below the pre-1914
rates of the United States (2.2 percent) and Sweden (2.2 percent), and only just above countries like Belgium (1.7 percent)
and Germany (1.7 percent). The comparison with the per-capita
growth rates of these industrialized countries today is even more
tragic. The most sluggish growth of a major economy in 1950–68
was in Britain, whose 2.3 percent was still above Latin America's, while the average rate for the major industrialized countries
mentioned in the last paragraph was 3.7 percent, almost double
the Latin American rate. Progress is shown to be almost illusory.
Obviously, there are economies growing faster than Latin America's, but countries like Iran, Taiwan, Israel, South Korea, etc.,
are so small as to be unrepresentative. And even they are faced
with the same population problems found elsewhere. By the end
of the 1970's, as the Third World's proportion of the world's
population increases from 65 to 71 percent, the gap between the
GNP per capita of the developed countries and that of the Third
World should rise from $2,517 to $3,641.[2]

Demography is a cruel science. As the World Bank's Robert
McNamara has stated, even if each couple in the world accepted

birth control and limited its offspring to two children, the present world population of 3.6 billion would still rise to 14 billion in seventy years' time. It is the survivors of the much smaller generations of 1910, 1920, and 1930 who are dying off, to be replaced by the offspring of the very much larger population of the 1950's and the subsequent mushrooming decades. Unfortunately, the bulk of governments in the Third World are still hostile or indifferent to birth control, often seeing it as an imperialist plot to restrict their numbers and thus their power, not recognizing that power really comes from wealth per head, not sheer numbers. Even where governments are favorable, the results are insignificant. In India the number of prevented births has risen from 32,000 in 1961 to 1.5 million in 1968–9. However, the Indian population still produces 12 million new mouths to feed each year.

Part of the problem is that cultures that were adapted to extremely high death rates have failed to adjust to the revolution in death control. Soap, detergents, insecticides, vaccines, and antibiotics were all introduced almost contemporaneously. A typical result occurred in Ceylon, where the first systematic spraying against the malaria mosquito dropped the mortality rate from twenty deaths per thousand people to fourteen per thousand in a single year (1947). Five years later the death figure was down to twelve, a drop in mortality that England took nearly a century to achieve during its early development. It is no wonder that this generation has been called the "DDT generation." [3]

The slow success in reducing the birth rate is only partly due to lack of technologies. The Indian experience shows that, whatever the device, Indians are more likely to stop using it than people in more developed economies. Although this is related to lower motivational drive to control family size, much of the problem is due to inadequate numbers of trained medical staff or technicians. The "coil," or intrauterine device, has been resisted because there was no staff to follow up the initial treatment and explain the side effects that sometimes appeared. As a result, stories of pain or heavy bleeding spread rapidly, leading to large-scale rejection of the device. Similarly, a full-scale sterilization program to reduce the Indian birth rate by 50 percent over five years would need 10,000 operations a day, seven days a week—and India just does not have the personnel.

The search is for simpler, more acceptable technologies. Long-acting injections, sustained-release substances, copper intra-uterine devices, and pill-a-month contraceptives are all in the clinical stages from various sources, but they are only part of the solution. Distribution into vast agricultural populations is such a problem that only governments can really solve it. The provision of the necessary number of doctors (in the poorer countries, one doctor per 13,000 inhabitants was the average for the early 1960's, against one per 885 people in the richer ones), and above all the provision of enough women doctors is a problem for governments, not for firms. The necessary revolution in cultural thinking on family size is something that will come only with time, economic growth, urbanization, and constant propaganda. Again, firms cannot contribute to solving these aspects of the problem.

The firms have a major opportunity to develop the necessary technologies, but here the multinationals' record is bad, though explicable. All the drug companies are being squeezed badly by the various watchdog committees, like the U.S. Food and Drug Administration, Britain's Committee for the Safety of Drugs, or the Australian Drug Evaluation Committee, all part of the general drift toward consumer protection. At the moment it may take a couple of years for a new contraceptive to go through the companies' biological and chemical laboratories, then another eight years of stringent clinical tests before the product is allowed to be sold openly. The total cost of developing a new product up to that stage may be around $12 million, and the drug firms are not always prepared to take this sort of risk. To some extent, these tough requirements explain why the firms are putting far fewer new drugs on the market than they did at the beginning of the 1960's, and observers claim that there is a declining interest in contraceptives on the part of the industry (existing brands excepted).

This antisocial trend merely illustrates a fact about contemporary capitalism. The profit-motivated firm is capable of handling only projects that will produce returns in a reasonably short period of time or that produce returns above a certain level. If returns are going to be low or long delayed, as in this case, companies cannot really operate as profit-making institutions and will be forced into other, possibly less socially desirable, fields. It means that non-profit-making bodies are doing much of the research. Bodies like the Ford Foundation, the International Planned Parenthood Federation, or India's Central Drug Research Institute are all active in trying to help those who might produce the necessary breakthroughs or in actually doing the necessary research and testing themselves. Of course, there are drug companies involved in these areas, but on the whole the industry is noted for its lack of interest. A glance through the 1970 annual reports of the majority of leading pharmaceutical companies turned up only Glaxo Labs Ltd. (India) and Wyeth Labs (part of American Home Products) who specifically claim to be producing oral contraceptives for and in Third World countries. Most of the rest find the American and European markets simpler to reach and more profitable, though this is not to deny that there are other drug firms active in the health field in the Third World. However, even here it is noticeable that few of them gear their research toward specific Third World diseases, though some like Parke-Davis (owned by Warner Lambert, Inc.) and Pfizer have extensive Third World production facilities.[4]

Agriculture and Food

Compared to an apparently uncontrollable population increase, the problems of agriculture at least look manageable; a change from the thinking of the early 1960's, when most experts could foresee only world famine. The Green Revolution has alleviated the general pessimism, but much remains to be done in order to achieve a global standard for adequate daily diet from birth. For one thing, productivity gains in the agricultural sector must outstrip population growth if the whole world is to be properly fed. This is not a simple problem of quantities but of quality. In some parts of the world traditional foods are nutritionally deficient, as with cassavas, widely found in West Africa. Although they provide sufficient nutriment for the immediate expenditure of energy, they are lacking in the crucial proteins essential for the body's long-term building activities. In fact, any simple diet will almost certainly lack crucial proteins or vitamins, and the job of agronomists and nutrition experts is to find ways of introducing these into the Third World's diet in a cheap and easily consumable form. Protein malnutrition is particularly crucial in a child's most vulnerable period, from six months to three years old, when the brain is being formed. Governments are starting to give child nutrition priority in their development plans, but the Indian government points out that even if there is a 3 percent annual rise in per capita real income it would be the year 2000 before just one third of Indian families are able to afford a minimally adequate diet, and even then there are likely to be iron and vitamin A deficiencies.

The lesson of the Green Revolution so far has been that private enterprise has not been crucial. The key events were the development of the "miracle" wheat and rice strains at the International Maize and Wheat Improvement Center in Mexico (for which Dr. Norman Borlaug received a Nobel Prize) and the International Rice Research Institute in the Philippines. Major support came from the Ford and Rockefeller Foundations; the agricultural multinationals were not much in evidence. A number of governments and aid agencies quickly saw the importance of these new high-yielding varieties and, since the mid-1960's, areas like Asia have actually increased their per capita production of food, and population increases and the increasing profitability of agriculture may make the whole process self-sustaining. However, we can now see barriers to the success of the Green Revolution, and they suggest that foreign investors may well have a role to play. The agricultural revolution cannot be reduced just to producing new, high-yielding seeds or improved animal strains. If it were, the existing international and state research stations could probably handle the whole business. But governments are unable to produce the necessary structural alterations in the rural sector, though land reform in Latin America may help the spread of new techniques, and the provision of new, cheap forms of credit may well be an essential prerequisite. The governments clearly can also play a role in seeing that demand for agricultural produce is maintained—after all, however badly people may need food, they will do without as long as their incomes remain static or decline. But there are also physical and organizational limitations to the Green Revolution that provide good potential markets for entrepreneurs, who are able to move into the areas left by government planners.

First, the characteristics of new seeds need to be adapted more closely to local tastes and conditions. Every country has its own particular problems—Iranians like to steam their rice and therefore need a long-grained variety—and taste and texture preferences will often vary within countries. Taking into account a variety of soils, climates, and even pests, the few central research stations that exist will be hard pressed to produce an optimal product for every part of the Third World. Local research stations obviously will be needed, but it will depend on their efficiency in individual countries as to whether private firms can find niches. Again, these yield breakthroughs need extending to other crops. In various parts of the world, wheat and rice are less important than millet and sorghum, or tropical roots and tubers, which in their turn need improvement. (Even hens and cows have to be specially bred to flourish under different local conditions.) The Green Revolution has so far been a revolution in crop yields. It has not started to touch the quality of the nutrition provided by these plants. And this opens up a new opportunity.

Crude inputs like improved seeds are not sufficient. The farmers can throw away one advantage of such seeds by failing to use improved cultivation methods. Many of these new strains will grow with their increased yields only if they are carefully irrigated and fertilized. Not only does this mean farmers have to change their habits (often a point of very major resistance) but it also means that a good proportion of the higher returns from the new yields are going into small pumps, fertilizers, pesticides, tools like hoes and tractors. Over the whole Third World agricultural sector this is already a sizable market, which can only grow.

The marketing and distribution problems are best illustrated by the Indian wheat stored in local schools in the absence of prepared warehouses or small local depots. Producing is pointless if rats get to the grain before it can be transferred to human consumers. There are also needs for new crop- and waste-processing techniques and industries, although, given the importance of keeping the rural sector out of the towns, a drive for small processing plants in the countryside keeping more of the value added might have extremely good social returns.

The Green Revolution is probably a misnomer. All that has happened is that the seed technology of a couple of important crops has been revolutionized, but what we have yet to see is the extent to which the rest of the agricultural system will evolve. Agriculture is a system in which the failure of any link can prohibit productivity increases elsewhere, so that, given the food crisis, it is unfair to expect state planners to get all the links of this system right the first time. It may be that the state should take control of key parts of the system, like banking, but there is plenty of room for private entrepreneurs to move in. And where private entrepreneurs have a role, the multinationals have one as well.

It is impossible to gloss over the social consequences of the revolution. The evidence is that the rich farmers will become even richer, since they have first access to available credit. In parts of India there have already been disturbances as landless workers have fought landlords whom they felt were not giving them their proper share of the benefits of these improved profits. In particular, the more conservative, uneducated subsistence farmers will be the victims, and it will be a challenge to governments to find a way to harness the advantage of these developments without social disruption. One possible solution is to use communes or cooperatives whereby the worst capitalist excesses can be avoided. However, both approaches leave plenty of openings for the more enlightened suppliers.[5]

Agriculture—the
Multinationals' Contribution

Just as the various aid agencies, like the World Bank, have become more aware of the agricultural sector, so have the multinationals, even if some are wary about the political risks. Some are following a "low-profile" approach by investing in this sector through multilateral private agencies. Thus they invest in a body like ADELA, a private investment bank backed by shareholdings from banks and other multinationals, that concentrates on Latin America. This body does pioneering opportunity detection and feasibility studies in rural areas, thus helping to circumvent one of the complaints of aid donors that often they have the money to give but not enough "bankable" projects to invest in. A typical study might be one carried out by a subsidiary, ADELATEC, which looked at actual and potential supplies of fresh fruits and vegetables for counterseason exports to European markets. For other bodies, like the Jamaican Development Bank or the Paraguayan government, ADELA has looked at industries like edible oils, fruit and vegetable processing, meat and poultry packaging, etc. Another body, in which ADELA itself has a shareholding, is the Latin American Agribusiness Development Corporation, founded in 1970 to make modest-sized, high-impact investments in the food-supply systems of Latin America. It explains that this could be in warehouses, transport lines, or distribution agencies, depending on the extent to which such investments would reduce waste and simplify marketing. This body's founder members included the Bank of America, Borden Inc., Cargill Inc., Caterpillar Tractor, CPC International (once called Corn Products), Deere and Company, Dow Chemical, Gerber Products, Monsanto Company, Ralston Purina, and Standard Fruit and Steamship. This is a combination of banks, chemical, tractor, processing, and transportation companies—a good cross-section of the kinds of industry that stand to benefit from increased productivity in the Third World's agriculture. However, what is even more interesting is that these companies find it worth their

while to invest in such joint ventures rather than to go ahead
with their own independent investments. This is perhaps a cheap
way of exploring a relatively unknown business sector in the
Third World. If the corporation's investments are successful,
then some of these companies will invest in their own independently produced projects.

Not many firms are yet involved in developing new high-yield
seeds in the Third World, perhaps because they feel so much
work is done in non-profit research organizations. Anyway,
IBEC's Brazilian subsidiary has had some successes with new
strains of maize but is having problems getting it adopted in
other parts of the world because of the extremely tough import
precautions in most countries. This is understandable, for Brazil's coffee crop was decimated recently by a disease accidentally
brought into the country on the clothes of a visiting African
delegation. Then there is CPC International in Mexico, where
a subsidiary has been working with a state seed agency to develop a local sorghum seed with the yields and economics of
imported hybrids. They have been reasonably successful, producing a seed yielding 20 percent more than the imported variety, and they are starting commercial marketing. In the animal
field IBEC's poultry subsidiary has been improving the stocks
used in countries like Argentina, where alternative meat sources
are urgently needed if some of the domestic consumption of beef
is to be reduced to allow beef exports to expand. It is a pity that
W. R. Grace, once so important in Latin America, is withdrawing from the continent, since as probably the largest force
in animal insemination in the world, the combination of its
technical knowledge and local experience could still benefit the
continent a great deal.[6]

Fertilizers will be one of the chief products to benefit from
the Green Revolution. The UN's Food and Agricultural Organization (FAO) reckons that about 45 percent of the Third
World's expenditure on inputs will be devoted to them (say
$45 billion during the 1970's). This will doubtless make them
prime targets for the economic nationalists, since imports involve
a great deal of foreign exchange and fertilizer technology is well
established, so it should not be too difficult to get turnkey plants

built. On the other hand, it is the fertilizer firms that will be most in touch with the farmers on a day-to-day basis, and it has been pointed out that, just as they run private agricultural advisory services in the United States for their customers, they are probably best placed of all the industrialists to instigate similar services in the Third World, where they would be really needed. Indonesia around 1970 was experimenting with a scheme whereby the chemical companies helped distribute agricultural aids and provided such advisory services, though it apparently had its teething problems. On the whole, though, the fertilizer companies do not comment on their Third World involvement too much, which could suggest a lack of self-confidence. They contrast strongly with the tractor manufacturers, who are much more "visible." [7]

The pesticide subsidiaries of the major chemical multinationals are much more expansive, and their work is important since it has been calculated that the proper use of pesticides could add one third to all farm products within the next fifty years. In a sinister spin-off from military technology, Dow Chemical has investigated vegetation and insect control and, with Monsanto, is producing herbicides aimed at controlling weeds among irrigated rice. The German firm BASF is also in the plant-protection business and runs research farms in Spain and Africa. The field of pesticides requires very specific research; the companies should be safe as long as they are supplying pesticides that are produced according to each country's needs. The development economists see the need to adapt existing methods of pest control to small-scale methods of storage and control, but there is also the problem of being careful about the ecological consequences.

This is a particularly touchy subject, since many Third World countries depend, at least in part, on agricultural sales to the increasingly "purity"-conscious food markets of the developed world. Already there are examples of "ecological imperialism," as when Argentina's failure to master its foot-and-mouth disease led to threats by the British to refuse to deal with the produce of certain packing stations. Australian meat firms, which are heavily dependent on the American hamburger, have found themselves facing similar threats. The pressures on all food producers are growing every day, and some authorities in Washington predict the time when American farmers will be licensed to use certain fertilizers or pesticides. Already many food-store chains have lists of "approved" pesticides, as well as ones they will refuse to handle. This is forcing the major food-producing companies like H. J. Heinz to stock up on things like gas chromatographs and atomic absorption spectrophotomats to spot traces of pesticide residues like mercury. This is blatantly unfair to the Third World. Just as it is starting to welcome the use of pesticides and fertilizers, it is suddenly informed that some very cheap and effective ones like DDT may jeopardize its agricultural sales to established markets. It will be very difficult for anyone in the Third World to produce new pesticides that will not affect their exports since, without the active assistance of an experienced multinational, they are unlikely to know enough about the testing and approving mechanisms of countries like the United States to obtain a clean bill of health. As long as the developed markets impose tighter ecological conditions, the multinationals based in those countries will have a definite advantage.

The best-known manufacturing multinationals have concentrated on the tractor market, where, in the past, the American and European firms have tended to offer standard ranges of four-wheeled models. This has infuriated many development economists who, as well as being worried about the labor-saving aspects of tractors (see the section on unemployment), have accused the companies of selling very expensive machines to small farmers who have neither the know-how nor the money to repair them when they break down. The distinguished agronomist René Dumont has argued that much more attention should be paid to improving hoes and oxen plow methods. Even though the tractors sold may be small and cheap by Western standards, they are expensive by those of the Third World. In Iran in 1970 a locally assembled tractor cost around $3,500, while the average rural cooperative would have savings of only $7,000.

By not developing models specifically geared to Third World needs, the Western manufacturers left a gap in the market into which the Japanese in particular have moved. In large parts of Southeast Asia, a four-wheeled tractor or large harvester is badly suited to wet and hilly conditions. Firms like Honda have been very successful with two-wheeled, walk-behind machines that in price come much closer to competing with the running costs of the traditional ox and plow. Other non-commercial bodies, like the International Rice Research Institute, or even young volunteers at the Swaziland Agricultural College, have been developing "mechanized water buffaloes," or simple tractors costing under $750 at the most. But now the major multinationals are moving in.

While British Leyland Motors has developed a twenty-five-horsepower mini-tractor, for which it has a contract with India worth $56 million, Ford has probably attracted the most publicity. Around 1964 Ford saw this tractor gap in their product line and approached governments and universities to find out what was needed. Their engineers were then given the task of designing a tractor that would be as simple, cheap, and reliable as possible. Using a seven-horsepower lawn-mower engine, Ford has produced a one-speed, rope-started model that can be easily assembled by local dealers. By 1969 the model was being field-tested in Jamaica, Mexico, and Peru among farmers who used a number of different methods, and in 1970 it went into test marketing in Jamaica. The company intends to sell it only through dealers who are willing to provide fertilizers and agronomic advice as well.[8]

Ford's strategy is shrewd, and it does show that multinationals can move on a scale that single research units are unable to match. By producing a tractor like this, as simple as possible (the Japanese opposition has gears and is therefore more expensive), it can be reduced to a price ($500 for the basic model, plus an extra $200 for a range of instruments) that will appeal to a number of farmers who are buying mechanical aids for the first time. Even if Ford does not make profits on this model, it has a good chance of selling larger models at a later date. On the other hand, the company's multinational spread made it relatively easy to test the machine and its equipment in different soil, climate, and cultural conditions at the same time, thus highlighting any problems that might arise. The greater the number of areas in which the final model can be sold without complicated modification, the greater its contribution to increasing Third World productivity. At a later stage it will be possible to upgrade it and develop variants better suited to specific conditions in different places. It should also be noted that the company is working with and through governments to some extent. The test market in Jamaica resulted from the particular enthusiasm of that government, and the company admits that it is heavily dependent on governments' cooperation. Finally, it should be pointed out that the company's insistence on selling only through distributors who are giving a total advisory service to the purchaser appears to be genuine. Reports of tractors rusting in idleness for the want of a single spare part have not been dismissed by the company, and it is genuinely determined to ensure that no attacks can be made on this venture.

The awareness that multinationals have a responsibility to do more than just sell hardware has been shared by some of the other tractor manufacturers. Massey–Ferguson provides full fellowships for Third World trainees, selected by their own governments, to attend courses at the company's regional training centers. The same company has gone further in setting up a School of Agricultural Mechanization with the cooperation of the Colombian government and the UN's Food and Agricultural Organization. This school is aimed at the whole of Spanish-speaking Latin America. A group of multinationals have got together, again under the auspices of FAO, to advise countries on farm-mechanization training. Inevitably, self-interest plays a part in their motivation (train a man and he'll probably buy your machines), but this philosophy is often pushed to the stage where the companies are wary about disclosing strategic commercial secrets, an indication that the companies are very concerned about the program.

H. J. Heinz—Portrait
of an Agribusiness

No one should underestimate the degree of technology and managerial know-how that goes into agriculture at its most productive. By the late 1960's it was almost a rule of thumb that for crops like wheat, maize, and rice, productivity in the United States, Canada, or Britain would be roughly four times that of countries like India, Pakistan, or the Philippines. Therefore, even when merely seeking ways to increase productivity in these last-named countries, it pays to ask what the major multinationals in this field have to offer. With regard to exports they cannot be ignored. In fact, the advanced organizations are busy integrating backward into the Third World, a strategy followed in the past by only a few special firms like Unilever or United Fruit. This procedure absorbs the experience of their relationships with farmers in the developed world, and countries unwilling to accept the discipline this entails may well lose agricultural exports, which will go to more compliant states. This discipline may be unattractive, but it can also involve company research into crops and export markets that the countries by themselves are not yet fully capable of developing.

The H. J. Heinz Company is one of the world's leading food processors, with strength in soups, baby foods, and tomato ketchup. It has had a checkered career; the American parent company was overshadowed by a phenomenally successful British subsidiary, but since the mid-1960's the American end has pulled around. Traditionally, a substantial portion of the American supplies have come from California farmers, and here the company has gone in for mechanized harvesting (the tomato crop is 100 percent machine harvested; cucumbers 40 percent), new planting methods (soluble plastic tapes from which the seeds are released at optimal depths and times), bulk-handling improvements (special vehicles mean many crops go from farm to factory without being hand-packed in individual containers), and research (tomato breeds more suitable for mechanical harvesting and less susceptible to disease). The company is starting to diffuse techniques such as these (increasingly commonplace in the United States) to the farms of their suppliers in Australia, Britain, and Portugal.

In recent years the company has started dealing with a large number of new supplying countries. The European operation has conducted growing trials in Morocco, has been expanding supplies from Turkey and Greece, where company technical experts have been helping, and is working with the Rumanian and Tanzanian governments to develop test sites for the production of navy beans. By 1971 it was experimenting with sugar purchased from Czechoslovakia for the first time, doing bulk-handling trials on Portuguese tomatoes, testing container importing of beans from the United States, and using shrink-wrapping techniques in Portugal, thus reducing costs further. Largely with the company's help, Portugal has become the world's largest supplier of tomato paste and is starting to produce other goods like dehydrated parsley and peppers. In Turkey the company is trying to ease the seasonal supply and price fluctuations that come from overdependence on tomato cultivation by bringing in pea-bean plantings for growth in the present slack periods. In Mexico the picture is the same: new products and rapid increase in purchases of pineapples and chili; new production methods like the introduction of machine harvesting of pineapple plants could double the pineapple crop. As a result of such attention, the yield per acre of tomatoes has increased from eight to twenty tons in a mere five years. The company is also involved with Peruvian fish meal and is experimenting with a pilot plant to produce low-cost fish flour, intended to alleviate the protein deficiency in the Third World that we have already noted.

These efforts are also backed up by some indigenous research. A research station in Portugal (admittedly a marginal country as far as the Third World is concerned) is looking at tomato strains with the color and firmness necessary for processing as canned peeled tomatoes, and is also working on vegetables suitable for dehydration. In Mexico there is another station that concentrates on pineapples and other tropical fruits and crops that have not previously been subject to scientific study.

Such a company is large and powerful. Southern Italy, long a tomato-producing area, is suffering from the Portuguese competition. Also, the whole agricultural sector throughout the world is notorious for its bad labor relations. Whether Heinz will be able to mitigate some of these excesses remains to be seen. On the other hand, the company shows just how research- and capital-intensive the whole industry is becoming. In many ways this is unfortunate. Do we want to see the rural sector becoming less labor-intensive, given the horrendous unemployment problems most of the Third World now faces? On the other hand, the markets in the developed world demand ever-improving quality and convenience. The drive toward pre-packaging, careful quality control, pre-processing will not be diverted. As long as a particular country wants to sell to such markets, it will have to deal with the H. J. Heinzes of the world, whether it likes it or not. Even in areas like the United States, agricultural technology is still not particularly "mature"; in large parts of the Third World one can say that the necessary technology is only just being discovered. The multinationals with their global experience will for some time to come still dominate the exporting sectors in particular.

The Search for Proteins

Whatever happens, there will be a world protein shortage for the foreseeable future. The drive to increase the volume of crops like wheat and rice will help little, since their protein content is still very low, while the consumption of animals as a source is problematic because they are expensive to raise and keep until slaughter, and the intensifying pressure on grazing land should lead to long-term price rises. So attention has been turning to more protein-filled oil-seed crops, like the soya bean, an important nutritional force in Asia and heavily used in animal feeds in North America. Other non-traditional sources under development are fish meal and oil by-products. In all of these approaches, multinationals have had and still have an important role to play.

The main problem that has defeated most firms in the field

has been how to find ways of making the high-protein products palatable, since people's tastes in food are depressingly conservative. We saw how the miracle rices were facing some consumer resistance because the taste and texture is not always "right," but the problem confronting the manufacturer of a totally new product, which it then tries to sell against traditional fare, is even greater. Thus, Monsanto produced a drink based on soya beans called Vitasoy in Southeast Asia. The risk was not great, since places like Hong Kong already have accepted the taste of soy. But as soon as traditional markets have been left behind, the taste and texture problem becomes acute. A staple drink like coffee has at least 160 identified components that affect the taste, and if this example is applied to traditional foods, the problems involved are readily apparent. Firms like the American International Flavors and Fragrances are already involved. It is, for instance, working on rice flavors and has had a measure of success with flavors for children's food in Algeria and Nigeria. But it and its few competitors are literally scratching at the surface of the problem. However, the relevant technology will be improving quickly as the developed economies also increasingly rely on artificially created foods. In the meantime, companies that have concentrated on producing new final products have had difficulties. International Multifoods worked with the United States AID agency to develop a wheat-based high-protein food for use in Tunisia that could be used in the indigenous diet. But it never caught on, so the project had to be terminated.

The second approach is to produce an intermediate product, like a flour that can be mixed into more traditional foods without affecting their taste. Even here trouble has arisen, with companies stopping experiments with fish meal because of problems of palatability and economics. Some companies feel that the technology of human taste is currently so complicated that concentration on animal feeds is the best approach for the moment. British Petroleum, which seems to have hit on a successful way of producing protein from the waxy by-product of certain oils, is concentrating initially on making animal feeds, since animals are more likely to eat what they are given and the final meat product from their flesh is not affected. It has carried out extensive tests on animals in independent research institutes to ensure that there are no harmful side effects. The first full-scale plant is to be built in Sardinia jointly with the Italian oil company ENI, and, as the economics become clearer, the interest of many Third World governments should result in the building of plants aimed specifically at the poorer parts of the world. Initially, these plants would produce animal foods, releasing more conventional nourishment for human consumption.

A modified approach is to produce traditional products with improved nutritional content. The technology for this food enrichment is becoming established, particularly in the United States, where consumer movements have highlighted the negligible nutritional value of some standard food products. The cereal firms in particular have responded to these pressures, and one of the larger companies, General Foods, has produced a food aimed specifically at the nutritionally disadvantaged in the United States and the Third World. The project began about 1968, and from the start General Foods realized it had to beat the problem of consumer resistance to unfamiliar products. It therefore went for a pasta product, since pastas are common in large parts of the world, and eventually decided on macaroni as a well-accepted form. It used common ingredients, two cereal flours and soya, then further fortified the product with vitamins and minerals. It paid attention to all the factors that determine acceptance, like initial bite, chewiness, elasticity, moisture release in the mouth, and flavor, then tested it thoroughly in disadvantaged areas of the United States, like Arizona (American Indians), Appalachia (poor whites), Atlanta (Southern blacks), etc. Feeding tests were also run in Brazil by the Brazilian National Commission on Nutrition, particularly as part of the school-lunch program; these showed that the product, Golden Elbow Macaroni, led to a significant decrease in malnutrition symptoms. Similar tests among undernourished children in Peru were also successful. Not only does Golden Elbow have more than seven times the protein of traditional macaroni, it has also been designed to require no special storage conditions and it cooks in five to six minutes, compared with the fifteen to twenty minutes needed for conventional macaroni.

These developments can be only a small part of the drive to feed the Third World adequately; the bulk of the work must come from Third World resources. However, it would be foolish to deny the fact that food production is becoming a more scientifically rigorous activity. A number of the world's leading corporations are heavily involved in key areas, and at this stage of development, refusing to deal with them would be criminal.[9]

Unemployment

After the problems of population and food, development planners are now most worried about the extremely high unemployment rates found in the Third World. Some estimates suggest that at least 20 percent of the world's potential work force is out of a job. Not only is this a tragic waste of resources but it poses some severe social problems that the multinationals can do nothing to alleviate.

Between 1967 and 1970 Latin American unemployment soared from 2.9 million to 8.8 million, partly because of the population explosion; during the 1970's 165 million Indian youths will enter the job market, compared with 117 million in the 1960's, despite the fact that Indian unemployment has already been rising from 11.4 percent in 1961 to 15.4 percent in 1969 (and this calculation is probably a conservative one). H. A. Turner studied fourteen Third World countries and found unemployment was rising 8.5 percent per annum, against a 7–8 percent rise in industrial output, while employment was rising at a mere 3 percent at most, barely enough to cover the population increase. Finally, it is even difficult to find jobs for those with qualifications, since there are at least 40,000 qualified engineers in India alone. In some parts of the world, employment is unfortunately a minority status and shows every sign of staying that way.[10]

Those who do get urban jobs become an urbanized labor "aristocracy" compared to those left behind. For instance, a nineteen-year-old girl working in a plastics-parts factory in Taiwan earned $300 per annum in the late 1960's, while her father, mother, and brothers *together* earned only $250 planting rice and bananas on the family farm. Such differentials between urban and rural work look more socially disruptive than they are. First- and second-generation urban workers are often still part of extended family, kinship, or tribal systems that ensure that a certain amount of their earnings will filter through to less fortunate members of these networks. But the pull of these high earnings is still a major factor behind the rapid urbanization taking place all over the Third World. The chances of getting an urban job may be low, but the lack of opportunity in the countryside makes the risk worthwhile. So we find higher and higher levels of urban unemployment as the shanty towns grow faster than jobs are created.

Now industrialization will not solve this problem in the short or medium terms. Nigeria is large (50 million population) but has a mere 2 percent working for wages or salaries, and even if this sector expands at a respectable 10 percent per annum, only 100,000 jobs will be created; yet in 1971 alone there were 700,000 leaving school. Puerto Rico is most often cited in connection with the benefits that accrue from private enterprise. Since the 1940's, local government has been attracting private investment by heavy tax concessions and the appeal of free entry into the United States market, since Puerto Rico is a Commonwealth attached to the United States. "Operation Bootstrap," as it is called, has been a key factor in the island's growth, providing 90,000 direct jobs and 175,000 indirect jobs since 1940, in an economy of 700,000 jobs in 1969, but still unemployment is high. There are 316,000 unemployed (31 percent of the work force), despite the fact that over a million of the islanders have already migrated to the States. "If we forced them to stay here," said a local political leader, "we'd find revolt inevitable." Once again it should be stressed that Puerto Rico is the case that is always cited when one asks what multinational investment can contribute to development. Yes, it has contributed jobs, but they are not enough.[11]

Employment creation will become a major development goal, but conventional approaches will only scratch the surface. Firms claim that it costs £2,000–3,000 ($5,000–$7,000) just to create a job in a low-technology industry, which would suggest that Nigeria alone would have had to spend $34 billion just to create the 700,000 jobs needed for 1971's school leavers. One approach tried by Kenya was an agreement among government, employers, and unions to boost employment by 10 percent, while keeping wages steady. Government and the firms all boosted their payrolls by 10 percent, but the main effect was to denude the coffee estates around Nairobi of workers, as they all flocked into the city to register as unemployed in the hope of being one of the extra 10 percent. Kenya is also trying to slow down the speed of farm mechanization, and when two firms put in roughly equal bids for tenders, the job will be offered to the one with the more labor-intensive scheme.

Multinationals are often the last to be in a position to tackle this problem, since, almost by definition, they come from economies where capital-intensiveness is the goal and they are not used to the concept of deliberately creating labor. In particular, they are not helped by the fact that most Third World leaders still want the most modern Western technology for prestige purposes, even though it will exacerbate the underlying employment problems. A few people have started to tackle the problem, like Dr. E. F. Schumacher, an economic adviser to Britain's National Coal Board. After leaving Germany in 1937, he spent some time as an agricultural laborer and since then has been instrumental in reminding us that 80–90 percent of the world's economic activity is still in agriculture. In 1966 he set up a private non-profit organization called the Intermediate Technology Group, which helps to spread knowledge of low-cost methods and equipment suitable for self-help in poor countries. Some of the tools are ones long discarded by Western economies, but which the group argues can do jobs as efficiently in Third World conditions as more capital-intensive ones, which may be more dependent on scarce spare parts or more sensitive to mistakes by the key operatives. Schumacher's opponents argue that his group has had more publicity than real impact, though he has been influential on a personal level with a number of Third World leaders, and the problem of appropriate technology levels is now seriously discussed by most development planners. The economists among them often dismiss his ideas as of doubtful value, since the amount of reinvestable surplus from discarded technologies will be less than from the most up-to-date ones, thus slowing economic growth. On the other hand, more open-minded economists suggest that there are obvious short-term social benefits in employment for the sake of employment, and also, in a low-skill economy, the marginal returns on given capital investment may decrease as the technology becomes more complex and sensitive.

Schumacher and his intermediate technologists should be considered in the wider framework of the search for more appropriate technologies in the Third World. Part of the development process is to discover the extent to which human and material resources can be wisely exploited, and the value of the intermediate technologists is that they stress that manpower in the agricultural sector is one particular, important, underused resource.[12]

Philips NV—Utrecht Pilot Plant

The only major company to take this kind of approach seriously has been the Dutch electrical giant Philips, which has always had extensive interests in the Third World, where its radios in particular have sold well. With the coming of import substitution, it was faced with the problem of setting up factories with production runs that were totally uneconomic by European standards. Its normal production techniques were beginning to look ineffectual, so in 1961 the radio, gramophone, and television section of the company created a small independent unit at Utrecht, some fifty miles from the company headquarters at Eindhoven. This isolation was deliberate, since it allowed the unit to look objectively at the parent company's technology and instructions. The unit was deliberately kept small (sixty-seven workers in 1970), since the average Third World factory making its products would have well under a hundred employees. This forced the management to study the managerial problems of small plants, and they devised ways of "doubling up" duties, so that the accountant may also look after personnel affairs. They also cut down on paper work, producing forms that were simpler and concentrated on essential information needed by management. They have also kept their work force as unskilled as possible, again to parallel likely conditions in the Third World.

The idea of the plant is to produce goods to be manufactured in the Third World, as far as possible under Third World conditions, in order to experiment with ways of simplifying the assembly process as far as economic viability allows. Starting only with radios (but now also dealing with more complicated products), Philips produced flexible production lines that can be added to others as a plant expands. It analyzed where components could be modified to make hand operations more simple. It tried non-traditional tools and sources of components. Thus, for certain operations, it found a domestic iron was a perfectly efficient hot plate. Likewise, it has found many ways of using the motor from the ubiquitous sewing machine, and at one point discovered that current passed through the kind of large wastepaper basket one finds in public parks would make an adequate shield against extraneous signals when tuning products. There are, of course, limits to this experimenting. Transistors, condensers, or capacitors are economically impossible to make in small quantities, but Philips did find a way to utilize an expensive mold for radio bodies by shipping it around between plants so that the cost is shared.

Now that the plant is well established, it has two main roles. The first is to consult with the parent company, helping to decide which new products should be transferred abroad and then to simplify the production techniques involved. The second role is to act as a kind of contractor to the factory managements in the Third World. Some of them are now well established with experienced indigenous managers, so they merely need reliable instructions on how to set up the new production line, what parts are needed, where they should be stored, the most common problems, clear pictures and instructions for all the important operations, and the estimated times of the operations. Some will want the line and components sent out to them, so the pilot plant will test them and pack them for shipment. Others want training done for them, and Utrecht claims that it is probably socially easier to train many Third World managers in a neutral place like Utrecht than in the field, where it may be socially unacceptable for a manager to be seen receiving training.

Since this operation has been running, other companies have moved somewhat in the same direction. The care with which Ford is approaching its mini-tractor and its on-off flirtation with the idea of an Asian Model T car that would utilize local materials and would be as simple as possible is similar to the thinking that has gone on within Philips. On the other hand, this particular approach has not actually led to much job creation because, while Philips has been simplifying existing operations, the whole technology of electronics has sped forward with the development of printed wiring and integrated circuits, which mean far higher productivity all around. Ultimately, it is up to the Third World governments to have a much clearer idea of what they want from multinational investment. If they want capital-intensive technology they will get it, since the multinationals already use it. But if employment matters to them, tax systems must be changed to encourage the use of labor, and pressure will have to be put on firms to adapt to more labor-intensive systems. Utrecht shows what a multinational can do in one of the basic manufacturing industries. But governments cannot expect many other companies to follow suit unless they are consistently cajoled.[13]

Export Creation

The "trade versus aid" debate has quieted down, probably because it is now clear that the expansion of either is severely restrained by the selfishness of the developed world. Idealists who once saw trade and aid as alternatives now wryly accept that they have to push for improvements from both sources as the situation changes.

Although the Third World's share of world trade has been falling steadily over the years, trade still provides four fifths of the foreign currency needed to mobilize its internal resources. Moreover, this is untied money that the countries can spend around the world as they like, thus permitting them to invest in projects they choose rather than those chosen for them by international aid donors. There are strong arguments for encouraging countries to work with bodies like the multinationals who can help with this push for new export markets, although there are also economists like Furtado who argue that reliance on exports for growth is eventually stultifying, since there is no motivation for changing the internal economic and social structure of the Third World country. Furtado has in mind the banana republics, Brazilian coffee, or Uruguayan and Argentinian beef. In fact, Argentina's economy is a classic example of bad economic management relying unthinkingly on traditional export sectors. Thanks to its beef, which fed the British workers in the late nineteenth and early twentieth centuries, Argentina had a standard of living equal to that of Italy by the outbreak of the 1914–18 war. Unfortunately, the proceeds of this boom period were plowed back neither into improvements in the cattle industry nor into sustained industrialization policies. Thus, when the British started to exclude Argentinian beef from the British market in the thirties, no one was capable of finding alternative markets, and the urban politicians like Perón allowed the industry to decay. By the late 1960's, the industry, Argentina's biggest foreign-currency earner, was in a state of perpetual crisis. It was technically inefficient compared to the industries of Australia and New Zealand, and incapable of meeting both local and foreign demand, though it was potentially able to do so with ease. This country provides an excellent historical example of the penalties incurred by a failure to build on export success, with its subsequent decline, compared to the European countries it once rivaled in wealth. Properly controlled multinationals can on occasion produce exports at a volume and price that local interests would be unable to achieve. This is not surprising, since the multinationals know their home markets very well, in many cases controlling the outlets through which the Third World products are sold. In trying to sell products on a world scale, Third World nationals will often be at a severe disadvantage. Multinationals may block a country's product completely from the developed markets. We saw how this happened to Iran in the early 1950's, when it attempted to expropriate the foreign oil interests. Today the problem lies in not knowing the international market well enough, so that products are wrongly packaged or designed, or prices are pitched at less than optimal levels. In 1969 Ghana's state marketing board for cocoa lost an estimated $60 million in potential earnings because of its lack of experience in spotting changes in the likely cocoa crop and thus charging prices lower than those which the market (well serviced by economic spies) could have borne. Likewise, the Hong Kong wig industry, which was flourishing in the United States and parts of Europe, was faced with severe slumps in 1971, in part attributable to the difficulty of keeping pace with trends in these markets.

The major breakthrough that multinationals are starting to make is the export of manufactured goods from the Third World. The extent of this is not yet clear for, though United States manufacturing subsidiaries in Latin America were exporting 10 percent of their output in 1966 against 3.6 percent a decade earlier, it would appear that a large proportion of these goods merely go to other Latin American countries. Only 18 percent of 100 major firms surveyed by the journal *Business International* in 1966 were shipping from Latin America to other world markets, while 64 percent were involved in trade between Latin American countries. This type of trade is of great help to the continent, provided that economies of scale are achieved and regional integration is strengthened. The multinationals can appear as the chief beneficiaries of the various common markets, but the same phenomenon was found in Europe, where American firms were quick to look upon the Continent as a single entity, though more recently European competition has been waking up. The claim that exports of United States affiliates in Latin America in 1966 formed 35 percent of all exports from Latin America that year is misleading, since only a small portion will go to the developed economies that are in a position to pay for them.[14]

Meanwhile, in the first half of 1971, Fiat exported over $2.5 million worth of tractors, trucks, etc., from Argentina to other

Latin American countries; the Japanese shipyard in Brazil, Ishikawajima, has already sold cargo vessels of up to 20,000 tons to the United States, which bodes well for an industry now accepting orders for vessels up to 400,000 tons; a Danish firm using air freight is shipping asparagus from an estate in Kenya to fill half the winter demand in Denmark; a British distillery company, Duncan, Gilbey & Matheson, has put together a consortium of African distillers from Gambia, Ghana, Nigeria, Sierra Leone, Tanzania, Uganda, and Zambia (some of these are state-owned) to invent, manufacture, and export a new liqueur named Afrikoko, based on coconut and chocolate; and Sears Roebuck saved the Panama hat industry in Ecuador of all places by persuading United States milliners to stock up. There are also cases where manufacturing multinationals use their subsidiaries in the Third World to manufacture components for the parent company. An example of this is the German company Bosch, with 6,500 employees in India, which is purchasing substantial quantities of its subsidiary's production. India as a whole is building up a reputation for reasonable-quality engineering and machine-tool production, and a number of other multinationals are assessing the situation to see if they too can benefit from this cheap source of supplies. However, this kind of development is a phenomenon in its own right and will be discussed in the next chapter.

In the short to medium term, even the most nationalist government stands to gain from marketing through the multinationals. Thus, the militant Algerians are not trying to sell their natural gas directly to the United States market but are happy to leave the smallish American company El Paso with the worry of tackling the bureaucratic and marketing problems involved. Similarly, the purely Saudi Arabian-owned Saudi Arabian Fertilizers Company has an agreement with Occidental Petroleum whereby one of the latter's subsidiaries will purchase and market all exports from Saudi Arabia's plants for seventeen years on a commission basis.

Even when governments do not directly own an industry, there is scope for putting pressure on multinationals, with local direct investment, to export more, as with the Mexican pressure on the auto manufacturers, whose ability to import will be increasingly tied to their exports from Mexico. The multinationals will not be happy with this kind of pressure. Normally, the local subsidiary was left alone, and provided the level of imports was not too high, no one was worried, so the problems of global coordination were not too difficult for the parent company. But if each manufacturing subsidiary is also expected to export, the parent has to find new markets and will have to increase imports—and this is contrary to accepted government policy. The coordinating and diplomatic skills of the parent companies will be more important than they have ever been. Multinationals may have to pull out of certain countries to concentrate on those where costs can be kept to the minimum, and this drive for higher exports will pose problems for many Third World governments who think that the companies can work miracles against all the laws of economics. Producing for a protected domestic market is one kind of problem; producing for world markets is something else.

One possible solution is the "complementation agreement" between companies and two or more countries, whereby tariffs are reduced or abolished on the flow of specified goods within the countries concerned. Companies can then rationalize their production among a number of countries, reducing costs as the production runs increase, with lower prices and greater chances of exporting to countries outside the agreement. In 1962 the computer company IBM signed the first complementation agreement within LAFTA, whereby Argentina, Brazil, Uruguay, and Chile abolished tariffs on punched-card data-processing machines, their components, and the paper for the cards, when produced in any of the four countries. This gave IBM a market that justified local production, so it built plants in Argentina and Brazil, and arranged for a license for Chile to produce the paper-card stock. Exports in these products from Argentina increased more than five-fold in the next three years, while Brazil's expanded rapidly from nothing. Other companies like Philips and RCA have since followed IBM's lead, and complementation agreements are proving more attractive to certain multinationals, who are able to take advantage of regional integration better than the local entrepreneurs themselves. If they reduce costs, the economies profit, but the region as a whole will benefit only at the expense of the rich nations if these reduced costs are translated into exports to the developed economies.

Education, Housing, Finance, Etc.

The problem of education in the Third World lies in providing basic facilities in villages and ensuring that syllabuses are relevant to the needs of that particular country. There are areas where high technology can help. For instance, there is the scheme for using a satellite to beam television messages on family planning, improved agricultural practices, etc., into some five thousand Indian villages. The American space agency NASA is providing the satellite, and the world's aid agencies are heavily involved. Except as subcontractors, there's not much room for the multinationals. Ford in Mexico and Argentina has persuaded its dealers to build and maintain schools for which the governments provide the teachers. So successful has this been that in Mexico Ford can even have its name on the schools, with the proviso that the company has no part in deciding educational policy. The only multinationals heavily involved here are the textbook publishers, who are charged with failing to produce locally relevant books. However, they face fierce competition from "pirates" in Taiwan who copy any successful book without the slightest hesitation. There are also schemes in practice whereby Third World customers pay no royalties to the original publisher or author. This obviously also cheapens the price at which books can be sold.

Housing

There is a decided need for cheap, lightweight structures made from local raw materials. It is unlikely that there will be any major opening by the multinationals here, though IBEC has a cheap device for making building blocks, and Automated Building Components is developing low-cost prefabricated buildings in the Philippines.

Banking

A crucial battle in the Third World today is to make the banking system more socially responsive to development needs that cannot be measured in normal commercial terms. Historically, the foreign banks have tended to be based in the cities, financing commerce but paying little attention to industrial or agricultural investment. Locally owned banks were no better, resembling the traditional moneylender who is unconcerned about how the loan is actually spent. Gradually, the emphasis has switched to the mobilization of savings, which will become less profitable the more it becomes a case of persuading farmers and peasants to bank their savings. The banks must assume a social role, as when a Mexican agrarian bank found itself keeping 300,000 people alive with "advances" when the world price of their produce dropped. A purely commercial bank cannot play this kind of role. This is not to deride the positive attempts by some multinational banks. Thus, Barclays DCO lost $4.2 million in the early 1960's, when it instructed its West African managers to expand their lending to indigenous African entrepreneurs. It also claims, however, that in over fifteen years in West Africa it pulled in small savings of at least £20 million, despite extremely expensive running costs. Then there is the Bank of America, which claims to be the only large international investment bank with extensive agribusiness experience (this stems from its California base). It has financed a number of large fertilizer projects and has been influential among aid bodies and investment banks just starting to think about this kind of investment.

Conclusion

To make a worthwhile contribution to the welfare of the Third World, multinationals must involve themselves with activities and approaches however alien to their traditional environment. Where they have been used to well-heeled, sophisticated, innovation-conscious Western bourgeoisie, they now find they are faced with near-starving, ignorant, conservative consumers. Where they were used to well-educated, highly skilled workers, they have to get by in an environment where workers lack urban, let alone industrial, experience and are often both physically and mentally affected by their extremely disadvantaged upbringing.

Many firms at the moment are totally uninterested in the development of the Third World, assuming that they will be able to survive in the richer and more comprehensible markets in Europe, the United States, and Japan. Others who would be willing to make a limited contribution point out that as commercial institutions they cannot profitably operate in population control or parts of the agricultural sector, despite their relevant technological and managerial expertise. This raises the question of whether aid bodies and governments need their help in such areas, and if they do, how they should work with such commercial, profit-motivated bodies. There are ways, but they will of necessity be controversial. Making profits out of the misery and starvation of much of the Third World can be justified only by an acceptance of an unchanging status quo. A number of multinationals do possess technology that could be useful to the development needs of the Third World. In the food and agricultural sector a purely non-profit or state-controlled approach will not work fast enough. Admittedly, the Green Revolution breakthroughs came from non-profit research institutes, but high-yielding seeds are only part of the whole wheat- and rice-growing systems, and a small, though important, part of the crops that feed the Third World. Developments are needed throughout each of these systems, and it is out of the question that the non-profit area can solve all these problems fast enough, since most of them demand the application of technologies that are still expanding rapidly. For better or for worse, the multinationals are among the leaders in some of these technologies, and here we have the central dilemma faced by the radical critic. In refusing to deal with the multinationals, one is slowing down growth in the one area whose rate of growth determines how many people will die or be crippled for life through malnutrition. However, like all technologies, food and agriculture will mature in time and become easier to acquire in other ways. And at that point the agribusiness multinationals can be tamed, just as those controlling the banks or the railways have been in the past.

Notes

1. Anderson, "The Changing International Environment of Development."

2. Kuznets, *Modern Economic Growth*; Ward, "Long Think on Development"; and an undated Stanford Research report cited in personal communication.

3. I first saw this term used in Lipton, "The International Diffusion of Technology." I've also used Sampredo, *Decisive Forces in World Economics*; Shearman, "Recent Advances in Contraceptive Technology."

4. Chenery, "Growth and Structural Change"; Seers and Joy, eds., *Development in a Divided World*; Shearman, "Recent Advances in Contraceptive Technology"; Ward, "Long Think on Development."

5. Advisory Committee . . . , *Draft of World Plan of Action*; UN: Ecosoc, *Panel on Foreign Investment in Developing Countries*; Wharton, "The Green Revolution." See also Brown, *Seeds of Change,* and Stikker, *Expansion and Diversification of Exports*.

6. Business International, *Nationalism in Latin America*.

7. Philip, "Southeast Asia: Investment and Development."

8. Business International, *Nationalism in Latin America*.

9. Glicksman, *Fabricated Foods,* and a large number of annual reports.

10. Elkan, "Urban Unemployment in East Africa"; Freeman, "The Challenge of the Seventies"; Rolfe, *The International Corporation*; Singer, "Dualism Revisited."

11. Foggan, "Youth Aspects of Unemployment"; Singer, "Dualism Revisited."

12. Business International, *The United Nations and the Business World*; Elkan, "Urban Unemployment in East Africa"; Freeman, "The Challenge of the Seventies"; ILO, *Toward Full Employment*; Oldham, "Characteristics of the Process of Transfer of Technology."

13. Advisory Committee . . . , *Draft of World Plan of Action*; Rolfe, *The International Corporation*; an interview with Philips management and company literature.

14. In part based on Herring, *A History of Latin America.*

7 : : *Runaway Industries: Cheap Labor Uncaged*

There are no laws of comparative advantage for the American worker in today's changing world, merely laws of comparative disadvantage.[1]

Some of us believe that the time is not far off when the underdeveloped countries will become net importers of primary products and new exporters of manufacturers.[2]

In 1924 an academic, Professor L. C. A. Knowles, described mid-nineteenth-century developments in transport and communications and their impact on imperialism as the "unlocking of the tropics," in that this revolution allowed European and American capitalists systematically to exploit the Third World's raw materials for the first time. With Nixon's trade measures of 1971 we see the first major ripples of a revolution that will be of less importance but of far greater subversive potential. For the first time in world history, our capitalists have both the physical and psychological ability to exploit the Third World's most basic resource—its cheap labor. Increasingly, they will do so, partly from choice but mostly from necessity, and this development is a rope with which many a traditional American or European multinational will be hanged—and it's not going to be so good for international union solidarity either.

Classical economic theorists like Adam Smith and David Ricardo put forward the theory that, under free trade, geographical specialization will permit production to occur where it can be carried out most efficiently. There are plenty of cases to support this, as when the British stole some rubber plants from Brazil, set up a new industry under a plantation system in Malaya, and wiped out the less competitive Brazilian industry. There is good reason, however, to think that industry is only just starting to be affected globally by the law of comparative advantage, which would suggest that labor-intensive work should locate where labor is cheapest. However, historically the position has never been so straightforward. Transport remained slow and expensive, though this did not concern tropical agriculture and mining, which were not in serious competition with American or European produce. The problem was more psychological, in that the colonial managers in Africa or the West Indies tended to use the natives solely for unskilled manual labor and never thought of trying to upgrade their productivity by training or installing machines. When they exhausted this local pool of labor, they imported Indian or Chinese laborers, in what was known unflatteringly as the "pig trade." The managers were interested only in meeting local needs with the cheapest, least troublesome labor force. No one thought of exploiting this force for the imperial powers' home markets. Where this might have happened, as in Indian textiles, the Lancashire textile workers were allowed to destroy the Indian industry in the name of "free trade," which, reduced to basics, meant "We Europeans produce the manufactured goods; you provide our food and raw materials."

The situation changed slowly. By 1950 over half America's imports were still crude materials supplementary to the United States output, but by 1965 nearly three quarters were manufactured goods competing with American jobs. This mainly reflects the international rationalization of production within the developed economies, but in recent years it is possible to see the rise of non-Western economies, led by the export of manufactured goods to the United States and, to a lesser extent, Europe, whose advantage has been cheapness, thanks to the low wages of the various labor forces.

The countries we are concerned with are Mexico, Hong Kong, Taiwan, and, to a lesser extent, India, South Korea, Singapore, and the Philippines. We must also mention Japan, whose early success depended on cheap labor, but whose continued prosperity now rests substantially on modern plants and long production lines. Whatever the precise figures, these are the economies that are causing the United States so much trouble. The deterioration of the United States balance of trade, in manufactured goods alone (ignoring Canada, which is a special case), from 1967–9, can be compared with those of Japan, which has improved its balance by $1.1 billion; India, by $212 million; Hong Kong, by $180 million, and Taiwan by $178 million. In fact, these four countries contributed 90 percent to the total deterioration of the United States position in manufactured goods ($1.9 billion) during this period, which was to culminate, in 1971, in the import surcharge designed to protect the United States economy from such ravages.

Economists in the past would hardly have expected these countries to have troubled the United States in manufactured goods, but the type of import flooding in has changed considerably. In the early 1960's it was decided to encourage American exports, and Section 807 of the Tariff Schedule allowed firms abroad to use American components in their products and then, if they decided to sell those products in the United States, there would be import duties only on the non-American parts and labor content. In one respect Section 807 has been a success. By the first half of 1969, the value of United States components let back into the country free was $151 million, roughly four times the annual rate of 1965. But at the same time, it looked as though many American firms were taking advantage of this provision to send components abroad for assembly. The finished product was then brought back into the country and sold by the same company. In its purest form, all the components might be American and only the assembly labor foreign. The American unions looked bleakly at Mexico, Hong Kong, Taiwan, and South Korea in particular. And in Mexico during 1969 nearly 70 percent of the exports going to the United States under this scheme consisted entirely of American components. The unions claim that parts of the Mexican economy survive solely by assembling products for United States multinationals. In other words, jobs that were once done in America are now done in Mexico, often within a mile of the border. American jobs themselves are being exported.[3]

The Flight of the Aging Particle

Classical economists are still not too worried. "Yes," they say, "some labor-intensive operations may be being exported, but by the law of comparative advantage, the United States economy will not suffer as a whole, because it will expand into those research-intensive industries in which it can keep a research lead." They are being too complacent.

The electronics industry, which covers everything from television sets and radios to computers and their components, ought to be such a research-intensive industry in which the United States can keep a comparative advantage. But even people within the industry have their doubts. In early 1971 Dr. F. E. Jones, the managing director of a subsidiary of the Dutch firm Philips, gave a talk in which he explained how the electron, founder of this century's communications revolution, is now an aging particle, known and used for seventy-four years and no longer producing any major surprises. As a result, he said, many jobs could now be routinized and subcontracted out to cheap-labor areas. In this era in which major electronic advances would be much reduced, where were the innovations to take over from color television, the last real consumer product of major economic impact? He could see none. Abe Morganstern, research director of the American International Union of Electrical Workers, raised the same question when I talked to him. He pointed out that one potential growth product was the video recorder, which allows the consumer to record television shows from his set, or else play TV programs through his set from the visual equivalent of the long-playing record. Certainly this has been developed from American research by firms like CBS, but, he claims, it is unlikely that a single video recorder will ever be commercially produced within the United States economy, since the company is licensing production out to Europe and the Far East. We thus find ourselves faced with a major development—the introduction of consumer products based on United States research but manufactured elsewhere. At least in the past, United States workers manufactured radios and television sets before their jobs were taken away from them by international competition. This time they may be deprived even of an initial period of manufacturing video recorders. Can the United States exist on royalty licenses alone, or can it really find alternative sources of employment?

This process was started, of course, by the Japanese. When transistors were developed in the early 1950's, the United States radio manufacturers envisaged no commercial use. Masaru Ibuka, the founder of Sony Corporation, with greater foresight, took a transistor license from Western Electric in 1954 and produced the first transistor radio in 1955. From the start he aimed heavily at the American market, maintaining quality, and between 1958 and 1963 sales to the United States multiplied fourteen times. Today, 91 percent of the radios sold in the United States are imported, often from economies even cheaper than Japan's. At the same time, the basic technology was being developed quickly. A simple transistor that might cost up to $11 in 1960 was down to about fifty cents by the mid 1960's, and with the development of integrated circuits around 1968, the cost per transistor was down to less than twelve cents, with the likelihood of even further reductions on the way.

This lowering of the cost of components meant that a gradually higher proportion of the final product came from labor charges, playing into the hands of the Japanese, whose labor might be well under a fifth of the cost of equivalent American labor. Of course, this was not the only factor at work, since the booming Japanese demand for radios meant that firms like Sony could get economies of scale not open to their United States competitors, who were faced with a replacement market.

The reaction of American firms was at first to fight directly, but gradually they started using imported components or even importing the whole product under their own names. But by 1960 one or two firms were starting to drift out to Southeast Asia, looking for bases to set up plants not only to compete with but to beat their Japanese rivals. Perhaps the first major electronics firm to emigrate was Fairchild Camera and Instruments, which was involved in the fast-changing field of microelectronics (the whole transistor field). It based itself in Hong Kong, and by 1970 had invested $200 million in the colony and was planning to increase this by a steady $500,000 per annum for the next few years. Its main competitors, like Texas Instruments and Motorola, were the next to arrive, and as the Japanese moved in on the black-and-white and then color television scene, the vast majority of American consumer electronics companies followed suit. Thus, in Taiwan, where labor is even cheaper than in Hong Kong, we find RCA, Philco (a Ford division), Admiral, TRW, General Instruments, Zenith Radio, and IBM (almost the cream of the United States electronics industry), with Fairchild in Hong Kong, Texas Instruments in Singapore, and the Dutch electronics firm Philips moving into Taiwan with the largest investment of the lot.

Already the television business is suffering from the same condition as radio. By 1970 51 percent of the black-and-white television sets sold in the United States were imported, as were 18 percent of the color TV's, and these are understatements, since the components of many sets assembled in the United States are also imported. What is even more important is that the softer parts of the computer industry are under attack. Already the crucial microelectronics come largely from Southeast Asia, but the Japanese are encroaching on the business electronic calculator market with firms like Burroughs and Friden importing from Japan and then selling under their own name in the United States. Meanwhile, Hong Kong is starting to concentrate on the manufacture of memories, subassemblies, and subsystems for computers. In fact, as the emphasis among Western computer consumers switches from the hardware itself to the software (i.e. programming, terminals, etc., that fit the consumers' needs as closely as possible), there seems little reason why much of the hardware side of the computer business should not go the same way as the rest of the electronics industry.

Hard economic statistics do not yet fully support an alarmist analysis. The trade unions' approach is to add up the increased imports in a field, calculate how many Americans could be employed producing them, and then claim that this number is the number of American jobs that have been "lost." Thus, they claim that 80,200 jobs were lost in the four years up to October 1970 in electronics component production alone, plus a further 47,300 jobs lost at plants manufacturing complete consumer electronic units. The hard-nosed economist argues back that more jobs are lost through normal increases in manufacturing productivity than through imports; that many industries with high import ratios are still increasing employment and exports; that many of these lost jobs were unfillable in the mid to late 1960's, when the imports were growing fastest; that there is remarkably little evidence of large numbers being directly laid off as a result of plants closing down because of foreign competition. At the same time, the normal economic adjustment process is still working and these lost workers are in fact working at other, more highly skilled work within the economy. And here the figures do support the analysis. Thus, in electronics the United States net balance of trade of exports over imports was $700 million greater in 1970 than in 1966, while employment had risen by 90,000.[4] Nevertheless, despite all the facts and figures, I think the alarmists are right.

The Range of Industries Involved

If only a few industries were involved, there would be no need to worry. However, the more one probes in the management journals, the harder it is to find an industry in which firms are not either already involved with a runaway investment or in the process of considering one. From airplanes and missiles to toy cars, the calculations have been made; from shoes and wigs to cameras, watches, and cars, the story is the same. Only the genuinely capital-intensive industries like oil and chemical refining seem to be holding out, but even here the development of new transport technologies like pipelines are making these companies more "footloose" and able to respond to the different incentives they are offered, even if differential labor costs are not particularly important to them.

Shipping is the granddaddy of all runaway industries. At the time of Prohibition, some United States shipowners discovered they could legally offer alcohol on board their ships if they registered them in places like Honduras or Panama. It was not until 1940 that official Washington investigated such schemes, after the 1940 Neutrality Act had stopped all official help to either side in the Second World War. The Lend-Lease administration discovered the virtues of "flags of convenience," whereby American shipping ran under other flags, and after the war one of the key Lend-Lease administrators went out to Liberia and helped it create a registration procedure that meant that by 1970 it officially had the largest merchant marine in the world, earning an easy $3 million a year in tonnage tax, with virtually no worries.

However, the rest of the world is genuinely concerned. Trade unions in high-wage shipping fleets see the "flags of convenience" as a way for the big shipowners to use cheap labor, undercutting high-wage American and European seamen. There is also an element of tax avoidance, since Liberia, Panama, and Honduras do not tax corporate profits, so although the taxmen elsewhere may catch up with the companies, the delays involved and the increasingly high subsidies offered by shipbuilding nations around the world mean that a shipping company paying taxes is almost by definition badly run! [5] There is also concern that ships under flags of convenience have lower safety requirements, and the fact that the oil tanker *Torrey Canyon,* which ran aground in the English Channel with disastrous results, was Liberian-registered (with an Italian captain, on charter to British Petroleum) only strengthened this suspicion.

At a more trivial extreme we can see the growth of "fad" industries like wigs, toys, or plastic flowers. Continually fluctuating, these industries depend on Western buyers, like department stores, subcontracting work to the numerous small entrepreneurs in places like Hong Kong. When the market breaks, the Asians are left to go bankrupt, while the Western firms look for some other product to sell. Even within these industries, a certain amount of stability can emerge. Hong Kong is now the world's largest exporter of toys, with American toy manufacturers like Mattel using the colony as a manufacturing base for its 1969 counterattack on British toy firms like Lesney and Mettoy. The sophistication of these minor industries should not be ignored. For instance, the wigs produced are not merely aimed at the cheap end of the Western markets. The world-famous hairdresser Vidal Sassoon styled a set of wigs to be produced in Hong Kong and sold in Europe. Again, in textiles, where a colony like Hong Kong is trying hard to move away from the manufacture of cloth into garment production, companies have taken to holding high-fashion exhibitions to show that they are ready to take on the top end of the market as well as the bottom.

More serious is the development of the camera industry as a runaway. By 1971 only one major camera (Polaroid) was being manufactured in the United States, with Kodak importing its top-of-the-line Instamatic Reflex (1970) from its German subsidiary. There are now clear signs that even the European industry is being driven out to Southeast Asia. Rolleiflex is building a plant in Singapore bigger than its existing one in Germany, while its competitor Zeiss Ikon has closed down its German plants, blaming low-cost imports. Rollei explained that labor costs make up 60 percent of the camera cost, and wages are six times higher in Germany than in Singapore. The camera makers are now close to the point where cameras will be so cheap that they will be given away with the film, on which the actual profits will be made. With watches the story is the same. The Swiss cannot make enough cases so, instead of importing cases and putting the mechanisms inside them, they export the mechanisms to Asia and allow the Asians to do the assembly. American companies like Timex and Bulova have been setting up plants on Taiwan. In fact, the list is almost endless. Even Haiti has got in on the act, making baseballs and bras for the American market.

But most significantly, there is evidence that major industries like cars, aerospace, and machine tools are starting to move. In cars, the onslaught of Toyota and Datsun on the American market can be compared to Sony's transistor-radio invasion of the late 1950's and early 1960's. The Ford decision to use European engines in its small car, the Pinto (even if it is switching to American ones), is like the radio manufacturers starting to use imported components. Chrysler's decision to use

British and Japanese models as its two small-car contenders in the United States market is one stop further forward (or backward, if you are an American unionist). The combination of pressures for more auto exports by countries like Mexico, and the greater involvement of firms like Ford in the Asian market (see the mini-tractor example), should lead to greater imports of automobile components. Thus, the early 1970's saw serious investigation by car companies all around the world of the economics of using Japanese parts, and anything that can be done in Japan can be done cheaper (after a time lag) in other parts of Southeast Asia. Some firms are already getting components from countries like India, Egypt, Brazil, and Yugoslavia. If Japan cannot open the market wide, nobody can.[6]

What Is a Labor-Intensive Industry?

If virtually all industries are open to some form of attack from cheap-labor sources, we are faced with the major problem of deciding which industries will not fall in this way. Conventional economists do not help very much, since we are in a fluid situation; analyses based on the 1960's have little relevance to this decade. H. B. Lary used value-added analysis to identify particularly labor-intensive industries like textiles, clothing, lumber, and wood. He also included a broad section of miscellaneous manufacture, which could include components of groups like motorcycles and bicycles, pleasure craft, and small boats. This is fine as far as it goes, but Chrysler has been importing whole cars from Japan; this suggests that the conventional wisdom about what constitutes a labor-intensive industry needs re-thinking. What we have is a continuum from the types of products Lary mentions to the real capital-intensive industries like nuclear power plants. In the past, only the extremely labor-intensive industries went abroad, while today the industry that can be exported has much more "capital-intensive" orientation. Ten years ago, the high labor content in textiles threatened the existence of the industry in the developed economies; today the labor content in small cars may be enough to force their manufacture in relatively cheap-labor areas. The question is, Which industries are at risk?

Air Freight and Containerization

What steam and refrigerated ships were to the previous un-locking of the tropics, air freight and containerization are today. Shipping components around the world makes sense only if they can be carried quickly, reliably, and cheaply, and both the established airlines and the new all-freight lines have moved in to create a booming air-freight business, without which the run-away industry in many cases could not exist. At the moment, only 1 percent of world trade is carried by air, but in Hong Kong 21 percent of all domestic exports were air-freighted in 1970, and 24 percent of all re-exports. Ninety percent of all wigs, 83 percent of electrical components, 93 percent of all precious and semiprecious stones, and 67 percent of all clocks and watches were air-freighted from the colony. In 1971 the American West Coast dock strike drove even more goods into the air. Air freight has already created new industries, such as the growing of pineapples in Kenya for sale in London three to four days after being picked. But the boom in air freighting has created companies that depend heavily on the runaway business.

One such company is the Flying Tiger Corporation, which sprang from a group of American mercenaries flying for General Claire L. Chennault in China against the Japanese (there's a John Wayne movie about this) in the Second World War. Through his widow, Anna Chennault, one of the formidable "China Lobby," the company has a fair amount of "political clout" in Southeast Asia, which has not hindered its expansion into the area. The company has picked up a lot of business from the Vietnam war, but more recently it has been doing well from the booming intra-Asian freight movements between Korea, Japan, Hong Kong, and Taiwan. Using the McDonnell Douglas "stretched eight" DC-8-63F, the company has been able to ship the Midwestern electronics manufacturers' components to Taiwan and back for less than the cost of having the work carried out in the United States. Even though the Vietnam war has ended, companies such as this would have a vested interest to ensure that the runaway phenomenon continues.

On the shipping side there is the development of containerization, which, by putting goods into standard-size containers, cuts pilferage and handling costs. Here progress is slower, but the ports of Hong Kong, Singapore, and Japan are all in bitter competition to get established as containerized bases. This is in some ways a smaller step than the growth of air freight, but it should help spread trade in more bulky, lower-value products and components, thus exposing a new range of industries to the runaway threat.

Tax Incentives and Export Processing Zones

Cheap labor is not the only attraction Asia can offer—there are some desirable tax exemptions as well. Most of the countries we have discussed have some form of "tax holiday" for incoming investors, modeled to some extent on the ten-year holiday offered in Puerto Rico's pioneering "Operation Bootstrap." In extreme form, such offers also permit the free import and export of materials and finished products, and even allow tax concessions on the earnings of expatriate managers.

Over the years, there has been much concern about such deals. There is the danger of "overkill" when incentives are offered over and above the level needed to tempt the foreign investors in. There is a feeling that countries will compete with each other, eventually reaching a stage where no country gains anything. This is what happened in the United States when tax-free municipal bonds were originally offered on a limited scale as an attraction to invest in certain authorities, but by the time everyone was offering them the general tax-revenue base had been eroded all around. Certainly we find firms, known as "dowry chasers," who go from government to government trying to get better terms. The Belgians and Dutch in Europe used to be adept at this sort of blackmail, while in the Far East a certain drug company shifted from the Philippines to Hong Kong partly because the Philippine authorities were not pliable enough. Finally, there is the suspicion that at the end of the tax holiday, firms will just pull up roots and leave for a new country willing to give them the right treatment. This does happen, but not as much as has sometimes been suggested. The Puerto Rican experience is that about 20 percent of plants shut down once the tax exemption period is over.

Governments are aware of the problem, though, in the absence of bodies like the European Common Market Commission, which has set a ceiling on the investment incentives their member countries can offer, there are limits to what single countries can do. Singapore, once thought to be offering overgenerous incentives to its "pioneer" industries (foreign investors bringing in new industries), has tightened up the conditions for granting full concessions. A firm now has to bring in at least $330,000 to qualify for pioneer status (five years of tax relief and controls on trade-union activities), with more favorable terms offered if an incoming investor brings over $50 million, contributes to local technology, and has 50 percent of its capital held locally; the technology and ownership clauses are dropped if the investment is over $330 million. This deliberate attempt to get away from the image of a "screwdriver economy" has been reasonably successful, and aircraft firms like Lockheed have moved in to do aircraft maintenance and repair; shipbuilding and repairing is picking up, and the larger electronics firms seem impressed with the high competence level of the local employees. Most other countries have similar schemes for "trading up," so that they move into more highly skilled industries, as Japan has done, leaving the very unskilled, labor-intensive work to newer countries. Furthermore, they feel that China will become the ultimate cheap-labor competitor, if and when it becomes fully integrated into the world economy.[7]

Many developing countries make life even easier for the multinationals by providing them with ready-built factories on industrial estates, many of which are pure export-processing zones. Originally, the idea came from estates built in Britain and the United States, but through Indian and Puerto Rican

pioneering, the concept has been adopted widely, to the extent
that commercial firms are now in the business of developing
tax-free industrial zones for certain Third World governments
(Gulf & Western for the Dominican Republic). The governments gain because they can concentrate their provision of electricity, water, sewage disposal, communications in a few locations. Firms gain because they can simply fly in their machinery
and are ready to start, unless they need a factory of unusual
complexity. However, Taiwan's experience with such estates
points out the need for caution. Its first export-processing zone,
opened in 1966, was a huge success. Only three years after it
opened, the Kaohsiung Export Processing Zone was employing
40,000 people, roughly twice the number predicted. So Taiwan
set up two more, but these have been progressing at a much
slower rate, as incoming investors got the political wind up. It
would seem that the type of firm attracted by these estates is a
marginal investor. Often it is investing for the first time and
lacks the confidence of the large, more experienced multinationals. Competition is increasing from similar estates in Singapore and South Korea. So these zones are no magic solution.
They require heavy investment on the part of governments, and
they can fail to bring returns.[8]

The Economic Worth of Runaway Industries

It is easy to become overenthusiastic about the impact of the
runaways on specific economies. A study of the Puerto Rican
experiment invites a bombardment of statistics. Since the
inauguration of "Operation Bootstrap" in the 1940's, the economy has grown at 10 percent per annum, which, despite rapid
population growth, has led to a healthy 5 percent per annum
growth per head. Average individual incomes are up from $118
in 1940 to $1,100 in 1969, the highest in Latin America. Illiter-
acy is down to 12 percent, and the number of doctors has risen
from one per 3,763 people in 1940 to one per 986 in 1961, comparable with Britain in 1960. However, even if one ignores the
vast disparities of wealth that still exist, or the high emigration
and unemployment rates, or the social tensions resulting from

the arguments of Black Power Puerto Ricans who have learned their lessons all too well in New York, Puerto Rico is still a special case, given its position inside the United States tariff borders. The commonwealth's population is still under 3 million people, negligible when one looks at the multitudes to be found in the rest of the Third World. The other countries normally cited as success stories tend to be special cases. Hong Kong, with its British colonial administration, is tiny and heavily dependent for food and water on the bland tolerance of China, which seems almost to welcome its existence as a commercial and technological window on the Western world. It is in foreign colonial hands, formally separate from Chinese internal politics, poses no direct ideological challenge to any Chinese leaders, and can therefore be treated pragmatically. There exists a kind of implicit "management contract" between the British and the Chinese that, provided the British do not treat the Hong Kong Communists too harshly, China will turn a blind eye and allow them to carry on as before. Then there is Singapore, dependent on the commercial acumen of its basically Chinese population and on its position as entrepôt for large parts of Malaysia and Indonesia. It is also relatively small—another rich enclave feeding on a large hinterland. Taiwan, South Korea, and the Philippines owe rather more to their special relationship with the United States and the political stability this is supposed to entail. But even they are insignificant compared to the Third World giants like China, Indonesia, and India. Until this runaway phenomenon takes roots in economies such as these, it will remain marginal to the development of the Third World as a whole but extremely valuable to those countries currently most attractive to runaway investment.

It would be a mistake to view this as a purely Southeast Asian phenomenon, though, since the United States economy was necessarily the first one to be hit by runaways, Southeast Asia was the logical recipient of their investment. There are now signs that parts of the European economy are being hit in their turn, and if the Japanese do focus their attention on Europe to avoid further American protectionist reactions, the search by European firms for cheap-labor reservoirs should begin in earnest. The situation is complicated because the Germans in particular have long used "guest workers" from low-wage economies like those of Yugoslavia, Portugal, and Turkey as temporary labor inside Germany. The long-term social implications of this policy, both on German society and on the nations being drained of much of their best labor, are frightening, and there are signs that European companies are starting to invest directly in these countries instead of importing the workers. Portugal (though relatively rich for a true Third World country) has been increasing its textile and electronics exports to Europe. Yugoslavia is inviting a lot of interest, though there are problems stemming from a Communist system, however enlightened, which means that direct investment is always likely to be difficult. Firms like Fiat and Daimler-Benz import Yugoslav-made components, and Japanese firms like Nissan, Toyota, and Mazda are sizing up the opportunities. In addition the Yugoslav, Spanish, and Portuguese governments are all aware of the potential attractions of free ports (basically export-processing zones located around specified ports), and there have been occasional rumors that the Japanese might locate a car-assembly plant in a Yugoslav free port from which to supply Europe. However, the action in Europe is still hard to pinpoint. Cameras, toys, textiles, and electronics have already been hard hit, and would have been damaged more seriously if the European Common Market had not discriminated against the Japanese. However, with protectionism increasing in the United States, the growth of the Common Market, increased competition within Europe, the spread of the number of Third World countries with "special" links to Europe, and the Common Market's pioneering acceptance of tariff-free imports of Third World manufactured goods, the scene is wide open for the runaway phenomenon to become a major force in Europe.

The major criticism of the economic impact of the runaways is that they call upon the simplest of skills and that, apart from wages, some local purchasing, and taxation as the tax holidays run out, the economy as a whole fails to benefit, remaining dependent on "screwdriver" industries, where the only skill lies in assembling the imported components. This is true in the early days of such investment, but there is clear evidence that economies can learn higher skills in the course of business. Japan has certainly managed this feat. Other economies like Hong Kong, India, Pakistan, Taiwan, and South Korea are busy improving textiles toward synthetics, while Singapore is using its incentive scheme to attract a more highly skilled kind of investment. The last-named country also sends its citizens, including Ministers, on sabbaticals to places like the United States to examine current trends at first hand.

There are major difficulties involved in "trading up." For one thing, much of runaway activity takes the form of either direct investment by the foreign company or specific contracting of work to local entrepreneurs, who are left little initiative in design and so on. But this is not too critical a situation. As this runaway investment becomes more firmly established, governments can start insisting on conditions, such as increased use of local components. The lesson from Japan, and to some extent from Hong Kong and Taiwan, is that these subcontractors soon become quite knowledgeable about conditions and styles required for markets. Japan easily made the transition; its entrepreneurs learned how to design products specifically for American consumers. In Taiwan and Hong Kong there are now plenty of ambitious, capable entrepreneurs who will soon be capable of doing the same thing.

Despite this, Third World governments will continue to have problems handling the phenomenon. The Mexicans have still not found the right answer. In 1965 the government decided to try to attract investment to the border area near the United States. This was intended partly to devolve the economy away from Mexico City and partly to integrate the border Mexicans, who looked strongly toward the United States, into the Mexican economy. On one level the program has been successful, with about 270 in-bond factories (i.e. the product cannot be sold in Mexico) churning out textile and electronic products. Twenty-five thousand border inhabitants, mainly women (typical of runaway industries everywhere), are employed, and $35 million has been added to the Mexican economy in wages, rents, taxes, and general services. The only trouble is that at least

65 percent of this is spent either in the United States or on American goods, meaning that these inhabitants are even less integrated with the rest of Mexico. Also, there are vicious inflationary pressures as the annual wage of a Mexican employed in one of these factories is $1,000, while the average Mexican worker in an indigenous plant will earn about $360. This sort of disparity cannot benefit Mexican society or competing Mexican entrepreneurs. It is all too easy for the multinationals to pay wages that, though low enough for their purposes, are wildly out of line with standard rates in the rest of the economy. In the past this kind of disparity has been found in other enclave industries, like oil and mining, and is probably one of the conspicuous differences between the kind of development taking place in parts of the Third World and the development that took place when the United States or Europe was economically young. Labor "aristocracies" as a sociological phenomenon can only prove a source of friction.

Trade-Union Responses

International trade-union solidarity has long been one of the untested creeds of the world's unions. The runaways are testing this for the first time, and the union movement is in some disarray. After all, everything the runaway movement stands for is anathema to a trade unionist. It stands for sweated labor, bad industrial-relations policies, competitive legislation by governments against workers' rights to organize. At the same time, though, the interests of the workers in the Third World and those in the developed economies are different; the greater the difference in wages and working conditions between the two kinds of economy, the more likely the Third World is to get jobs, and in a world where unemployment can mean starvation this is important, however much exploitation is involved.

Work conditions in the Third World can be atrocious. Wages in South Korea, currently about the lowest in the runaway economies, are about a dollar a day, or around $7 a week. Hours are worse in Hong Kong, where 60 percent of its male workers work a seven-day week, while 52 percent of all employees work ten hours a day or more. Each year some 34,000 children between twelve and fourteen are forced to find work, and a case in which a ten-year-old girl started work at 6 a.m. and was still working at 8:50 p.m. is not exceptional. Official estimates are that at least one in four factories in Hong Kong uses child labor and a U.S. consulate official flew home from the colony to run for Congress in order to expose this practice, after a twelve-year-old foster child he had sponsored left school to go to work.

Western unions have spent well over a century trying to eradicate such conditions, and they are not happy to see good work undone by Western multinationals who shift into the Third World to take advantage of conditions outlawed in their parent countries. The Western unions are even more incensed when they see Third World governments competing to make life as difficult as possible for fledgling union movements. In dictatorships like Taiwan unions have no chance at all, but in other countries where unions have had some rights, there have also been serious government inroads. The incentives for pioneer industries in countries like Singapore and Malaysia specifically guarantee freedom from union trouble for a given number of years, and in 1970 there was the unedifying spectacle of Malaysia tightening its anti-union measures to bring them into line with those of Singapore. In Hong Kong the British administration has a bad record of siding with employers and was responsible for introducing controversial restrictions on picketing.

It is not surprising that Third World union movements are weak. High levels of unemployment do not help matters, and the average government is hostile, seeing the unions as "annoying pressure groups for higher real wages and more advanced social services than the economy can afford at a time when investment is a critical need." [9] When a militant union wrote to the International Labor Organization in Geneva complaining about a new piece of anti-union legislation in its country, the complaint reached the ears of the government, which promptly called the leaders to a meeting with the relevant Minister. The unionists were forced to write another letter to the ILO withdrawing their allegations. Having signed, the unionists were told that they

would be driven out of office and their union would, to all intents and purposes, be closed down.

The multinationals themselves do not always help, since they
normally appoint a local citizen to handle labor relations. One
advantage of such an appointment is that he usually is sensitive
to local feelings, but on the other hand, he will often see the
management position more like that of Henry Ford, Sr., in the
1930's than the smoother operators of today. As one manager
put it: "The condition of labor relations in Argentina when I
was down there six years ago was strikingly similar to that in
the United States back in the thirties. We have learned so much
about labor relations since the thirties. Had I been able to
see the parallels involved and to convince our men in Argentina
of these similarities, we would have done a much better job of
handling our labor relations in that country." [10] Thus, United
Auto Workers officials like Victor Reuther, who were themselves
beaten up by the auto companies' goons in the thirties, saw that
the practice of having armed foremen in Latin American car
plants is only just dying out. There are also stories about how
the managements of some well-known multinationals have co-
operated with General Franco, not just to get leading local
labor organizers jailed but to attempt to smash the whole Spanish underground union movement.

The standard strategy of the Western unions has been to
build up the strength of their Third World counterparts. During the late 1940's and early 1950's this process had strong
and rather unpleasant ideological overtones, with bodies like
the AFL–CIO and the CIA working closely together to set up
non-Communist unions to fight those created by their Communist opposite number, the World Federation of Trade Unions.
By the end of the 1950's, individual American unions, like the
United Auto Workers (UAW), foresaw the danger of Japanese competition and tried to create a united front with the
relevant Japanese unions. Despite personal attempts by the
union's president, Walter Reuther, they made little initial progress, but gradually they have managed to persuade the frag-
mented auto unions in Japan and Mexico to present a more
united front against the companies. There has also been scope

for financial assistance to unions too weak to stand on their own feet, and the American unions and various international bodies like the International Metalworkers Federation or the International Chemical Workers Federation (both Geneva-based) have started preparing computer printouts of, say, collective bargains agreed to by the leading auto multinationals throughout Latin America, country by country and plant by plant. In this way, negotiators can see what a given company is offering throughout the rest of the continent or how a specific offer compares with those of other parts of that industry in the same country. There has also been scope for simple tactical advice, as when the United Steel Workers helped the bauxite workers in the Caribbean set up the Bauxite Federation of the Caribbean to coordinate bargaining. They were thus able to make points about the type of issue that they, the Americans, felt was symptomatic of exploitation by the bauxite firms. When negotiations with the bauxite companies in Jamaica broke down, local leaders flew to the United States for tactical discussions, came back home, and won a satisfactory contract the next week.

Where the help involved merely requires decisions and action of the union headquarters in America or Europe, there are not too many problems. When a British Leyland subsidiary in Chile fired some union organizers in the late 1960's, British unions were alerted and lobbied the company headquarters to reinstate them. Grants of money to help carry on with a strike may not be too grave a problem, since strike pay in the Third World is small compared to that expected in the developed economies. But more direct action may be difficult. The Western unions want their Third World counterparts to win wage increases, which will narrow the gap between the two sets of economies, so that jobs in the developed economies will be preserved. Their Third World comrades would be foolish to push wages up so far that investors stopped coming, or transferred to more pliant economies. Once the two sets of unions have worked together in strengthening the institutions of Third World unions, there will probably always be conflicting aims and ideals. Both want the best-paid jobs for their members, and it may be that only one side can win. When a delegation from the Denki Roren (the Japanese Federation of Electrical Industry Workers), representing 400,000 workers, came to the United States in 1969, it "agreed to disagree" with its American hosts the Electrical Workers and the Machinists, who had hoped to get agreement on common policies toward runaway industries. It was simply impossible to reconcile the conflicting interests of the Japanese and United States electronics workers.

The Western unions have a perplexing problem—unless they narrow the wage differential between the developed world and the Third World, they will steadily lose jobs. Some of their solutions are just absurd. I have seen the suggestion of an international minimum wage to be achieved through some body like the ILO; within three to four years the average hourly wage in every industrialized country should not be lower than the United States minimum wage; rapidly industrializing nations like Mexico and the rest of Latin America would have five years; the rest of the Third World would be given six to ten years. Certainly such a plan would save American jobs, but even if it were politically feasible, the social tensions within the countries concerned would be incredible, and there is no device for solving the balance-of-payments problems that would result. Probably the most attractive concept to emerge from the union movement has been the call for some international fair-labor standard. This idea has been current for some time, after Walter Reuther introduced it at a meeting of the International Metalworkers Federation way back in 1956, when the idea had been proposed that trade expansion could result from "unfair competition." It is a shady concept, which assumes that it will be possible through bodies like GATT and ILO to push up the social standards of Third World economies so that competition would become "fair." Demands are made that such countries should recognize the right of workers to associate, and there is a current feeling that runaway multinationals should contribute to the Third World economies the equivalent of the United States minimum wage, or some such arbitrary sum, for each person they employ. Thus, if it would be disruptive to pay the individual employees what, to them, would be a vast sum, the difference should be contributed in further investments of some sort in infrastructural improvements.

Again this is an admirable scheme, and there could be ways of enforcing it. Companies wanting export credits, risk insurance, or tariff concessions (as under Section 807 of the United States tariff code) could be required to follow some such policy; the Swedes do have strings attached to their government insurance scheme for commercial risks in the Third World, requiring recipients to follow a positive labor-relations policy. But there are also inevitable holes in the argument. There are already firms in the United States that have moved from New England to the Southern states explicitly to employ non-union, black, female labor. Despite the fact that this is the cheapest labor to be found in the United States, they have not been able to match Southeast Asian competition and have been forced either to move out or close down. We are, therefore, discussing a policy that makes no economic sense as long as firms from other countries are operating under different rules. Even if all countries agreed, and the agreement could be enforced, would any firms find it worth their while to invest in the Third World at all? If the answer is no, the developing nations get neither the vital jobs nor infrastructural improvements.[11]

I have great sympathy for the union leaders in Europe and the United States who have to deal with this problem. Even in Europe, with its relatively long history of trying to guide industrial location so that dying industries are replaced by new ones, the lessons are not encouraging. It is a long, slow process, requiring coercion on industrialists as well as incentives, a lot of expensive infrastructure and retraining. But there will still be disruption. In the United States the problem is worse, since the country's long tradition of non-planning and the split between federal and state powers inhibits even the most interventionist government from forcing new industry to go where it is needed. If unions accept the demise of certain industries, they automatically condemn their members to a future without jobs, or the retraining facilities needed to get different work.

But Third World labor forces have a case, too. However

badly they are being exploited by Western standards, they are making definite advances with jobs that many of them would not otherwise have, and if unemployment pay is bad in Europe and the United States, the unemployed are in a better position than those of, say, Taiwan or India. American union leaders justifiably argue that some of the development of the Third World is taking place at the expense of the American or European working man. It is unfair that the rich in America should sit back and let the poor whites or the blacks suffer for the Third World. But this is a problem of American domestic policies, not one of the Third World's creation. America and Europe are rich enough to provide decent unemployment pay, retrain workers, and force industry to locate where it is needed, while the Third World is not. Looking at this through Third World eyes, the internal political problems of the United States and Europe are not a good enough excuse for sabotaging one of the few hopeful developments in the Third World.

It is easy to understand why the American unions have recently moved heavily into the protectionist lobby. It's a moot point whether they should have pressed for conventional measures like quotas or for a devaluation of the dollar against the threatening economies, but either way, the aim is to slow down the process whereby jobs are lost to the world's reservoirs of cheap labor. The unions have a duty to protect their members' jobs, whatever the cost to the Third World. Only the system that forces this behavior is at fault.

The Final Impact

The most impressive and frightening aspect of the runaway phenomenon is the speed at which it has spread. In 1960 it was rare for an American company to think of switching any manufacturing operations abroad for reasons other than the growth of protected markets overseas, which could be tackled only by local manufacture. When American companies were forced to accept such a step, most of them seem to have viewed the process with reluctance, manufacturing outside the United States only those goods that would otherwise create losses or low profits. Even in 1970 it was unusual to come across an American company that had screened all its products to see which could be manufactured most profitably abroad. The rule is still to manufacture in the United States wherever possible. This is a straight case of capitalist motivations conflicting with nationalistic ones, and nationalism is proving a potent factor in investment decisions.[12]

Nevertheless, *The Wall Street Journal* could comment on "sourcing" from abroad in mid-1971: "What's new is the breadth and depth of the effort. Of more than 40 manufacturers interviewed in recent weeks, all but a half dozen report they're looking harder for overseas opportunities to buy or manufacture components to be sold in the United States. Many say the change involves a whole new corporate philosophy." [13] What is even more thought-provoking is how few companies already using runaway facilities seemed worried about the 10 percent surcharge on imports announced by Nixon in 1971. *Business Week* quoted a number of such companies that said it just did not make any difference to their general strategy. These included Rohr Corporation (Mexico: rapid-transit cars), Remington Rand (Italy and Latin America: typewriters; Japan: calculators), Bulova (Taiwan: jeweled watches), General Instrument (Taiwan: television components), Bell & Howell (Japan: cameras), and Ampex (Hong Kong and Taiwan: computer core memories). There were a few companies like Singer that talked about the possibility of moving some operations back to the United States, but the general lack of reaction is as significant as the dog that did not bark in the night in the Sherlock Holmes story. At this stage of the game, a 10 percent rise in import costs in the United States is irrelevant to companies using labor some fifteen to twenty times cheaper than American labor. The one point that worried some of them was that American customers might well be shocked to discover how low the landed prices of many components or products really were compared to their final selling prices.

All the evidence shows that the psychological and technological revolutions that have produced the runaway phenomenon will leave the United States and other high-wage economies in extremely exposed positions. There are indications that the United States economy is now becoming totally nonviable in traditional terms of international trade and will spend the next ten or twenty years learning to live with this unpleasant reality. In the past, America has been able to maintain herself as a high wage, high standard of living economy through a number of factors that were once unique but are no longer. It avoided wars on its territory, had an extremely large domestic market, possessed copious supplies of raw materials, was protected by vast oceans from significant foreign competition, and was thus able to build up an extremely productive economy that could compensate for the high wages paid. As the years have gone by, the cheap stocks of iron, oil, copper, lead, and bauxite have been eaten away, costs have risen, and dependence on imports has increased, exposing United States industry to more equal competition with companies elsewhere. The growth of Japan and the expansion of the European Common Market mean that there are now other really large, reasonably integrated markets in the world. Finally, the communications revolution has reduced the once awe-inspiring Atlantic and Pacific Oceans to mere puddles. We are not yet in McLuhan's "global village," but for business-men, at least, the concept makes sense. What Detroit, Ralph Nader, American youth consumers, or Salvador Allende do one day is known the next by all the best-organized firms around the whole world. Oceans are barriers that add to transportation costs but pose few other major problems for the business community.

In the past, the high productivity of American workers saved them from the competition that could overcome the other ad-vantages of the United States economy. But this, too, is chang-ing. Other economies are mechanizing quickly, and they gain from the leapfrog effect, whereby a new Japanese industry, aimed at a vast market of first-time consumers, will have newer and more efficient plants than elderly American or European counterparts, whose consumer growth has slowed down as the replacement market takes over. Raw materials like steel and oil can often be purchased cheaper by non-American companies, who can buy on unprotected world markets. Plant construction costs may well be lower outside the United States, and then there are the ever-present investment incentives to be found all around the world. All this means that non-American firms may now have productivity levels similar to those of United States companies. If one takes RCA and the Japanese electronics firm Matsushita, one finds rough parity in sales per employee ($24,775 versus $20,220 in 1969), pretax profits per employee ($2,196 versus $2,326), capital invested per employee ($7,875 versus $7,782), and pretax returns on profit (27.9 percent versus 30.0 percent). The only real difference is that RCA wage rates in America are five times those of Matsushita in Japan.[14]

It is often claimed that the American economy will survive because the payments it receives in royalties will balance the outflow of cash needed to pay for the manufactured goods it imports. It is predicted that by 1975 the other countries will be paying the United States $17 billion a year in dividends, fees, and royalties from foreign investments, while the United States will be exporting only $6.5 billion. In terms of the American balance of payments, this is a lot of money, but the prophecy is probably optimistic. Since non-American firms are growing faster than American ones, the amount of money foreign companies have available for research will grow in comparison to American funds. This would suggest that the gap will soon begin to close. Again, it is not clear if useful research can be done separate from the manufacturing process by firms that may be distributors rather than manufacturers. Productive research, which provides the profitable licenses and patents, is more likely to be done close to the manufacturers in areas like Southeast Asia. After all, research costs are just as subject to runaway pressures as any other operating expense. Some American multinationals like Exxon are finding that European research workers are just as good as American—and considerably cheaper. As the standard of university education rises around the world, research work will doubtless drift to less expensive areas, just as record companies are finding that orchestras from lesser European countries can play classical music as well as American musicians but, again, for considerably less money.

Like it or not, America is being hustled into the "post-industrial society" beloved of futurologists like Daniel Bell and Herman Kahn. This condition, which is to be marked by the importance of service industries, leisure, and education, is the next logical step from present-day society, which still rests heavily on the direct production of goods. Company spokesmen like Henry Ford II claim: "I frankly don't see how we're going to meet foreign competition. We've only seen the beginning. We may become a service nation one day because our manufacturers could not compete with foreigners."

The futurologists consider the switch to the post-industrial society a logical evolutionary process. In fact, it will be no such thing. The United States, and perhaps Europe behind it, is being pitchforked, kicking and screaming, into the future, long before society as a whole is ready to make the transition. For instance, there is no system for dealing with structural working-class unemployment. Both unemployed and governments are still stuck with the idea that man has a right to work —and, in fact, ought to work. As a result, unemployment and retirement benefits are totally inadequate, and there are no schemes for equipping people with the skills needed to endure what may be decades of unemployment. If the work ethic proves too strong, there will be a need for well-planned public-work projects aimed at employing the low-skilled, while making sure that the particular jobs are not so degrading as to become another alienating force. In any case, no one has yet thought out the balance-of-payments implications of a switch to such a service economy. The whole of our international system of trade relies on the production and swapping of goods and services so that each country's trade balances the inward and outward flow. The only thing that a service economy is really geared to produce is knowledge, which can then be sold, but as we have seen, it is an open question whether it is possible to produce enough knowledge of value in the international market. Also, one of the by-products of moving into a post-industrial society is leisure-time travel, which is bound to eat into the United States balance of payments.

The economic and social picture looks bleak, and for the next twenty years at least, United States political leaders are surely going to be faced with a deteriorating economy, which will force a series of devaluations of the dollar against competitive currencies. European economies will face the same predicament, starting in the mid-to-late 1970's.

As a result, domestic American politics will be affected for the worse. It is very difficult for a politician to accept that his country's power is declining, and it is going to be particularly difficult for Americans, who have been brought up since the last world war to believe that this is the "American Century." That dream was already fading in the mid-sixties, but the American psyche has not yet adjusted. Nationalist Americans will face the same psychological shock that has hit colonial powers like France and Britain since the mid-1950's, when it became clear that the colonial era was dying. The dangers consist either of following the French pattern of fighting colonial battles when all is in fact lost (Algeria and Vietnam), with resultant right wing–left wing clashes, or of following the British model of pinning national pride to the value of one's currency, trying to preserve insupportable values in changing circumstances. Britain condemned herself to perhaps ten years of stagnant economic growth in futile attempts to preserve the parity of the pound. This kind of "stop-go" era can lead to an enervating political period in which all worthwhile social change is put into cold storage, while attempts are made to right the trade balance. Either way, the struggle to eliminate urban decay, racial discrimination, or poverty will be just as hard as long as there is a situation that is perceived as a financial "crisis."

The implications for international relations are equally disturbing. The whole dogma of free international trade is due to be tested in the most ruthless manner. In the past, the system worked reasonably well. The idea that countries should adopt fixed parities that they would stick to unless circumstances changed drastically was understandable, predictable, and a great deal more attractive than any alternative system of a steadily rising tariff-protected market. The escape clause allowing occasional devaluations or revaluations also began to work more efficiently, allowing economies that were out of line to be brought back into balance without too much disruption. In fact, as the multinational revolution gained ground in the late 1950's and mid-1960's, the system was improved by companies' speculative or precautionary financial planning, which led to ever-increasing flows of temporarily unemployed money across national boundaries, finding out those situations where a currency was obviously over- or undervalued. These ever-increasing flows of "hot" money forced the hands of national governments, like the British or German, who were clinging to old parities for symbolic rather than economically defensible reasons, and led to devaluations of the franc and pound and revaluation of the deutsche mark. Many economists were quite happy that parity changes were becoming more automatic, but by the late 1960's the whole system was in trouble because it could not cope with the dollar.

Devaluations or revaluations of any currency, except in the dollar area, are relatively easy. Once a new price is announced in dollars and cents, the issue is settled; the currency is now worth more or less in international transactions. Unfortunately, the system is not geared to handle a situation where the dollar itself is badly out of line with a large number of currencies, as it was in the late 1960's. The only solution was to try to persuade large numbers of countries to revalue their currencies together against the dollar, thus in practice devaluing it. The rest of the world was unenthusiastic about bailing out Americans. The Germans, having endured revaluation twice in the sixties, felt that they were in danger of pricing themselves out of world markets, which would not please their firms, and were as reluctant to revalue as were the Japanese, who argued that the inflow of American investment they were halfheartedly encouraging would help the Japanese cut back their huge trade surpluses. The Americans had no alternative but to present an ultimatum to the rest of the world saying, "Key currencies, revalue against the dollar—or else." This is what Nixon did in mid-1971, and again in early 1973—getting results like the revaluation of the yen but leaving considerable ill will in the rest of the world. The argument in this chapter would suggest that the parity changes resulting from the 1971–3 dollar crisis will have only temporary effects and that the long-term erosion of the United States economy will continue. We can therefore expect, within the next twenty years, at least three or four international financial crises.

These international clashes provoke uncertainty in world trade, as firms wait to see what final settlements are reached, and the use of quotas and special tariffs, tempting weapons when imports are flooding in, causes economic distortions and international resentment. This would suggest that international relations are going to be far rougher than one expected in those balmy days of the early 1960's, when the Kennedy round of tariff cuts went ahead in a blaze of idealism. One helpful decision would be for all the world currencies, including the dollar, to be tied to a neutral yardstick, like the International Monetary Fund's Special Drawing Rights units, which could make a useful alternative to the dollar. This would mean that should the dollar continue to be overvalued, the United States authorities could make their own unilateral decision to devalue in relation to the world's currencies, without having to hold crisis meetings whenever speculative pressures get out of control. The most likely alternative is that the major trading blocs in the world— Europe, Japan, the United States—will squabble over trading patterns that are felt to be disruptive. Japan, in particular, will be bullied and cajoled by the other two into restricting its activities, and attention will be concentrated on the cheap-labor economies of South Korea, Taiwan, and Hong Kong. International trade relations will remain bitter, and the chances of further extending trade concessions to the Third World in the form of generalized preferences for their manufactured goods in developed countries will diminish, even though the European Common Market has agreed to one such deal.

Whatever happens, the relationship between the Third World and the developed countries will become more violent because, for the first time since the turn of the century, economic forces are starting to work in favor of the Third World. In the past, economic forces have served only to harm it by, for instance, forcing the collapse of prices in commodities like cocoa and coffee. Any intervention to prevent such calamities has been an act of magnanimity on the part of the developed economies. The forces behind the runaway phenomenon are working directly in the immediate interests of the Third World, so any interference will be positively hostile to the poor of the world.

Every time quotas are slapped on imports from the Third World, a further brick is removed from the crumbling façade of the rich countries' official dogma that they really have the interests of the Third World at heart. With the advent of the runaway industry, we may be forced to admit that the selfishness of the rich nations is incurable—that any help or redistribution aiding the Third World will remain marginal on the rich countries' list of priorities.

Conclusions and Recommendations

These recommendations are listed in declining order of ideality.

1. The runaway phenomenon should be actively encouraged, and the drive to remove tariffs on manufactures and semi-manufactures from the Third World should continue. This involves a change in the status quo, but as far as the Third World is concerned: "The status quo is when you stand on me. When I try to get up, that is violence." Most objections to the runaway phenomenon come from those people who have profited from the old status quo. It is time for a change.

2. The long-term implications of uncontrolled competition must be considered. It is possible that there will never be enough productive work for the world's idle hands, and this is a blueprint for starvation. We may well need to produce a series of "commodity agreements" for manufactured products in which the plight of the American, Hong Kong, Indian, European workers would be examined in multilateral conferences and shares of the world market would be allocated by agreement.

3. In the meantime, there will be social dislocation in the developed economies. This can be slowed down by reaching for unilateral quotas or tactical devaluations. The latter are to be preferred because quotas reflect the industrial power structures of the past, thus making adjustment to newer industries a messier, less rational business.

4. The unions should accept that there is probably a genuine conflict of interest between workers in America and Europe, and those in Southeast Asia. Critics of the unions should also

realize that even the idealists in the union movement who are aware that the plight of the Third World worker is basically more serious than the plight of an American or European one are forced by the structure of their situation into protectionist positions. There is nothing reprehensible about such split loyalties.

5. The unions have a genuinely social role to play in the Third World. They should continue their help to fledgling Third World union movements, but should also accept that there is evidence from studies, like that of the ILO on Colombia, that overambitious working and social conditions for workers can actually lead to a decline in total employment. If this is a common phenomenon, they should concentrate harder on trying to improve the overall social policies of the governments concerned. They should try to make the aid programs of their parent governments more socially responsible. Sweden, for instance, now has a policy whereby aid is restricted to those countries whose governments show they have the interests of the majority of their populace at heart and not just those of a privileged minority. In societies where employment is a minority status, the urban trade unions may be elitist, and though they are still deserving of support, Western unions might seek to back organizations in the Third World that also look after the interests of the unemployed and the rural worker. They might also pressure their home governments to refuse export credits, or even government contracts, to multinationals that fail to observe above-average industrial-relations policies in all the Third World economies in which they invest.

6. Governments in the developed economies should accept that substantial structural unemployment is imminent and make their plans accordingly. Any competent manpower economist can supply breakdowns of the major industries likely to be affected by competition from cheap-labor economies over the next five to ten years. Plotting the geographical areas that will be worst hit is not difficult. What is needed is the political will to push new industries into these areas before the decline has set in, and no government can come close to solving this kind

of problem without using some form of coercion over the location policies of companies. Without such new industry, all retraining programs for unemployed workers are a waste of money. It may also be that governments should start devising labor-intensive public-work programs for such areas, or even that they should accept that unemployment is an inevitable status and deserves an adequate salary.

Notes

1. Hanningan and Morganstern, *A Trade Union Program for Expansion of International Trade*.

2. Professor W. Arthur Lewis, quoted in Barnes, *Africa in Eclipse*.

3. Schedule 807 statistics from Ericson, "An Analysis of Mexico's Border Industrialization Program"; Myint, "The 'Classical Theory' of International Trade"; Shelton, "The Relationship between Changes in Imports and Employment in Manufacturing."

4. For a good non-alarmist summary of arguments, read Sanford Rose in the August 1971 issue of *Fortune*.

5. Boczek, *Flags of Convenience*.

6. Many press reports plus Baranson, *Automotive Industries in Developing Countries*.

7. Daniel, ed., *Private Investment*; Kindleberger, *American Business Abroad*; Servan-Schreiber, *The American Challenge*.

8. England, "Labour Policy in Hong Kong."

9. Galenson, *Labour in Developing Economies*.

10. Skinner, *American Industry in Developing Economies*.

11. Barovick, "Labor Reacts to Multinationalism"; Hero and Starr, *The Reuther–Meany Foreign Policy Dispute*.

12. Stobaugh, "The Multinational Corporation."

13. *Wall Street Journal*, September 10, 1971.

14. Dr. F. E. Jones of Philips, quoted in the *Financial Times*, March 25, 1971; Rhodes, "The American Challenge Challenged."

Further Reading

The literature is expanding fast. Some recent references: Adam, "New Trends in International Business"; Balassa, "Industrial Policies in Taiwan and Korea"; Cohen, "The Economic Impact of Foreign Investments for the Export of Manufactures"; Harrod, "Multinational Corporations, Trade Unions and Industrial Relations"; Helleiner, "Manufactured Exports from Less Developed Countries"; Hopkins, ed., *Hong Kong: The Industrial Colony*; Kassalow, "Trade Unionism and the Development Process"; Leontiades, "International Sourcing in the LDCs"; Levinson, *Capital, Inflation and the Multinationals*; Little, Scitovsky, and Scott, *Industry and Trade in Some Developing Countries*; Power, Sicat, and Hsing, *The Philippines: Taiwan. Industrialization and Trade Policies*; Rose, "The Poor Countries Turn from Buy-less"; Shaw, "Foreign Investment and Global Labor"; Vernon, ed., *The Technology Factor in International Trade*; Watanabe, "International Subcontracting."

8 : : *Tourism—The Most Subversive Industry*

Lord Jesus Christ, Son of God, have mercy on the cities, the islands and villages of our Orthodox fatherland, as well as the holy monasteries which are scourged by the worldly touristic wave.

Grace us with a solution to this dramatic problem and protect our brethren who are sorely tried by the modernistic spirit of these contemporary western invaders.

A new prayer recommended by the
Greek Orthodox Church

The national bourgeoisie will be greatly helped on its way toward decadence by the western bourgeoisie which comes to it as tourists . . . If proof is needed of the eventual transformation of certain elements of the ex-native bourgeoisie into the organisers of parties for their western opposite numbers, it is worth having a look at what has happened in Latin America. The casinos of Havana and Mexico, the beaches of Rio, the little Brazilian and Mexican girls, the half-breed thirteen-year-olds, the ports of Acapulco and Copacabana—all these are the stigma of the national middle class.

Frantz Fanon in The Wretched of the Earth

Tourism As Industry

Tourism is not just a big business. For large parts of the Third World, it is the fastest-growing "export" trade. Ironically, it depends on the sun, which, along with a starving, unhealthy labor force, has long been blamed for the "scourge of tropicality"—that mind-numbing lethargy that has helped condemn the Third World to grinding poverty. But today that sun, instead of draining the productive energy from ill-fed, malaria-ridden natives, beats down on beaches filled with the tanned bodies of Scandinavian nudists, beach-bumming hippies, jet-set beauties, and elderly retired couples. Among them, these bodies account for between 6 and 7½ percent of total world trade—$15 billion worth of business per annum, growing at between 10 and 16 percent each year.

A growing number of economies would fall to pieces if it were not for the tourist. Mexico made its tourist chief a member of the cabinet to acknowledge that, whereas income from this source in 1950–3[1] was equivalent to a mere 46 percent of the value of exports, by 1960–3[2] it had climbed to 68 percent and by 1967 to 83 percent. Soon, then, the Mexican tourist industry will be worth more in foreign exchange than the whole of the conventional export industries. Without this source of income, Mexico would have been wracked by inflation and would have had to grow more slowly. Tourism is also a much more stable industry than most conventional Latin American export industries. Similarly, in Europe the Spanish and Yugoslav economies are becoming just as dependent on the "Golden Hordes." Mexico's earnings from tourism reached $1.2 billion in 1969, while Yugoslavia, part of a poorer continent, took in $360 million in 1970. This was $100 million more than she received from the hundreds of thousands of Yugoslavs working in Western European industry.

It is a deceptively enticing industry. Planners look at the Third World's measureless stretches of sun-baked beaches and the apparently unlimited willingness of the world's rich to lie upon them. Moreover, it is a clean, safe industry compared to traditional mines and manufacturing. Tourism does not kill or maim its workers, nor does it seriously pollute or devour material resources. All that is needed is to house and feed a few foreign tourists and the money will roll in. Surely this is industry without chimneys? But this is to gloss over the drawbacks.

Above all, it is a capital-intensive industry. The less developed the economy, the more money will have to be invested in bringing the infrastructure up to the standards required by the tourists. Airports, hotels, roads, sewage systems, tourist guides, cultural and amusement centers all have to be provided before the tourist will come. In some cases, new towns have to be built from scratch. In their lack of impact on the rest of the economy, these investments can often become the 1970 equivalent of the railways built in previous generations for the exclusive use of foreign-controlled enclaves. They can be justified only if they generate high returns that actually stay in the Third World country. In practice, the profits still tend to seep back to the rich countries.

United States citizens provide the bulk of the billion dollars earned by the Mexican tourist industry. They come to Mexico by plane and car, they tour in coaches, they eat in restaurants, buy souvenirs, stay in hotels. Ultimately, most of these services are owned or controlled by American companies like Pan Am, Coca-Cola, Hertz, or Sears Roebuck. A study of the impact of this Americanization of the tourist industry in Jamaica in the late 1950's showed that at least 39 percent of the tourist receipts left the country again.

The Pressures on the Third World to Develop Tourism

Multinationals have a vested interest in this industry. They have learned one of the new laws of economics: the more someone earns, the greater proportion he will spend on travel and tourism. World expenditure on these is inexorably growing faster than per capita incomes, and thus a growth industry that the multinationals cannot afford to ignore is indicated.

The established airlines should have been the prime beneficiaries—their jets extend to a range of countries that can be reached comfortably and cheaply. In practice, they have made an almighty mess of their involvement. Vacationers are very easy to fly. They tend to book well in advance, and they can be put together in groups, thus allowing the airlines to fly expensive aircraft at 90–100 percent capacity. This compares favorably with the normal scheduled flights, which are priced to become profitable once they are about half filled. The sharper operators used their computers and calculated that such high utilization of aircraft meant they could profitably cut prices and generate still more business.

However, the airline giants like Pan Am, BOAC, and Lufthansa belong to what must be the world's clumsiest cartel —IATA (the International Air Transport Association). This body sets the rates on all major international routes. It has traditionally kept these high to allow various pygmy airlines to stay aloft and has incidentally allowed giants like Pan Am to go on mad purchasing sprees that would have bankrupted them in any other industry. The whole high-fare IATA establishment tried to wish the problem away and did nothing. This allowed a number of industry newcomers like World Airways, Universal, Britannia Airways, or Spantax to build up cheap-fare, charter businesses outside the auspices of IATA. They bought or leased aircraft only if they were guaranteed tourist business, and they rapidly lured away much of the most profitable trade of the established airlines. However, by 1972 the giants were responding. They, too, started slashing key fares.

Whatever this does to airline profits, it can only stimulate the tourist industry. Cheap fares will open up areas that are now relatively expensive to reach, such as the Caribbean for European vacationers. It also means that the airlines are going to have to fight harder to fill their planes. They will thus get even more heavily involved in related activities like running hotels.

Some independent hotel chains like Holiday Inn still exist. ITT has its Sheraton subsidiary, and oil companies like Exxon have dabbled with motels. However, most of the significant action has come from the airlines. Hilton International turns out to be a subsidiary of Trans World Airlines, Inter-Continental of Pan Am, Western International of United Airlines' holding company, and so on. During 1970 and 1971 it was hard to pick up any financial paper without reading of some airline getting involved with new hotel ventures. BOAC, BEA, Lufthansa, Alitalia, and Swissair came together to build a chain of hotels in Europe; Third World companies like Pakistan International, Air Congo, and Air India struck similar deals with foreign partners. There are virtually no major lines left without hotel interests.

Their logic is impeccable. The people they fly have to have

somewhere to stay at the other end. Often the development of a new route depends on the building of hotels of the necessary standards. But even more, the airlines control worldwide booking organizations, which make it extremely easy to book the traveler into hotels at the same time he books his air tickets. The airlines can thus guarantee their hotels a relatively high rate of occupancy. Moreover, these hotel chains can make or break a tourism project. Their hotels symbolize the willingness of a major multinational to put its reputation at stake, so that other minor investors can commit themselves with more confidence. In this way, the multinationals can often find eager local investors who may well put up the bulk of the money in order to get the lucrative rights to well-known international brand names. The multinationals may provide only design and operating expertise, along with the guarantee that the hotel will be put into its worldwide marketing operation. So the Third World countries get 1970's status symbols—a Hilton or Inter-Continental hotel—while the airlines have accommodation waiting for their passengers. Both sides apparently win.

Not only commercial bodies are backing tourist schemes. Many international aid agencies are becoming extremely interested. For instance, the United Nations Development Program, which specializes in basic infrastructural investment, helped the Yugoslavs in 1967 to prepare a long-term economic growth plan with tourism as an essential element. An Italo-Polish consortium, Tekne-Cekop, was brought in to help draw up a regional plan for the South Adriatic, with Dubrovnik as the pivot, taking into account the area's coastline, cultural history, and ancient architecture. The following year, Mexico got $100 million from the Inter-American Development Bank for "tourist infrastructure" around the Mayan ruins in the Yucatan peninsula and on the Pacific coast. This was believed to have been the first loan for tourist activities from an international development bank. A year later the International Finance Corporation (the World Bank subsidiary investing specifically in private enterprise) joined with various European, Middle Eastern, and United States companies in a $39 million project to promote and finance a wide range of Tunisian tourist projects. At least 10,000 jobs then depended on this industry, and it was hoped to create another 15,000 by 1973. American Express was the only household name, but the Aga Khan was involved through his Swiss company, Industrial Promotions Services. Some Arab oil money also came through the Kuwait Foreign Trading, Contracting and Investment Company. Finally, the World Bank has become involved in its overall capacity, creating a special Tourism Projects Department, which by early 1971 had yet to approve any projects, though several were in the pipeline.

The Social Implications

Tourism will undoubtedly have some beneficial consequences. The average tourist is sensitive to issues like pollution, so governments will have to keep this in mind when planning their industrialization policies. Growth rates may well be slowed, but at least if governments should opt for maximum growth, there is more likely to be public debate about the consequences than there was in the days of the earliest industrial revolutions. Some countries are even finding that conservation can pay. Tanzanian game reserves like the Serengeti are a major tourist attraction and are therefore carefully maintained. Zambia has leased 2,500 square miles of the Zambesi River Valley to a non-profit-making United States society called Wildlife Conservation International for twenty-five years at $1 per acre, on the understanding that the society provides its own management for the park and the necessary game guards, roads, and welfare facilities for rural communities. Again, the search for picturesque tourist attractions often leads to a search into the country's past to preserve indigenous dances, legends, and folk arts. Even if some of this culture reaches the foreigners in bastardized form, it does mean that rural traditions, in particular, will not be totally destroyed during the industrialization process, as often happened in equivalent stages of European and American economic growth. The local nationalist thus benefits from work done initially for the tourist industry.

On the other hand, much of the business is extremely unattractive. In particular, it is unlikely to develop any worth-while social or political consciousness. For one thing, key management like headwaiters, chefs, tour guides, golf and tennis professionals will all tend to be foreigners, since tourists tend to flock to hotels that have the sign "This hotel is English/ American/Japanese/German managed." At best, this layer of employees will be minimally interested in the country's wider development; at worst, they will bitterly resist measures that hit at their rights to import luxury goods or send their savings to safer climes.

Since tourism is essentially a seasonal industry, we are likely to find the pattern established in existing tourist areas that attract apolitical drifters and marginal workers or, as many Western hotel managers put it, the "scum" of society. This already unpromising material is then split up into numerous small work places (cafés, bars, beaches, bus driving, etc.)—the classic formula for producing an apathetic work force, since there is so little opportunity for traditional political solidarity to evolve. Finally, and perhaps most importantly, these workers are forced to adopt a role that requires them to show ingratiating servility toward the foreign guests on whom they have to wait. It is rare to find a radical headwaiter.

Is There a Critical Mass?

The planners swarming into this field are blandly confident that the industry is politically "safe." They assume that McLuhan's global village has actually arrived, that we are all tolerant cosmopolitans—especially at a glimpse of foreign exchange. These technocrats are too easily impressed by the miracles of communications technology. They tend to forget the evidence of Third World tragedies, like Biafra, Bangladesh, Burundi, and Indonesia in 1965, which suggest that many parts of the world are still wracked by tribal, racial, and religious divisions. United nationhood is difficult enough to achieve, let alone internationalist status. Where the structure of a society is so tenuous, the tourist is more likely to aggravate than to soothe the situation.

A case can be made that there will be a critical point beyond which a tourist industry becomes so big that it starts producing a significant backlash in the host culture. Even Switzerland, for centuries the hotelier of Europe, has exhibited a profound resentment at the number of foreigners who have invaded her country. A xenophobe political movement has been rapidly growing. In 1970, to the horror of the Swiss establishment, an ex-journalist and publisher, Dr. James Schwarzenbach, launched a referendum calling for a substantial cut in the number of resident foreigners, who now total around 1 million among barely 6 million Swiss. Almost half the votes were in favor, and the government started cutting down on the number of foreign workers allowed into the country. Ironically, as well as American managers and United Nations personnel, there were large numbers of Italians and Spaniards brought in to handle those jobs in the tourist industry now considered too menial for the Swiss. So when the cuts were felt the hotel industry was particularly badly hit, and in some cases, prices went up by almost 90 percent in a single year. The pressures on Switzerland will continue as wealthy Europeans try to buy into the lucrative tourist industry or take advantage of the country's generous tax breaks for the rich. The Swiss are now finding that this means competition for available housing and land, and that the prices they pay are affected by the ability of wealthy foreigners to afford more. The situation seems to be worsening, although a government ban on any new foreign workers seems to have delayed any immediate challenge from the xenophobes. However, it is still possible that a referendum could be held, calling for a 50 percent cut in the total number of foreigners living in Switzerland (up from 10 percent in 1960 to 17 percent in 1970). Whatever happens, the dispute has shown that there is a limit to the number of foreigners as tourists or residents that even a society like Switzerland's can tolerate. For societies less stable, the situation looks more critical.

Tourists do not present quite the same problems as foreign residents. The atmosphere and climate that attract foreigners as tourists will draw a smaller number as permanent residents. A single foreign dweller may make more social impact than a single fleeting tourist, but there will be more of the latter, and their inflationary impact may be more severe, since they have more money to spend per day of stay than the residents. However, some countries' capacity to absorb tourists is remarkable. Spain received 25 million tourists in 1971, which comes close to the country's total population of 33.5 million. But there have been violent incidents involving hippies in Ibiza, and demands have been made that the country opt for "better-quality" tourists who would spend more and behave discreetly. However, the vast majority of these tourists go to holiday ghettos like Benidorm and remain isolated from Spanish society. The situation in Greece is more complicated, since the local culture and historical relics are an important attraction in their own right. By 1972 Greece was receiving 2.5 million visitors (from 394,000 in 1960), equivalent to just under a third of the total population of 8.9 million. Already some observers are concerned about congestion in this small, mountainous country, especially as the bulk of these tourists want to visit historical sites like the Parthenon and Delphi. The planners blithely predict that there will be 10 million visitors by 1980. However well the influx is controlled, both tourists and Greeks will find their patience taxed.

The hippies test the system first. Most countries really want Spiro Agnew's "silent majority," who will pay their money and keep to the guided tours. But they also get the kids from California, the students, the dropouts for whom work is of marginal importance, who seek pleasure and self-fulfillment as primary goals. Such attitudes are far more disturbing to societies in which work is a privilege than the dollars of staid vacationing businessmen. Countries as far flung as Taiwan, Singapore, and Tanzania have regular drives to keep their youth uncontaminated by decadent Western customs like long hair and minidresses. And there is an inevitable spin-off toward the less ostentatious members of a different culture. A year ago in Singapore I was politely pulled out of an incoming airport line and had my ticket stamped so that I could not sell the return half in the city and "go underground" on the proceeds. This treatment was friendly enough, but the culture gap can manifest itself much more unpleasantly. The Turks, for instance, put young drug purchasers into jail for well over ten years for offenses that, if committed in their home countries, would merit a fine or suspended sentence at the most.

An equally serious problem for conventional tourists is a traffic accident. In Uganda, one is allegedly allowed to report an accident to the police station in the next town rather than hang around the scene of the crime and thereby risk the wrath of the local inhabitants. A traffic offense may lead to imprisonment for months in a strange land. Consular officials in countries like Turkey have been known to advise their nationals in this kind of situation to leave the country at once, rather than stay to face a trial where it is judged that the odds are stacked against foreigners.

Such legal differences are likely to become a major source of conflict. This follows a long historical pattern, in which the old colonial powers would always insist that their citizens be tried in courts they could control rather than in local courts. Foreign army bases provide a history of soldiers, accused of crimes against local citizens, who are whisked out of the country before local courts have a chance to hear the cases. Incidents involving American army personnel were still being reported in 1970 and 1971 in Okinawa and the Philippines. Tourists, however, are much more vulnerable. We can expect a series of cases in which the host country prosecutes tourists for offenses that do not exist in their home countries. On the other hand, if tourists are let off with nothing but warnings, the local citizens will become justifiably incensed. It is likely that we will be faced with a growing number of *causes célèbres,* involving tourists and alien legal systems. These will infuriate the host countries, who will be lectured by the tourists' home countries about the "barbarity" of their laws—but it will be tragic for the tourist victims.

Race and the Caribbean

A significant part of tourism involves shipping rich white pleasure seekers into some of the world's poorest black societies, so it is not at all surprising to find racist reactions to the industry in various parts of the world. They seem strongest in the Caribbean, where riots in Jamaica (October 1968), Curaçao (May 1969), and Trinidad and Tobago (April 1970) convinced many American tourists that the whole of the Caribbean was unsafe and bubbling with resentment against them. In fact, tourism was not an important factor in any of these riots, which stemmed rather from existing deep divisions in these societies, exacerbated by the import of Black Power ideology from the United States. However, the industry is a central point in the argument raging between the "Afro-Saxon" (i.e., "Uncle Tom") elites of the area and their militant opponents. After all, what clearer evidence can there be that these rulers have "sold out" than the erection of luxury hotel and restaurant complexes that exclude local black citizens? The old banana or bauxite industries were bad enough, but at least the beneficiaries were enjoying their dividends back in the United States. But their successors are the people who stay in the expensive Caribbean holiday complexes. They are sitting propaganda targets for anyone wanting to link the area's grinding poverty to the workings of capitalism. Rich, white, and capitalist, they lie in the sun, unconsciously symbolizing the whole structure of oppression as understood by local radicals.

In Georgetown, Guyana, foreign arrivals were being advised in mid-1971 not to venture out of their hotels on foot, even during the daytime, as attacks on whites grew in numbers. This was not necessarily a manifestation of racism but showed that any white person was likely to be worth robbing. As urban unemployment grows in all the expanding Third World cities, the ostentatiously rich foreigners will become more and more in danger. In Jamaica armed guards now patrol hotel grounds, and in Puerto Rico the independence movement regularly bombs American-owned hotels and businesses. Despite the fact that the average tourist in the Caribbean will encounter none of these tensions, the stories multiply, and whether the story is true or not, it is said that in the Bahamas tourists who have a flat tire in the countryside drive to the next town before changing it. A riot, whatever the cause, does mean a heavy drop in tourist bookings. To some extent the tourist regimes can cover up some potentially harmful incidents by very careful control of the press. Thus, the Greek colonels, after the 1967 coup, were soon able to reassure worried European tourists, despite the fact that for the next couple of years bombings continued in Athens and Salonika. But in the long run the tourist himself must become the prime target of the dissident groups.

As explained above, he is a symbol of the inequality of the world, and the inequality he represents is far greater than that seen in any European or American society. After all, a Kenyan or Tanzanian peasant is earning at the most about $100 a year, while the tourists he sees lounging on the beach will be earning about $25,000 a year (a cheap package two-week vacation from Europe will start at about $450). Even at the height of the robber-baron era, few businessmen were earning that much more than their fellow citizens, and the Protestant ethic taught the poor that everyone had the chance of success. But there is no equivalent Third World ethic to teach the vast pool of un-employed that they, too, can become chairmen of General Motors.

So far most anti-American attacks have been on stores or factories, which are relatively easy to protect, but the tourist is a sitting duck whenever he wanders off the beaten track or mills about a crowded airport waiting for his plane. Even a police state cannot hope to protect every tourist when they are flooding into the country in the millions. At some stage, an opposition group in one of the countries dependent on tourism will say to itself that tourism is the only major industry it can hit with reasonable impunity. It might well lose some middle-of-the-road sympathy in the countries whose tourists are either killed or assaulted, but it would also embarrass its government considerably. The current urban guerrilla tactic of kidnapping diplomats or businessmen does not hit anyone in the pocket, but sabotaging the tourist industry would, since it is readily sensitive to such scares. Uruguay's Tupamaros (urban guerril-las) have adopted this tactic by threatening the resort of Punta del Este, the "in" place for South America's rich, but have had little success so far. Once jumbo jets start flying the tourists in droves, the job will be easier.

The Golden Ghettos

There are only two approaches to the problem of cultural rape. One is to control the quantity and quality of the incoming tourists by providing facilities that price the area or country beyond the pockets of the hippies and other low spenders. The second is to segregate the foreigners in tourist ghettos, located well away from centers of population, so that cultural disruption is kept to a minimum.

So far few countries have set about using the pricing mechanism deliberately, though areas like the Caribbean have traditionally been exclusive, because the cheap end of the American market was satisfied with readily accessible California, Florida, and Mexico. Thus, there was no need for the airlines and holiday firms to develop the mass-produced "package-tour" industry for the Caribbean on the scale that has led to the colossal expansion of the tourist industry in Spain and other Mediterranean countries. Spain is in the middle of a debate about the quality of the tourist it attracts and is beginning to regret the cheap, mass-produced image its industry has acquired. In particular, it is very much aware that package tourists spend little compared with those visiting countries like Britain and is, therefore, starting to think of ways to attract more liberal-spending individuals. It is worried in case it loses this upper end of the market to countries like Portugal which can see some of the problems facing Spain and are deliberately trying to keep their tourist developments more exclusive. There is greater emphasis on the building of apartments for leasing or purchase, and thus greater attention to the more wealthy Northern Europeans looking for a second house or a place to retire. The Portuguese have also begun television programs to instruct their citizens on how to behave toward tourists, stressing politeness and etiquette. Among other habits they are seeking to eradicate is the accepted Portuguese practice of spitting in public places—

it disconcerts the tourists. This kind of instruction is nothing new. Japanese governments over the years have drummed into their citizens that certain local customs are found odd by foreigners, while Uganda has been trying to persuade one of its tribes to don clothes for the first time to protect the country's international image. It is cheering to report that the tribesmen have been resisting bitterly.

The best-known luxury tourist development around the Mediterranean is the Aga Khan's Costa Smeralda in Sardinia. He controls some 6,000 acres on part of the island's most spectacular coastline that he helped develop into what is known as Europe's leading millionaires' playground. In recent years there has been an attempt to downgrade the image slightly by encouraging select "residential" tourism, where the wealthy businessman builds himself a vacation mansion. One smaller, but newer, elite development has no hotels at all, and it is opening golf courses, which in Europe cater strictly to the upper classes. It has developed an exclusive image that the Spanish would dearly love to emulate.

An alternative approach is to develop tourist ghettos. Large numbers of tourists want just a couple of weeks of sand and sun, and provided there are a reasonable range of recreational facilities and a number of compatriots around them, they show little interest in moving far into the surrounding countryside. It has thus been possible to create artificial towns consisting entirely of hotels, restaurants, and bars, with no provision for permanent local residents. Alternatively, holiday camps or villages can be created in the beachcombing image developed by Club Méditerranée. Only a few local citizens work in the tourist industry, and thus cultural shock is minimized. This device is used intelligently by some of the Eastern European countries, which want Western European tourist money without any political trouble. Bulgaria arranges that most Western tourists go to the Golden Sands resort on the Black Sea, and although there are a lot of East German, Czechoslovak, and Bulgarian tourists there as well, the problems of such transideological meetings are limited to this one resort. Of course, it is impossible to rule out some touristic influence, for such ghetto resorts obviously attract all those in the country who are most receptive to the foreigners' way of life, but this is a controllable problem. So, for countries where the cultural shock may be even more severe, as in Africa, this ghetto approach is probably the most sensible. But it will not solve all problems. Tanzania, for instance, has had to instigate a two-price system for its game reserves, with local Tanzanians paying a cheaper entrance fee than the tourists. The tourists may complain, but when income differentials are so high this is a reasonable arrangement.

However, attempts to limit social corruption are easier to formulate than to carry out. If the industry depends entirely on incoming planeloads of tourists who are all booked through the same travel agency, it is possible to channel them all into fairly restricted areas. But if they are mobile from the start, difficulties will arise. Mexico is plagued with the problem of towns like Tijuana, Nuevo Laredo, Matamoros, and Ciudad Juarez, whose red-light districts are an irresistible magnet for American "twenty-four-hour" tourists. In 1970 these "boys' towns," or "zones of tolerance," raked in some $879 million in foreign exchange by official calculation, so it is unlikely that any Mexican government can yet afford to close them down. If it should try, the underground figures flourishing there could be as hard to eradicate as a force in Mexican society as the Mafia has been since the ending of prohibition in the United States. A number of the newer touristic nations are trying to emulate Monaco, whose success has always rested heavily on the existence of its casino. They are deliberately providing gambling facilities as an added attraction. But they are becoming involved in one of the industries that is most difficult to control. As the British discovered when they legalized gambling in the early 1960's, Mafia-related interests are quick to infiltrate such new ventures, which are safely beyond the reach of the American authorities. Unless the local government is extremely alert, it will find the casinos falling into the hands of crooked operators. The alternative of keeping them under state control is no guarantee, moreover, that criminal elements can be thwarted. Not only do casino operators have to be able to spot which of their employees is trying to cheat them, but they need an encyclopedic knowledge of the industry to know which gamblers can be granted credit facilities and which will default on their debts. This kind of skill comes only with experience, and it is a fact of life that many of the best advisers or managers will be linked with the Mafia. The Bahamas once accepted this fact by calling in Meyer Lansky, a Mafia-linked gambling boss, as technical adviser when setting up their casinos. The danger, however, is not that the Mafia will wander the world picking off the less experienced countries one by one; after all, local criminals are as nationalistic as any honest businessman worried about incoming foreign competition. The danger is more that indigenous operators will move into positions of such economic strength that they will become major political forces in their own right.

Bali—Last Paradise or New Waikiki?

Bali is a small Indonesian island of 2.3 million inhabitants lying just off the end of Java. A fertile combination of animist religions and the Hindu pantheon has created a range of gods and ceremonies on a scale rarely found elsewhere. The islanders have developed into natural artists—wood-carvers, painters, dancers, and actors—of such originality and talent that the island has long fascinated anthropologists. Now, however, the island is attracting the more adventurous (and wealthy) tourists who have exhausted the delights of Europe.

The Indonesian government is not going to disappoint them. Trying to repair the economic damage done by former President Sukarno, the technocratic, pro-Western regime of President Suharto is not in a position to turn down any project that promises badly needed foreign exchange—and Bali could prove a gold mine. Bali's airport was expanded to take jets in 1968, and the ten-story Bali Beach Hotel (owned by the government, managed by Inter-Continental Hotels) has been doing turn-away business ever since. Other operators have been rushing to add to the mere 645 first-class hotel rooms available by 1971. A Hilton is due to be built, while the Dutch and Indonesian airlines, KLM and Garuda, are involved with another large hotel scheme. There may be some delay while the local authorities decide whether to permit such hotels to be built higher than the local coconut trees (by early 1972, the cynics were being proved wrong as the regime held fast against the hotel interests who prefer skyscraper designs), but according to plan, there will be an extra 1,300 hotel rooms in time for the 1974 annual conference of the Pacific Area Travel Association, due to be held on the island. By 1985 the number of first-class hotel rooms should be up to 8,500 and the number of incoming tourists should reach a million per annum, roughly the number that Greece's larger population was accepting at the end of the 1960's. Meanwhile, countries like Singapore, with the region's pivotal international airport, are cheerfully assuming that they will profit from this boom.

To give the Indonesians their due, they backpedaled on any major developments until a French team financed by the World Bank and the United Nations Development Program had completed a study in 1971 of how the island should be developed. The report specifically examined how a tourism boom can be achieved with minimum harm to the overall culture of the island. A number of younger travelers who base themselves on Kuta Beach have been involved already in lurid incidents like naked dancing in the sacred Monkey Forest, which for a while led to careful rerouting of the tourist trips in that area. In principle, the official study suggests that the tourists should be kept to given parts of the island and that the dances and arts should be brought to them, rather than the other way around. This will allow the genuine student of strange cultures to prowl off the beaten tourist track, without having the islanders too contaminated by less dedicated vacationers. In the meantime, the government has also started programs of cultural education in the public schools, where young Balinese will be taught traditional dances, art forms, and music. They will learn the meaning of the legends and myths that are an integral part of Balinese creativity. A new force is thus intruding itself on this unique culture. What criteria will determine which dances are chosen for special attention? To what extent will these choices be influenced by a selective perception of what the tourists are capable of appreciating? A new cultural influence is going to impose itself on Bali's richness.

Tourism, like many other industries, provides foreign exchange, which can be used to provide significant numbers of local inhabitants with materially richer and securer lives. In the process, inevitably, tribal or national cultures will be modified, and it is right to show concern. No one eats religious ceremonies, but one can buy medicine, food, agricultural equipment with the money brought by foreign spectators. In deploring their impact, we can come close to arguing that cultures like Bali's should be preserved forever, unchanged, in a kind of social aspic. It is like arguing that American Indians should have stayed technologically at the level of their forefathers. Just as today's Indians would not take kindly to such a suggestion, it is doubtful that the Balinese will appreciate being "preserved" to salve the consciences of the world's sentimentalists. The key argument is that Bali is now capable of entering the world economy through tourism. The rich and "civilized" have no moral right to deny them. But we do have the duty to ensure that the maximum amount of the industry's material proceeds reach the Balinese themselves and that the industry be regulated to make as little cultural impact as possible, until the day when the Balinese formulate their own policies.

Conclusion

Most planners in the industry give only token attention to these issues. They tend rather to see it in politically "neutral" (i.e. purely financial) terms. There is, though, a real chance that the growing number of tourist projects backed by aid agencies will have a radicalizing influence on Third World politics. Tourism is an industry running directly counter to one of the chief survival tactics used by the rich to hang on to their privileges. As his wealth increases, the rich industrialist moves first to a suburb, then to a country estate, and finally perhaps to a Greek island. In the meantime, the poor are unaware of the true life-styles of this absent upper class and so tend to judge their own progress purely in terms of their personal histories. Since they will probably be doing better in absolute terms, they do not see the proportionally rapid rise in the rich man's position. They thus find it hard to believe that they are still relatively just as badly off.

Tourism reacts to this process in two contradictory ways. In the tourist-generating countries, the industry is merely a continuation of this politically moderating trend. The poor in the urban slums of Europe, North America, and Japan will be even less affected by the conspicuous-consumer indulgence of the rich when it takes the form of around-the-world cruises, second houses, or retirement in faraway sun traps. In the tourist-receiving countries, the situation is completely different. Here the industry does the reverse of the process described above. It is basically shipping the world's richest citizens into some of the world's poorest societies. In itself this is dangerous for the politically neutral development theorist, since the vast separation between the world's rich and poor is forcibly demonstrated daily to all those living in areas affected by the industry. This must result in some political radicalization. But it also makes structural change in these countries more difficult, so that change, when it does eventually come, will take a much more violent form. It is unrealistic to expect Third World elites to ignore luxuries like indigenous car industries for the overall good of society when every day they see tourists displaying their privileges, like cars and leisure, which they might be able to achieve for themselves, provided they can keep their relatively privileged status. On the other hand, these elites will become more aware of how they, too, are underprivileged by global standards. Their chances of getting the good things of life will be improved if they put the pressure on foreign companies in their midst to give a better financial split to local businessmen and government bodies. So the pressures pushing the Third World elites toward economic nationalism will also be increased.

Tourism is unleashing a highly complex set of pressures on Third World societies. Economically it is extremely attractive, but the political and cultural implications are extensive. On balance, it is more likely to polarize Third World societies than unite them, and when the resultant tensions finally bubble to the surface, tourists will be not only symbols of the issues but extremely vulnerable targets. The indiscriminate slaughter of travelers in Tel Aviv airport by a Japanese execution squad in 1972 is only the beginning.

Further Reading

Tourism is a much-neglected industry. The few books dealing with it tend to underplay the social consequences. Try Cohen, "Arab Boys and Tourist Girls"; Forster, "The Sociological Consequences of Tourism"; Gray, *International Travel—International Trade*; Peters, *International Tourism;* Sigaux, *History of Tourism.*

9 : : *Free, White, and Beleaguered— Corporations and Southern Africa*

IT was an unfortunate slip of the tongue. The Episcopal Church and the Project on Corporate Responsibility were hammering at General Motors's top management to try to get it to withdraw from South Africa. Pressed by a minister attending the hectic annual general meeting, General Motors's chairman, James Roche, was arguing that the company management was responsible to the shareholders. "Yes," Roche said, "we are a public corporation owned by free, white . . . [the audience gasped, waiting for the clinching "and over twenty-one"] and, and, and, and, black and yellow people all over the world."[1] Roche was smart and experienced enough to know how to wriggle out of his blunder without too much loss of face, though newspapers all over the world cited this use of an archaic, basically racist expression as a symbol of the generation gap that now challenges large corporations. But down at the operating level, where managers face the racial problem firsthand, they are not always so guarded.

In 1970 Tim Smith, a young researcher for a United States organization, the Council for Christian Social Action of the United Church of Christ, wandered around South Africa interviewing representatives from about twenty American multinationals about the racial problem. Since he was preceded by letters from the parent companies, he was seeing people at the managing-director level, often along with labor-relations officials. He returned with some quotes that, if coming from an equivalent manager in America, would have led to riots. For instance, he asked the director in charge of Ford's South Africa operation, if he had any friends or acquaintances in the African, Asian, or

Cape colored communities (this was a standard question in all interviews). "No," came the reply. "I didn't mix with them in the States; I don't mix with them here, and if I went back to the States, I wouldn't mix with them there either." Similarly, he was chatting with the South African director in charge of International Harvester's operations, about the Bantustan policy of the South African government (the creation of all-black reserves in various parts of the country). "This Bantustan thing," said the director, "I agree with it 100 percent. It is economically and politically sound. I am sympathetic with what the South African government is trying to do. I don't want hundreds of Africans running around in front of my house." The rest of the study, if not always as sensational as this, merely served to confirm that this kind of view is typical of the average multinational manager in South Africa. Not one manager admitted to having a non-white friend or acquaintance, but many were willing to talk authoritatively on the customs, culture, superstitions, and problems of the non-whites, though their closest acquaintance with them seems to have been as servants.[2]

A similar study was done in 1971 by an English newspaper, the *Sunday Times,* of the social policies of British firms there. Probably because they were talking to a newspaper reporter, the managers did not express any of the overt racism that Smith uncovered. However, a Unilever director was perceptive enough to see that even a straight factual report could cause trouble. He suggested to the reporter that "the article will be so controversial you should consider whether you would be loyal to British interests by publishing it." His company in 1971 had a soap factory in Durban, in which African laborers started at £7 a week ($17), with two clerks earning the top pay for Africans there of £64 a month ($202). Admittedly, elsewhere in the Unilever system there were African salesmen who reached £146 a month ($350), but the general principle that the Africans worked only at those jobs not reserved for whites, who were paid on an altogether higher scale, was clearly borne out. Elsewhere in the interview the director was asked if whites ever worked under blacks. "Silly question" was his answer. "The laws and customs are such that it never happens. Not that we don't want to, but we don't have to." [3]

South Africa is a police state in which about 4 million whites live off the backs of some 16 million non-whites. In the manufacturing industry there is precise evidence of discrimination. In the twenty-five years after 1945, the ratio between white and African workers' pay widened from 4–1 to 6–1, while colored workers (descendants from interracial relationships) have seen their average wage decline from 42 percent that of the white worker to 25 percent. Manufacturing wages alone are misleading, since the bulk of work is agricultural and extractive, and in mining, there has been no rise in real wages since 1911. A large proportion of Africans are still without any work in a society where the whites earn an average £ 1,000 ($2,400) per year, while the black Africans pull in a measly £ 53 per annum ($127). The Africans as a whole could do better in any one of ten other states south of the Sahara, including the Ivory Coast, Ghana, and Zambia. It is a brutish, repressive society with over 2,000 arrests a day for offenses connected with the passbooks every African must carry with him at all times, and one hundred judicial executions (almost entirely non-whites) each year, a good half of all the world's known executions. The rule of law is twisted to favor the whims of the security services, so that a prize-winning press photographer of the *Rand Daily Mail* has twice had cases against him dismissed by the courts, only to be rearrested in court and detained again. One such occasion was in March 1971. By June the security police had still not made any comment, and under the Prisons Act, the *Rand Daily Mail* was not even allowed to print his picture. When states go this far in creating "non-persons" and denying the basic rule of law that all civilized societies aspire to, it is not unreasonable to predict that the tensions that are thus created must eventually result in a violent reaction. It is still possible that the white South African police state can maintain its hold, since the technology of repression (weapons, planes, identification systems) improves yearly, but it is unlikely that it will ever be anything but an unequal, extremely racist society in a world where racism is the only real clear-cut evil against which significant numbers of people will rally. The multinationals in South Africa should have very good reasons for their investments.

The Polaroid Case

On the morning of January 13, 1971, readers of *The New York Times* and *The Christian Science Monitor* found themselves looking at full-page advertisements from a camera manufacturer, the Polaroid Corporation. Instead of plugging one of their models, the company announced that it had just sent a multi-racial, four-man team to South Africa to examine the situation and then advise on future policy. The team interviewed some hundred non-whites and found that they mostly wanted the company to stay, providing the opportunity for the increased use of black talent and recognition of black dignity. The company announced that it had, therefore, decided to continue selling cameras there for the moment (though it had previously announced it would not sell to the South African government), but that through its South African distributors it would carry out a one-year experiment. There would be a crash training program to boost the skills and jobs held by non-white employees; part of its South African profits would be spent on encouraging black education; a black-run Association for Education and Cultural Advancement (ASECA) would be supported; a gift would be made to a foundation to underwrite the expenses of five hundred black students at various levels; it would also investigate the possibility of creating a black-managed company in one or more of the free black African nations.

This came as no surprise. The company had worked hard on the image of an "equal-opportunity employer" in the United States, and coming from the Boston area, it saw itself as a corporate counterpart of the liberal universities. Nevertheless, it did not announce this new policy out of any altruism; the policy was forced upon it.

A year or so earlier an employee had come across an inter-office memo dealing with the sale of Polaroid's identification system to South Africa. This system, known as ID-2, would take and develop pictures of a person in two minutes, sealing them in an unbreakable plastic holder, which could also contain names, addresses, or other information. It was likely that some of this equipment was being used to produce the passbooks, an integral part of the coercion of the African in South Africa. A black group, the Polaroid Revolutionary Workers' Movement, sprang up in protest. This kind of action was nothing new. There had been a Dodge Revolutionary Union Movement, which in 1968 had managed to shut down Dodge's main assembly line with wildcat picketing. The movement started with a rally in October 1969 at which they handed out leaflets saying, "Polaroid imprisons blacks in just sixty seconds." At first the company denied their products had anything to do with the passbook system, but after some inquiries, it had to admit that about 20 percent of the hated documents were in fact produced with Polaroid equipment. The company's founder, Edwin Land, said that it would immediately stop such sales, and the company came out with a formal condemnation of the apartheid system. But this was not enough for the Revolutionary Workers' Movement, and they increased their demands that Polaroid get out of South Africa completely, a demand that sent shivers down a number of corporate spines. It was not as though the South African market was important for Polaroid (less than .5 percent of the company's $444 million sales in 1970), but there was a general feeling that if Polaroid could not fight off the "unreasonable" demands of such militant groups, no one could. So three of the Revolutionary Workers' Movement were fired, and the multiracial team was sent to South Africa to come back with its recommendations.

It is still far too soon to say whether Polaroid will be satisfied with its experiments, but it has pushed up African wages for its South African agents, Hirsch & Frank, by between 13 and 33 percent. Minimum wages for blacks are now around $98 a month, which compares favorably with the fact that only 5 percent of black workers in Johannesburg earn over $81 a month. It should still be put beside a figure produced by the Association of Chambers of Commerce, which reckoned in 1970 that an African family of five living in the Johannesburg African satellite town of Soweto needed a minimum of £43 ($103) a month to keep above the poverty line. It has also promoted several non-white workers into supervisory positions and will eventually try to encourage them into managerial positions.

So far, white South African resistance has been muted. Hirsch & Frank, being a commercial undertaking, does not have any white unionized workers, and while there is no law saying one shall not pay one's African workers high wages, it has not tried to breach the law forbidding black workers to give orders to white ones. So, given the fact that the Polaroid challenge is not especially controversial, the South African government was not going to risk scaring off foreign investment, now badly needed as economic growth slows down.

To some extent, Polaroid was unlucky to be singled out for treatment, and its handling of the situation has shown a degree of sensitivity. There is a lesson here for other companies, for Polaroid's relatively small involvement in South Africa has led to an expenditure of money and managerial time that could have been avoided. It may be that the cost of the fact-finding tour of South Africa, some $20,000 in donations to Boston's Black United Front and the hundreds of thousands of dollars spent on the advertising campaign are minimal. But on top of that should be added the sheer waste of managerial time, as top managers like Land himself have had to work out a co-herent strategy. There is also the question of image. Firing the leaders of the Revolutionary Workers has not shut them up, and the notoriety of the case has supplied a platform from which they have been heard in many parts of the world. Some of the attacks on the company are excessively vicious, considering that there are ten or twenty multinationals more deeply concerned with the preservation of the apartheid system. Caroline Hunter, one of the sacked Revolutionary Workers, in Britain to get Anti-Apartheid to move against Polaroid's British interests (it adopted the cause), accused the company of "technological fascism." She pointed out that the company has a world monopoly in identification and that we now have a society in which even high-school kids are expected to carry their tags along with them. In this way, Polaroid is emotively identified with a Big

Brother society of computerized data banks and universal identification systems. It is difficult to put a market value on such
a change in image, but it is doubtful whether a market of
$1,500,000 has really been worth all this trouble for Polaroid.

Polaroid—Not Alone

Polaroid is not the only company faced with this dilemma. The
British sugar and general trading company Booker McConnell
pulled out in the late 1950's because an essential part of company policy was that there should be no discrimination on race,
color, and creed. The British civil engineering firm John Laing
pulled out in 1961 after the Sharpeville massacre. Another construction company, Bovis Holdings, made an informal decision
in the late 1960's not to get involved with South Africa, and in
a bid it made for another company, Cementation, it decided to
dispose of the latter's South African interests should its takeover
bid succeed. Then in 1970 Neil Wates, the managing director
of his family construction firm, Wates Ltd., turned down an
invitation to franchise its industrial building system to a South
African company. Challenged to look at the situation firsthand,
Wates went there and on his return issued a blistering attack
on apartheid: "The idea of doing business in South Africa is
totally unacceptable; we could not be true to the basic principles
on which we run our business, and we should lose our integrity
in the process."

To a certain extent, these are smallish companies still closely
controlled by managers who do not have to worry too much
about outside shareholders. Wates and Bovis were merely considering first-time involvement with South Africa, which could
easily be refused. Critics say life is very much more complicated
for those firms who find themselves there for historical reasons,
although this did not stop Booker McConnell from pulling out.
Nevertheless, these companies made their decisions with very
little outside pressure. Neil Wates is a liberal Christian. The
Booker management has always been politically left of center, so
doubtless there were ideological reasons for their early departure.
They may also have done their sums and realized that in the

long term black Africa would provide a larger market than white South Africa, but even today, there is little evidence that black Africa has the will to refuse to deal with companies involved with South Africa.

Public pressure groups have also been making themselves felt elsewhere. Probably the leading *cause célèbre* in recent years has been the Cabora Bassa Dam, which is being built on the Zambesi River in the Portuguese colony of Mozambique within one hundred miles of white-controlled Rhodesia, black Zambia, and the rather less militant black country, Malawi.[4] It is a huge project costing about $350 million, with a planned output roughly double that of the Aswan Dam in Egypt, and much of the power will be sold to South Africa. At the best of times this would have been a controversial project, since the dam is placed right on the border between white- and black-dominated Africa, but what really makes it a major issue is that a large part of the materials will be coming from Rhodesia, contravening the 1968 resolution of the UN Security Council banning UN members from activities promoting the export of Rhodesian goods. Such sanctions were widely flouted, with many goods from this white-supremacist country being rerouted through South Africa. But the Swedes in particular take their responsibilities to the Third World seriously, and a law was passed in support of the UN resolution, while their radicals focused on ASEA, the big Swedish engineering firm, which was planning a heavy commitment. The government could not guarantee that ASEA might not be prosecuted if it went ahead, so ASEA withdrew. A British company, GEC–AEI, then prepared to step into ASEA's shoes, but a similar storm arose in Britain and the company backed out, saying that it had "been thoroughly embarrassed by the publicity accorded to our attempts to get involved with Cabora Bassa." The action then transferred to Italy, where, in May 1970, the Italian government decided not to grant export credits to Italian firms supplying the project, and strong trade-union pressure forced the Milanese firm Società Anonima Electraficazione to remove its South African subsidiary from the project.

Construction still continues, despite the withdrawals and the threat of guerrilla action. After all, it will be the fifth largest dam in the world and a huge source of business for potential suppliers. The South Africans are involved, with Harry Oppenheimer's Anglo-American Corporation leading the consortium that won the final bids. A number of West German firms like Siemens, AEG, Telefunken, Brown Boveri, and Hochstieg are involved, as are a number of French firms, headed by Alsthom and CGE. On the fringes, various South African subsidiaries of British firms are setting up operations in Mozambique, presumably to take advantage of the project.

So far there has been little pressure from black Africa. Countries like Zambia and Tanzania have been giving support to the freedom movements, but this hardly worries companies that are well protected behind some 60,000 Portuguese soldiers and unspecified military aid from Rhodesian and South African sources. One British company, United Transport Overseas, had its branch in Zambia expropriated for refusing to pull out of the project, but retribution ends there. Nevertheless, other firms have suffered considerable embarrassment in the course of the action.

The British bank Barclays (world's fourth largest in 1970) got caught up in the general flak. Through an affiliate, Barclays DCO, the company has always had a strong base in South Africa, with significant business in parts of black Africa like Nigeria. It had nothing to do with the basic financing of the dam, which was handled by various official South African loans and a group of French, German, Italian, and Portuguese banks. However, in the course of its normal South African business it extended a line of credit to one of the dam's subcontractors. One report suggested that the client was actually the consortium leader, Anglo-American, or a subsidiary (Barclays is certainly Anglo-American's bankers), but be that as it may, the bank was involved, despite the fact that the line of credit has allegedly not been called on.

This dispute raised the whole question of the bank's general role in South Africa itself, where its activities are on a scale that dwarfs Polaroid's. Barclays spokesmen pumped out facts in its defense—that it had 700,000 non-white customers there, who were 60 percent of its total customers; that there is no provision of separate branches or separate tills on racial lines; that the company had a record of pioneering work in black Africa, both in lending to black entrepreneurs and in opening up rural savings accounts. Above all, it argued that the impact of its withdrawal on South Africa would be minimal (which does not say much for its British headquarters), since its branches would merely be taken over by local interests. (A report from the Franzsen Commission suggests that the government might require foreign-controlled banks to dispose of a certain proportion of their assets to South African citizens anyway.) Besides which there is the famous "bridge-building" argument used by so many businessmen involved in South Africa; as Sir Frederick Seebohm, chairman of Barclays DCO, put it at the 1971 annual general meeting, "When changes come to South Africa, as they surely will, our long and worldwide experience will stand us and all the people there in good stead." None of this kept the bank's critics happy, and there have been a number of attempts to get universities to use banks other than Barclays. Occasionally the bank's mask slipped, and Sir Frederick spoke at the same meeting of political groups "bent on destroying our society in order to impose their minority ideology on the rest of us." One of their aims, he said, was to "bring about bloody revolution and they see in South Africa a chance to do just this." Whatever the truth of such allegations, the businessman is not absolved from some moral obligations.

The Polaroid decision added to the pressures, and in August 1971, Barclays and Standard Bank (the other big bank in South Africa—British but linked with Chase Manhattan) announced that they accepted the principle of equal pay for equal work without consideration of race. Only about three hundred non-white employees were due to be affected by the decision, but the banks became the first large-scale employers of labor in the country to accept the principle.

The various actions of companies like Polaroid, Barclays, Wates, and Standard Bank are coming at an interesting time in South Africa's development. Its rapid growth since the Sharpeville massacre of 1960 is starting to slow down. Its mines are aging and expensive to run, and major new mineral discoveries are becoming hard to find. An increase in the price of gold would help, but it is difficult to envisage any new mineral success story. If the country has to rely solely on the manufacturing industry, it will be in trouble, since the internal South African market is too small to support a full range of economic mass-production industries. It could attempt to combat this state of affairs by raising the general standard of living of the African population, but such an action would endanger security, social superiority, and job preservation for whites. The other alternative is to sell widely to black Africa, which to some extent explains why South Africa is currently conducting a diplomatic blitz on the friendlier black African states like Malawi. If neither strategy works, the economy is in trouble.

Already South African industrialists are worried. Harry Oppenheimer, whose family controls the vast mining companies Anglo-American, De Beers, and Chartered Consolidated, has been a particularly bitter critic. A long-time supporter of the Liberal Progressive Party with its lone Member of Parliament, Mrs. Helen Suzman, he publicly blames bad education and job reservation, integral parts of the apartheid system, as prime causes of many of South Africa's ills. "I do not think," he has said, "that the economy of a country which deliberately sets out not to train or make proper use of 80 percent of its potential working population can be described as basically sound." Bitterly hated by large segments of South African society (the Afrikaners tend to call him "Hoggenheimer"), he was threatened by one extreme Minister during the 1970 election campaign with discriminatory sanctions should his companies be used to promote racial integration in the republic. Nevertheless, other businessmen follow his lead, which stresses the economic drawbacks to apartheid and implies that the economic contradictions of the whole apartheid system will lead to its eventual dismantling. Their optimism may be unfounded, but the attacks on the system are symbolic of some of its ills.

Meanwhile, the foreign-investor community is less enthusiatic about the country. In September 1971 a government attempt to borrow money from the Dutch banking community was igno-

miniously undersubscribed. The South Africans were also reported to have tried to raise a medium-term Eurocurrency credit
from a group of international banks, but apparently the American ones in particular were nervous that publicity could lead
to broken windows back home in the States. Earlier in the year,
after a certain amount of picketing, Chase Manhattan Bank
had backed quietly out of a consortium providing $40 million
revolving credit to the South African government. However,
the company already had a 15 percent share in the second largest
bank in South Africa, Standard Bank, dating from the late
1960's. The general feeling in a number of companies seems
to be that if the projected returns are the same as for an investment somewhere else, the non-South African one should be
preferred. Life would be quieter.

South Africa's responses to these pressures are inevitably
complicated. It has an understandable grievance that its dependence on multinational investment is imposing political pressures
on South African society from the parent companies. This is
similar to the situation when American anti-Communists ham-
pered European governments as they tried to persuade the subsidiaries of United States multinationals to take an active part
in trading with Eastern Europe. The defenders of multinationals
have always tended to pooh-pooh the importance of such developments, but the South African case is clearly an instance
where pressures through foreign-owned multinationals are building up as time goes by. Also, the kind of leverage that Zambia
exerted on United Transport Overseas (get out of South Africa
or else) is akin to the threats from the Arab Boycott office to
those multinationals that insist on doing business with Israel,
or the December 1971 Libyan expropriation of the local assets
of British Petroleum in retaliation for alleged British involvement in some Iranian maneuverings as Britain withdrew her
troops from the Persian Gulf. All are clear cases of political
pressure being imposed both on and through multinational
companies, and they expose the myth that multinationals are
always neutral, purely economic forces. It would be convenient
for their managers if this were the case, but the realities of
world politics will not let them alone. In the mid-1960's South

Africa was more confident of dealing with such threats. In 1966 the Canadian government stopped Ford from selling a quantity of four-wheel-drive vehicles through its Canadian subsidiary. In retaliation, the South African government boycotted the company for two years until Henry Ford paid the country a visit to make peace. Today things are less easy for the government. Threats against Harry Oppenheimer are still possible, but an open conflict with a foreign company over some aspect of the apartheid laws would merely increase anti-apartheid pressures on the companies already in the country and would help to scare off international investment, which, as we saw, is losing confidence in the country anyway. So Polaroid has apparently not been officially pressured, and the Barclays and Standard Bank moves were accompanied by unofficial mutterings but no open action, for, after all, they were breaking no laws. The crunch will come if some company tries breaking one of the apartheid laws, such as job reservation, in such a way that the government can no longer turn a blind eye to infringements that can, at the moment, be officially overlooked.

Namibia

The fate of Namibia (or South-West Africa) has created new problems. Both the United Nations Security Council and the International Court at The Hague have decided the country should no longer be run by South Africa, which has been ruling it since the end of the First World War under a mandate from the League of Nations.

The firm involved here is the British mining company Rio Tinto-Zinc, which announced in 1970 that it was going to start a $200–300 million open-cast mine to produce uranium. The deal is a joint one with the South African Development Corporation and was given the official blessing of the last Labour government, which allowed the nationalized United Kingdom Atomic Energy Authority to sign a deal for 7,500 tons of uranium between 1976 and 1982 (worth about $90 million). The Minister involved, Anthony Wedgwood Benn, trotted out the bridge-building excuse, despite the fact that this deal ostentatiously ignored international legal opinion. Originally, there also was to be a long-term contract with the German company Urangesellschaft for supplying the needs of Euratom, but on this occasion the German government had qualms about the potential damage to relations with black Africa and withdrew financial backing, forcing Urangesellschaft to back out of the deal.

RTZ will probably get away with this gamble. Namibia is a large, sparsely populated country, whose local chiefs seem safely in the pocket of the South African government. Successful guerrilla movements are unlikely, since the nearest black-ruled country is a long way away, in contrast to the Cabora Bassa Dam, where hostile borders are a mere one hundred miles away. However, in 1972 the unexpected strike by the Ovambo tribe, which was one of the province's chief suppliers of labor, showed that political tensions were far closer to the surface than analysts had suspected. However, mining companies are notoriously insensitive to political pressures, since, apart from their corporate headquarters, they have little property accessible to demonstrators. The companies are vulnerable only if they depend on government finance like export credits, or if they decide to open up major investment in a hostile country. RTZ has centered its activities on a small Australian-controlled island in the Pacific called Bougainville and in Labrador. Neither of these projects is likely to run up against insurmountable local objections, though it is interesting to note that part of the incipient nationalism in Papua–New Guinea, of which Bougainville is a part, is turning against the company's mining activities. Otherwise, the company is in the running for some of the major contracts likely to be available when the Soviet Union hands out contracts to develop some of Siberia's mineral resources. It is unlikely that the Soviets will make an issue of the company's involvement in Namibia.[5]

Gulf and Angola

In fact the South African government is having an easy time of it, since the Portuguese are acting as a buffer between it and militant black Africa. A long time ago, in the era of Henry the Navigator, the Portuguese were a leading imperial power. Like many other nations Portugal waxed fat off the slave trade, but over the years its empire has been eroded, until today it consists mainly of two vast plots of land, Mozambique and Angola. Although the ratio of whites to blacks is 1 to 22 in Angola and 1 to 69 in Mozambique, the Portuguese have refused to bow to the coming of African independence, sadly convincing themselves that these colonies are essential for national survival and that their policy of "assimilation," whereby Africans are converted into "good," civilized Portuguese, will somehow or other see them through. Wars broke out in Angola in 1961 and in Mozambique three years later. By 1971 Portugal had between 130,000 and 150,000 troops committed to its colonies and was spending 6–7 percent of its gross national product on defense, the highest figure for any West European nation.

By the mid-1960's the financial strain was beginning to tell, and in 1965 Portugal lifted the tight controls on investment in the colonies in the hope that private investment would facilitate its struggle—which it did. We have already seen how the South Africans, with some European help, rallied around the Cabora Bassa Dam in Mozambique. In Angola Krupp, the German steel giant, came in to head an international consortium to develop iron-ore deposits at Cassinga, but the major investor and savior has been Gulf, the American oil company. Gulf had apparently been an investor in Mozambique before this step, but once foreign investment was fully liberated, it intensified exploration and found large reserves in the particularly insecure colony of Cabinda, which has frontiers with two black-governed powers, Congo (Brazzaville) and the old Belgian colony Congo (Kinshasa). Once the Cabinda strikes were made, Portuguese troops were sent to help keep order, and the local Africans were relocated in what looked suspiciously like the strategic hamlets of Vietnam and Malaya.

Many believe that Gulf's operations in Angola facilitate the Portuguese policy of repressing the armed revolts of various freedom movements. The contract signed with the Portuguese government specifies that all foreign companies must help secure "peace and order," which involves contributions for the construction of military barracks. In particular, Gulf is subject to a special defense tax, which, since 1963, has required graduated payments by foreign companies rising as high as 28 percent for companies with gross earnings of $1.7 million or more. As one study put it: "The importance of the corporate-military alliance is dramatized by the story of the governor-general of Angola traveling around the districts of the colony talking to the white-settler population, assuring them that although they had to pay heavy taxes to aid the war effort, the burden would eventually be lifted from them and absorbed by none other than the Gulf Oil Corporation." [6]

Of course, the company stresses the good that it is doing—the high wages, the purchase of local products, the development of infrastructure, etc. This is a genuine colonial situation, where the ruling power might well have had to concede defeat had it not been for the influx of investment. As it is, Gulf's investments in Angola have allowed the Portuguese government to spend more on crushing freedom movements. The company has poured easily $200 million into the colony, and royalties on investment reached $5 million per annum in 1970. Since there is a chance that Gulf Cabinda may become the fourth largest field in Africa, these royalties are likely to keep climbing and will be used to keep the white Portuguese in power.

However, Gulf will soon be alone no longer in Angola. A *Financial Times* report in mid-1971 gave a lengthy list of companies either searching for offshore oil or entering bids for new concessions. There are a number of obscure Portuguese names that may be fronts for some well-known companies, but we still find Texaco, Total, Société Nationale des Petroles d'Aquitaine, Ultramar, Standard Oil (the report does not identify further), Union Carbide, Shell, British Petroleum, Tenneco, and Mobil. The royalties from such companies should make the Portuguese position almost impregnable, as long as domestic dissension can be held in check. Protest groups in countries like America have a limited amount of leverage, since they can only picket or disrupt the companies' service stations. The oil companies, however, are less sensitive to such attacks than banks, whose vulnerability is that they must pay more attention to young, highly educated protesters. These are the banks' most profitable future customers and if, through idealistic motives, they open their first accounts with the competition, it is very difficult for the offending bank to persuade them to switch business in later years. This is not to say that the mainly American campaign against Gulf will not have its long-term effects—even the most hard-nosed management cannot be happy about campaigns to persuade educational and religious institutions to sell their holdings in Gulf stock, and its image is not improved by people wandering around with badges saying GULF KILLS. The only hope is that black African oil-producing states like Nigeria will wake up to their continental responsibilities and refuse to do business with companies involved in Portuguese Africa. There are precedents. Libya has kicked out British interests in retaliation for British policies elsewhere, and Zambia was responsible for forcing the Italians to back out of the Cabora Bassa scheme by threatening action against the substantial Italian interests in Zambia. Nigeria's oil reserves are attractive enough to minimize the danger of boycotts by other oil majors, and Gulf does have extensive interests in Nigeria. Unless Nigeria takes such a step, it looks as though Gulf and a number of other oil and mining multinationals will get away with investments that are ethically indefensible.

The Future

Anyone planning strategies that deal with South Africa should assume that the most likely prospect for the year 2000 is that the whites will still be in power. In the more distant future is the chance of a black African regime that has come to power by a successful campaign of violence. Way down the list of probabilities is the possibility of some compromise regime, where the whites have gradually conceded political power to the blacks. Most liberal businessmen assume that the last of these scenarios is not only possible but likely. They deceive themselves. The world is filled with the graves of moderates who thought that reactionary regimes could be persuaded to relinquish their power peacefully. The South African whites have nowhere else to go, and thus the situation differs from that found in the former imperial colonies.

The most convincing scenario of future developments is as follows: the South African government will continue with its policy of separate development but will make a few concessions to its non-white urban workers. The traditional, mainly conservative chiefs in the Bantustans will be upstaged by more politically conscious Africans who will be influenced both by black political movements in the United States and by some militant black African governments to the north. Tensions will arise in the Bantustans over just how much independence they can actually have and in the cities, where increasingly politicized non-whites will be dissatisfied with their slow progress toward political power. Some non-whites will become impatient, taking advantage of any liberalization by resorting to violence on a limited, and probably unsuccessful, level. White fears about what would happen if they conceded political power will be strengthened, and so repression of militant non-whites will again be increased, thus polarizing society still further. Unless the technology aiding armed uprisings makes some dramatic breakthroughs, a successfully repressive white police state will remain in power.

Multinationals who argue that they are building bridges are undoubtedly kidding themselves. There is, however, an excellent case for their staying on—as Trojan horses, which can be used to help black Africans in their political struggle. Withdrawal of investments would currently be a politically regressive step. The South African government would be able to find replacements for the multinationals from somewhere, even setting up government-owned enterprises if necessary. The economy as a whole would become less efficient, but this would not be politically significant and the anti-apartheid forces would lose one of their best chances of affecting conditions within South Africa. No locally owned company is ever going to pioneer schemes like giving blacks equal pay and equal job opportunities with whites, but the multinationals can be pressured in these directions. This is important for two reasons. First, it matters that the absolute wages of black Africans get pushed up as high as possible, since political activities become easier the less one has to worry about providing for basic needs like food and housing. Second, the multinationals are much more likely than locally owned companies to get into well-publicized confrontations with the government on issues like the job-reservation laws. The more important the companies concerned, the greater their impact on political awareness both within and without the country. Black Africans who feel tempted to argue that the system will evolve in their favor will find it harder to make a case, while outside attempts to stop other nations from selling strategic goods to the South African government will become more effective.

The correct strategy for anti-apartheid forces is thus to pressure multinationals into significantly improving the conditions of their black workers and into confrontations with the government. Much can be achieved by simple publicity. The companies are vulnerable to journalistic and academic exposure. After all, their policies in South Africa would be indefensible if carried out in their home countries, so they have a genuine concern to prove that they are liberal employers, in order that Polaroid-type concessions can be won more generally.

Attention should also be directed toward companies that are trying to maintain a low profile. Du Pont, for instance, exports sizable quantities of chemicals and man-made fibers to South Africa, but makes sure that none are sold under the Du Pont name. This is an interesting reversal of the usual brand-name policy, but as Du Pont put it to a reporter: "We haven't had any situation where we've been forced to reappraise our position in South Africa." [7]

We also need to know far more about which companies play an important role in the defense and security activities of the government. The British chemical giant Imperial Chemical Industries (ICI) owns, for instance, 43 percent of the shares of African Explosives and Chemical Industries in conjunction with De Beers. Not only is this the largest manufacturing concern in South Africa but the munitions business is making ICI more deadly to black South African interests than Polaroid or Barclays Bank. Other wholly or partly owned British companies include Shell, British Petroleum, and British Leyland, which makes Land Rover vehicles for the army and police.

American investment is smaller, through having started later, but had reached some $755 million by 1970, which amounted to 14 percent of all foreign capital. The key firms here are IBM, Ford, General Motors, Chrysler, Gulf Oil, Mobil, and Eastman Kodak. Of these, IBM is the most interesting. If it controls well over half the computer market, as it is claimed it does, in all non-Communist countries but Japan and Britain, it is probably the most strategically placed company. The South Africans are not going to be able to manufacture their own computers, and they would find it genuinely difficult to replace the company should it withdraw. *Fortune* judges IBM's employment policies as "unbelievably" good, but if Polaroid is under attack for having sold some cameras to help produce the passbooks, it would be interesting to see a detailed analysis of IBM's South African activities. A company spokesman has denied that the security forces use IBM computers, although the government is apparently a customer.[8]

Finally, the activities of the French in South Africa need closer scrutiny. Through companies like Marcel Dassault's, France is now South Africa's main arms supplier, despite a UN Security Council resolution calling on all nations to stop the sale of arms to this country. The French make a distinction of sorts between weapons that can be used against internal insurgency and those for use against external aggression, but this has not apparently stopped the Rhodesians using, since 1967, armed helicopters originally sold to South Africa for "medical purposes."

What successes have been achieved to impel the multinationals in more liberal directions have been the result of pressures from American and European anti-apartheid groups. The role of black governments in other parts of Africa has yet to make itself significantly felt. Zambia (4 million population; per capita income $180) and Tanzania (13 million; $80 per capita) are the two most important countries, and clearly they are not economically attractive when compared with South Africa (21 million; $590 per capita). After the addition of white-controlled countries like Rhodesia and the Portuguese colonies, the attraction of black Africa wanes. The balance could be tipped back toward black Africa should Nigeria ever decide to play a militant role in this issue. This country possesses a booming oil industry and 60 million inhabitants, even if its per capita income is currently only $80. Nigeria's size makes it strategically important should it ever be possible to create an African equivalent of the Arab Boycott list. The Arabs have more purchasing power to deny offending companies, but it would be possible for the African states to pressure United Nations and aid agencies into refusing to work with companies that do business in South Africa. On a purely national level, these countries could start trying to persuade bodies offering export-credit guarantees to limit their involvement to companies following certain minimum practices, among which should be racial equality of job opportunity.

It is important, though, not to become too optimistic about developments. Only a few companies have been persuaded to improve standards in their South African activities. The indications are that more multinationals may follow their lead. If this should be the case, it may be possible for anti-apartheid movements to engineer significant developments within the South African system. As long as this racist regime relies on multinationals, it is not entirely master in its own house.

Notes

1. *Guardian,* July 2, 1971.
2. Smith, *The American Corporation in South Africa.*
3. Herbstein, "The Bridge Builders."
4. Marchant, "The Dam at Cabora Bassa."
5. RTZ has recently been examined in West, *River of Tears.*
6. Committee of Returned Volunteers, *Gulf Oil.*
7. *Sunday Times,* January 17, 1971.
8. Blashill, "The Proper Role of U.S. Corporations in South Africa."

Further Reading

American Journal of International Law, "Round Table: Foreign Investment in South Africa"; Bowman, "South Africa's Southern Strategy"; Ersmen and Gardlund, "In Sweden, Investment Abroad Is a Moral Issue." A view on aid more radical than the Swedes' is expressed in Lodge, "U.S. Aid to Latin America: Funding Radical Change."

10 : : *Multinationals and Malthus—The Future*

If the creation of the world begins last Sunday midnight, then the age of reptiles does not begin until four on the following Saturday afternoon. Five hours later are the redwoods and the pelicans, then, just three minutes before midnight, Man. A second-and-a-half to midnight, formal agriculture. And then, in the last fortieth-of-a-second before midnight, the Industrial Revolution. We cannot go on behaving as we have behaved in the last fortieth-of-a-second. For all the attempts to reassure us, we see in any direction we care to look that we're in trouble.[1]

FOR many people, growth is the answer to the Third World's ills. Despite the population explosion and vast social inequalities, the future is not altogether bleak. Absolute growth rates are impressive by historical standards; the competence and confidence of Third World planners and managers grow year by year; factories open, mines and wells open, consumer booms for transistor radios convert into demands for cheap bicycles and then for scooters and cars. The recipe for prosperity would seem to be successful population curbs, more aid, and better access to the markets of the developed nations. Some planners, in considering parts of Southeast Asia, have debated whether there is an optimum growth rate for countries beyond which their social fabric will be ripped apart by the industrialization process. We are gradually realizing that such commitment to growth rests on precarious assumptions about the resilience of nature.

The Resource Eaters

The implications of universal unrestrained growth are disturbing. We would have to assume that the whole world's population could catch up with and surpass the living standards presently enjoyed by countries like the United States or West Germany. But as Paul Erlich has pointed out, an American child is fifty times more a burden on the environment than an Indian one. The Americans, with 5.7 percent of the world's population, currently consume 40 percent of the world's production of natural resources, using a quarter of the world's output of steel and fertilizers, 40 percent of the wood pulp, 36 percent of the fossil fuels, a fifth of all cotton, and a tenth of all farmlands outside the United States. Another American authority, Harrison Brown, calculates that for the world to attain the American standard of living, every mine and factory would have to work around the clock for a full sixty years just to produce the capital stocks required.

Barry Commoner has made the point that even if growth on this scale is possible, it will be accompanied by increasingly destructive patterns of production. Since 1945 American population has grown by 40 percent, per capita growth by 50 percent, the gross national product by 126 percent, and pollution levels by 2,000 percent. We have switched from natural fibers to synthetics, from soap to detergents, from increased use of land to fertilizers, from rail to road freight—each of the old technologies being replaced by one making greater demands on power, or having more disruptive side effects. Just two of the major post-1945 industries, aluminum and synthetic chemicals, accounted in 1967 for some 27 percent of the total industrial use of electricity, which in turn is a factor in creating the need for Alaskan and North Sea oil, strip mining, and radioactive nuclear power. The message is transmitted stark and clear. If the Indians of the world can catch up with the American standard of living only by resorting to such destructive technologies, the world will be unable to meet the demands on its resources.

The Club of Rome and World Dynamics

The best-known statement of the pessimist's position has come
from work done under the auspices of the Club of Rome. This
body was created by Dr. Aurelio Peccei, who is very much part
of the Italian industrial establishment—vice-chairman of Olivetti, board member of Fiat, managing director of Italconsult,
a large management "think tank." [2] By the mid-1960's he had
become seriously concerned about the world's future and so
created the Club of Rome, an informal association of about
fifty industrialists, humanists, scientists, economists, and planners devoted to warning the world about the "predicament of
mankind." An odd body, they see themselves as background
figures with a mission to save the world by using their establishment connections with the world's power centers. They became
interested in the work of Jay Forrester of the Massachusetts
Institute of Technology, who constructed an interactive computerized model of the predicament allegedly facing the world.
Forrester had done previous models on the birth, growth, and
death of cities, and his new model took into account rates of
capital investment, resource depletion, pollution, population,
birth and death rates, and some factors relating to the quality of
life. All these were linked in ways meant to reflect life—as
population increases, capital investment grows, making higher
demands on natural resources and leading to higher levels of
pollution, which at some point will affect birth rates and so on.

In 1970 the Club of Rome got support from the Volkswagen
Foundation, which commissioned Dennis Meadows (also of
MIT) to extend this work, run it through computers, and
modify the model as necessary. The results from the computers
were grim. They suggested that we are living in a golden age,
where the average standard of life is higher than it ever was in
the past and ever will be in the future. No cultural or technological progress that will allow the globe to sustain as many as
14 billion people is seen within the next hundred years. Since
we are due to reach this number in only sixty years, the model
suggests that population growth is due to undergo a profound

deceleration. In this case, arguments about bringing the Indian living standards up to those of contemporary America are obviously out of the question, and there is every chance that the developed economies will be forced (particularly those heavily dependent on imported raw materials) to take a severe drop in their living standards as well.

It is very hard to know how much weight to put on such findings. Critics have maintained that it is presumption to feed relationships into the model involving, say, pollution levels and the birth rate, when established demographers through the years have had enough trouble predicting population without taking pollution levels into account. The model, the critics say, has been built around simplistic and arbitrary assumptions which a priori support the pessimistic views held by the Club of Rome members.

The Closing-Vise Scenario

It is too soon to side with one particular set of conclusions, but it is worth speculating what will happen if some of the pessimists' predictions do come true.

The simplest assumption made is that we will inexorably run out of raw materials. At the moment, the world's metal consumption is climbing at 6 percent per annum. Even if this rate were cut to the 2.5 percent at which world population is growing, known reserves of mercury, lead, platinum, gold, zinc, silver, and tin will be gone within twenty years; copper and tungsten would last thirty years; molybdenum, nickel, aluminum, cobalt, manganese another seventy; while steel would last a century. But new deposits will be found through satellite surveys of world resources; more metals will be recycled; there will be substitutions as scarcer materials rise in price; new techniques will be developed to process lower-grade reserves. Strip mining has already made a number of copper and uranium projects economic where traditional mining would have been too expensive (on the other hand, the ecological cost of strip mining is high).

Much of the debate centers on how fast and effectively one

expects such developments to spread. Optimists point out that there is little evidence that raw materials' prices are rising as one would expect if shortages were imminent. Copper prices, for example, are so low as to render uneconomic existing high-cost mines like Zambia's. Prices are stagnant in a wide range of other metals, like platinum, lead, and zinc. The only industries of note where prices are rising are gold, which has a strong speculative element, and oil. Even here, however, the rises reflect the special situation created by the Suez Canal closure and the growing confidence of the producing countries, rather than any significant turnaround in the basic relationship of world supplies to world demand. This does not mean that the industry has no worries. During the 1970's it will have to provide £200 billion ($500 billion) for new investment in exploration, recovery, refineries, pipes, and tankers to satisfy expected world demand. Much of this oil will come at first from established sources like the Middle East, where it is still cheap to expand production. Once oil personnel are asked to speculate about the 1980's, they become less confident. They must increase the amount of oil they get from the seabed, and this increases the danger of disasters like the major underwater seepage at Santa Barbara. The industry will also have to spread into oil shales and tar sands, where production is currently fifty times more expensive than conventional oil drilling. After that, it will have to move into oil-from-coal schemes, which would require massive strip mining, and here it is reluctant even to start talking about cost.

At some future point, the rising cost of oil should meet the downward prices of nuclear power, which should start making inroads into the markets currently held by oil. Nuclear power is not limited much by raw materials or even heat barriers in general, for a 10 billion world population could use up to a hundred times more energy than we do before hitting the ultimate heat limit when the polar ice would melt. There will, however, be severe local problems, as in Southern California, which can only double its energy requirements before running into perhaps unsolvable trouble with heat effluents. If other industries follow oil's pattern, it is likely that the world will be able (and will thus probably choose) to muddle on for another decade or so as though things have not changed. It will take steps to limit pollution, and costs will gradually creep upward, but the emphasis will still be on growth.

The first trend that will stem from this is that large parts of the Third World will gain in power. As raw materials become more scarce, world prices will rise, and those lucky countries possessing them will be able to call the tune as the oil producers have done in recent years. The disputes will spread to other industries like copper and bauxite, and the countries concerned will show greater solidarity in the terms and prices they ask for their products. In many ways the situation will resemble the collective-bargaining situation found in labor relations, with "trade unions" (alliances of producing countries like OPEC and CIPEC), "strikes" (attempts to block sales of key materials to developed countries during key bargaining periods), "lockouts" (refusal of developed countries to buy certain products that they have stocked up with before the trouble starts), "blacking" (refusal of developed countries to buy products from specific countries that have pushed their luck too far), and "collective bargains" (formalized agreements between one or more producing countries and one or more developed economies specifying the terms and conditions under which raw materials are sold).

If the conflict between producers and consumers becomes really bitter, the role of the companies in the bargaining process becomes marginal. If the producing governments band together in bodies like OPEC, the companies can bargain efficiently only if they too are allowed to band together to negotiate as a unit. But this is a decision that can be taken only by consumer governments, since it runs against all our concepts of what companies are about. Again, the success of the companies in resisting the demands of the producer governments may be achieved only if the consumer governments can credibly show that they have sufficient buffer stocks of the product to get through any disruption of supplies without difficulty. A group of individual companies acting independently cannot put together an adequate buffer stock, since it costs money to keep, say, nine months' reserve of oil, and in a situation that stresses competition, any company keeping less will have a competitive advantage. So, if the consumer governments have to come to the help of their companies, the independent free-wheeling role of the companies will have to change. They will increasingly become agents who come in to run the industry between the major policy rows, which have to be settled government to government. They will retain this role as long as they have knowledge or technology unavailable to individual governments at either end. Above all, the multinationals have a flexibility that national governments rarely possess. The producing governments have the problem of maximizing their returns from a fixed range of local resources; the consuming governments have the task of buying from those sources that are cheapest at any one time. Multinationals today are trying to fulfill both roles. As the owners of oil fields they are trying to find new markets for that oil, which will explain why they have gone into petrochemicals or even the development of artificial proteins from oil. As sellers to the energy consumers, they have an interest in moving out of oil into nuclear power and oil-shale technology as soon as the economics of the energy market change, and the evidence shows that they are fully prepared to do just this. They have already bought their oil-shale reserves and their coal mines and set up their nuclear-power subsidiaries.

As the conflict between producer and consumer countries becomes more clearly polarized, the ambiguous role of the multinationals must change. It is nonsense to think that they will be allowed to perpetuate the myth that, as both producers and consumers of oil, the terms they agree on with the producer governments are those that really militant producers would try to obtain. So the multinationals will probably have to choose between one part or another of their double role as producer and consumer. Most will choose the consumer role, which, in this rapidly changing era, will allow them to pick and choose their supplies with relative freedom. This will mean that the push by producer governments to gain more control over the production of their own facilities will meet only token resistance. No oil multinational is going to fight to the death over the decade for the inalienable right to produce oil if oil is a declining product and nuclear power appears to be a better bet. In the vacuum, state companies or local entrepreneurs will take a greater interest in selling oil in the world market. This will prove a more difficult task as the decades pass, and so the producer governments would be sensible to put oil sales in the hands of bodies that are committed to oil as their first priority. The multinationals will be too busy juggling their nuclear power and oil-shale interests to be fully committed to the interests of the oil-producing countries.

A further argument suggests that this polarization between production and consumption would lead to situations where the producing governments refuse to sell their raw materials to the rest of the world, on the grounds that they want to hang on to what they have. A more extreme scenario shows countries fighting each other for raw materials. This assumes not only that a modern state will collapse without a few key raw materials but also that one or two governments could bring their supply to a halt. The fact that materials are substitutable is ignored, and the one lesson from the gloomy forecasts about loss of raw materials is that the search for substitutes will become highly sophisticated. In any case, the days have gone when only one or two sources supplied a single raw material. It seems extremely unlikely that governments would find themselves in situations where they could not buy some supplies of a crucial input somewhere on earth. If they were forced to pay well above what the non-cooperative producing government would normally get, it would be surprising if the latter did not re-enter the market. It is just possible that South African policy might invite a worldwide boycott of supplies; in this (probably unlikely) situation, it might be tempted to seize nearby territories that produce necessary materials. A more likely development is the growth of "Biafra-type" situations, since the rising value of mineral resources will make mining areas extremely desirable sources of revenue. They might be annexed by more powerful governments, or the relevant regions might secede rather than share their wealth with other parts of the same country.

It is easy to forget that serious rises in world prices for raw materials hit the Third World far harder than the developed economies. The price increases won by oil-producing governments affect the Third World as well as the richer countries, and whereas the United States and Europe may grumble, the burden of their extra oil payments is minimal compared to the impact these same payments make on oil-importing Third World governments like India. We may, therefore, see a breakdown in the apparent unity of Third World governments in bodies like UNCTAD. Power will move into the hands of the producers, and the consumers will lose—but this split occurs within the Third World as well as between the Third World and the developed economies. The issue of whether OPEC countries are willing to give preferential terms to other Third World countries will be an interesting test of the degree of solidarity found between less developed nations. In the absence of inspiring leadership from the richer nations in other fields, it is hard to ask the oil producers to be charitable.

The Third World, however, is not dependent only on oil and may itself be living in a golden age. If the pessimists are right and material prices increase rapidly, they are trapped in a vise that will be far more serious than that likely to grip the developed economies. The latter have already enjoyed the products from car and domestic-appliance industries and, should times get hard, could always cut back on the size or sophistication of these products, or could engineer them to last longer. But Third World elites may find themselves chasing such industries, whose rising basic costs put them permanently out of reach. If their rising expectations are thus thwarted, they will become more deeply resentful of the developed world's good fortune. Their attitudes toward the activities of the foreign-controlled multinationals will therefore harden, and the drive toward economic nationalism will become more widespread.

The only optimistic outlook for the Third World in this gloomy future is that the need for runaway industries will be increased. The more expensive the raw materials, the greater the need for the reintroduction of labor-intensive technologies —and the one shortage no one is predicting is that of labor.

The Ecological Pressures

If future economic developments can be seen only in rough outline, ecological ones are even less clear. All we can be sure of is that our actions may be pushing the regenerative powers of the eco-system beyond the limits where recovery is possible. Scientists like Barry Commoner put forward depressing scenarios —the world will run out of oxygen as the oceans, the source of most of our supplies, are contaminated by DDT, a chemical retarding photosynthesis (the oceans contain 25 percent of all the DDT ever produced). The chances of such major disasters are higher than we can tolerate, especially since we lack a clear understanding of the key relationships that maintain our present life-bearing system. Certainly the drive to control pollution will increase, and the attention currently being paid to auto emissions will be a forerunner of similar assaults, which could even lead to certain industries being put out of business. The richer countries will tend to export their more dirty industries to countries too poor to resist the attractions of the jobs they offer. But where precautions are taken, they will be extremely expensive. Even in the developed economies there is evidence that smaller, less profitable companies cut back more on pollution control than bigger, more profitable ones; when extended to a global scale, this would suggest that the temptation to skimp on such spending will be nearly overwhelming for governments whose survival depends on immediate production levels, not on the votes of the next generation.

The two "worlds" will thus be brought into a symbiotic relationship not hitherto understood. The Third World now has the power to destroy global society, even if the richer nations take all the necessary measures to ensure that their own production becomes environmentally neutral. These richer nations have only two strategies open to them. They can either try to persuade the Third World countries to lower (or reverse) their growth rates, or more probably they can try to buy the latter's cooperation.

Persuasion will not work. Third World spokesmen will point

out how unfair such arguments are when the developed economies have achieved their current privileged position under ecological standards far laxer than those they are now asking the
Third World to adopt. In any case, the internal political pressures on the latter's governments to go for growth at all costs are
virtually irresistible. Telling Indian farmers that they cannot
use DDT because of some unimaginable disaster in twenty or
thirty years' time is difficult when they know that American
farmers have been using it for years. Thus, we may well find
governments politically unable to stop the polluting processes,
in which case the richer countries are left with an uncomfortable
problem. Rather than using coercion, they will probably try
to find ways of buying off the offending countries. They might
give general aid to those governments willing to tighten their
general standards, or they might subsidize the prices of products
or processes that are of less long-term danger to the world. Thus,
if the rich cannot make a global ban on DDT politically acceptable (the World Health Organization's antimalaria campaign is
dependent on it for this decade, at least), they will have to bring
down the price of competitive technologies, subsidize research
into substitutes, or, if there is no satisfactory substitute, make
up the Third World's lessened output with cheap or free supplies of food from elsewhere.

In any event this implies that the rich nations will have to
acknowledge the Third World's existence in an unprecedented
way. A new form of bargaining will arise, and the Third World
will have a new card to play in the general balance of world
power. It will become very much harder for the rich nations to
maintain their position of privilege when their survival depends
on the actions of every other country in the world. So, provided
the Third World governments realize this, demands for greater
redistribution of the world's wealth should find a much more
receptive audience than they have in the past. Of course, the
internal tensions within the rich nations may cause formidable
problems to governments willing to make the necessary concessions to the Third World. Even within their own borders,
they will have to sell policies calling for slower growth, which
may lead to the closure of certain plants or industries that are

major polluters. At the same time, the United States, and perhaps Europe, will be hit by a general feeling that it is losing power as the runaway phenomenon gets into its stride. It may very well be difficult for such governments to sell to their electorates the idea that it is necessary to buy off Third World countries with extra aid payments. Redistribution is hard enough when growth is taking place, but with a stagnant economy it will be very difficult to achieve.

A Role for Multinationals?

Multinationals thrive on complexity; the more complicated the mix of raw materials, labor reserves, ultimate markets, and financial resources, the greater their potential role. There is no reason why any foreseeable ecological crisis should limit their activities. For instance, their search for new raw-material supplies is driving them into new areas like Siberia; a number of multinationals are waiting to see if the Soviets will call them in to develop untapped mineral riches. The spread of the runaway phenomenon means that ultimate markets and the production process will be increasingly separated, thus creating coordination problems whose complexity will be more easily handled by the multinationals. The increase in aid flows creates new sources of finance to be tapped. The growth of new economies inspires the development of new, non-traditional markets. It will be rare for non-commercial or purely national organizations to have the experience to manipulate this rapidly changing environment with the desired speed and flexibility. Firms will become, to use Howard Perlmutter's term, "transideological," working with Communist countries or helping with Third World development on a scale hitherto outside the experience of capitalist institutions.

There is no sign that the supply of new, complex technologies is going to dry up. As new supplies of raw materials become difficult to discover, the drive for substitutes or for ways of extracting from previously uneconomic reserves will maintain a constant stream of new technologies. By mastering these thoroughly, the better multinationals will carve themselves an assured place in the world economy, where the discovery of and production from reserves will be in circumstances even more hostile than those found in the Alaskan and North Sea oil discoveries of the late 1960's. In manufacturing industries, the call is for extensive modifications or innovations that reduce the social cost of products. If we take the car industry, we find an industry that has matured to the extent that the U.S.S.R., for instance, is buying turnkey auto and truck plants. However, the technology is far from static, what with government demands for cleaner emissions and crash-proof cars; and rises in oil prices could still render the internal-combustion engine uneconomic, stimulating moves into other forms of propulsion, like electric or steam motors. Urban congestion is also spurring the development of mass-transit systems flexible enough to replace the private car. The car firms are not tied to an aging technology but are increasingly being forced into new technologies, which will give them future competitive advantages over industries experienced with only current auto technology. The multinationals will thus lose ground rapidly where their industries are technologically routine, but will compensate by reaping the profits that result from ecological necessity. Thus the mineral-extracting companies will make sure they dominate the discovery and extractive parts of their industry; and the car firms will move into pollution-free urban transport.

On the other hand, many of the projects that will become necessary will increase both in size and in the length of time over which returns can be achieved. This means that the risks the multinationals are taking will increase and, paradoxically, that they cannot be allowed to fail. A good example of the issues at stake can be seen in the Lockheed saga. It entered a new market, that of the airbus, where there was room for only one or two models at the most. In the middle of producing its plane, it ran out of cash (as did Rolls-Royce, the British engine manufacturer). By traditional capitalist practice it should have been allowed to go bankrupt, and that would have been that. However, both the American and British governments could not allow such large bodies to go bankrupt—the resultant unemployment would have been politically disastrous and the governments needed various other products from both companies—so they were allowed to survive. The aircraft industry is in such a precarious position that where the stakes are so high and the payback is so long, individual companies are gambling their whole survival on the chance that a particular project will go through without any mishaps.

The pharmaceutical industry is currently unwilling to do serious work on developing new contraceptives because of the delays and uncertainty created by the need for rigorous testing before a final product can be put into service. It may well be that fertilizer manufacturers will find themselves under similar surveillance, which will increase the chances they are taking in trying to develop major, non-polluting products. The extractive industries will certainly be affected by this trend, as the quality of material reserves declines; the capital investment required and the size of project must increase in order to make the extraction process profitable. Already the oil companies, which have long prided themselves on being self-financing, have started borrowing heavily in order to develop their more recent discoveries.

However, all these developments increase the risk for multinationals at a time when profits, and the resultant money available for developing new products, are stagnant. The multinationals are caught in a vise of their own making. In the old days they supported the development of new products from the profits made from current ones—they could afford a few failures, and the proportion of successes enabled them to finance the development of further new products. The extended time span needed for the development of new projects implies a higher chance that current products will become unprofitable, so that the company runs out of funds halfway through the new venture, or else that the ultimate market environment changes and the company finds itself producing an unwanted product. The odds are against the multinationals who must finance all such projects out of retained profits or sums they can borrow from world markets. If the multinationals want to stay independent of government finance in this environment, they will be obliged to form consortia with other companies to handle a specific project together. This is a way of reducing the risks they face and is a kind of arrangement now found widely in the extractive industries and in international finance. The spread of such arrangements indicates that the scale of international economic activities is outgrowing existing economic institutions. Fundamental questions are thus raised about the future of an allegedly competitive system, where the companies and their state-controlled opposite numbers are linked with each other in an ever-spreading number of consortia agreements around the world. This means that in case after case the rhetoric of antitrust authorities about the virtues of competition is being offended. Events in the oil industry in 1971, when the oil companies were allowed to form a common front against the OPEC nations, were perhaps a pioneering instance in which governments accepted that there is a community of multinationals that can act as arms of national policies. One might therefore expect both consuming and producing governments to take a growing interest in consortia agreements in this and other industries. The multinationals may still officially be commercially motivated bodies, but they will be left in no doubt that they must reconcile the interests of a growing number of governments. By accepting such limitations on their commercial activities, they will acknowledge that the international business environment is increasingly circumscribed by complex patterns of political cross-pressures.

The more successful multinationals will try hard to avoid becoming too closely tied to the goals of any particular government, because this is to lose the flexibility that is one of their chief competitive advantages. However, some of their weaker brethren will be unable to survive the tougher environment and will fall into the hands of governments politically unable to let them go bankrupt. They will exist as extensions of single states, serving to warn the multinationals of the political facts of life.

The way for companies to avoid such a fate is to recognize their limitations by acknowledging that certain projects are too large or risky to be financed commercially and therefore have to be financed by public funds. We find companies accepting this on a national level, where urban services, hospital administration, and education are controlled by public agencies, with companies supplying subsystems for fixed fees. Thus, companies profitably provide the trains used in rapid-transit systems, the textbooks used in schools, and the computerized monitoring systems used in hospitals. With rare exceptions, the companies do not try to move in as overall project initiators, planners, or financiers where the scale is too big, or the prices charged for the final product cannot be pitched high enough to give a company running the whole sector an adequate profit.

It looks as though we may see the same pattern evolving in the aid field, where the amount of money available is certainly tempting some of the more clear-sighted firms. Total aid from public sources is now running at around $6.8 billion per annum, so that any firm that can get a slice of this can notch up quite a healthy business. The managing director of a Swedish civil-engineering firm, Norconsult, put it this way in 1969:

The United Nations invests every year over $150 million in its development program. The World Bank finances annually projects amounting to over $1,200 million. The regional development banks are approaching a total capital investment equal to 50 percent of the World Bank. All these figures are increasing and the international institutions require an increasing supply of consulting engineers to solve and supervise these various programs and projects. Furthermore, equal amounts are available from the receiving countries as their share toward the cost of solving the projects involved.

The case that best illustrates the path developments might take is the United Nations agency the Food and Agricultural Organization. FAO was born in 1945 to help overcome the world food shortage, and it has always had much closer links with industry than most other UN agencies. For instance, in 1961 the Fertilizer Advisory Panel was formed, in which firms like Exxon (Chemical), ICI, and BASF worked with FAO officials to promote the efficient use of fertilizers and to think through the role that fertilizers should play in development policies. This initiative was symptomatic of the frustration of many aid experts as they saw aid projects being advanced to the point of making modification difficult, before the eventual industrial investors were called on for comments. As a result, the overall efficiency of many aid projects was suffering. So in 1966 the Industry Cooperative Program was created to bring aid administrators, government planners, and firms together at the beginning of agro-allied projects, rather than toward the end of them. Firms can contribute only if they are already involved with the Third World in some aspect of agricultural production (suppliers of capital equipment are eligible). A fee of $3,000 a year is charged to help keep membership down to those who are serious, and in 1971 the program had eighty-four members from nineteen countries, including Mexico, Brazil, Japan, Hungary, and Poland. Many of the world's leading multinationals are represented: chemical firms like Dow, ICI, Bayer, Hoescht; tractor firms like Massey–Ferguson, Caterpillar, and Ford; food companies like Del Monte, Brooke Bond Liebig, and Nestlé; oil companies like Shell and British Petroleum; heavy-engineering firms like Thomson Houston–Hotchkiss Brandt and Kloeckner–Humboldt–Deutz. These firms are allowed to initiate projects that they feel need the backing of one or another of the United Nations agencies—these agencies might be asked to contribute related infrastructural developments, extension services, the development of information about resources, etc. Provided such schemes have the FAO's technical approval, various other UN agencies will now cooperate with the firms.

The British sugar firm Tate & Lyle, for instance, developed a process for turning the sugars in carob beans (found widely in the eastern Mediterranean) into microbial protein, which could then be used to feed animals. They therefore proposed a cooperative industry/UN system pilot plant in Cyprus, where carobs are plentiful, to test the viability of the technology under full-scale working conditions. The UN Development Program came in to finance the plant and the FAO's services; the government of Cyprus provides the buildings and necessary power and water; the company provides the technology and key technicians free of charge and, with the agreement of the government, is subcontracted to design, construct, and operate the pilot plant under FAO supervision. After some intermediate research, which covered nutritional tests, economic studies, and fermentation efficiency studies, the go-ahead was given, and the pilot plant was being constructed in 1971. One major problem did come up over copyrights, over which Tate & Lyle wanted to keep control. Eventually a formula was agreed upon that would give FAO a resonable amount of flexibility to get the technology used in other countries in the region. There is no guarantee that other parts of the United Nations system will accept private enterprise as readily, and it will be understandable if many Third World governments are actively hostile. On the other hand, the U.S.S.R. now seems fully reconciled to dealing with the multinationals, as shown by the deals it has made with Italian and American companies for new auto and truck plants. Since industrial leaders like Henry Ford II have visited Moscow on official business, it would seem unlikely that the Russians will be too dogmatic in rejecting such companies as suitable partners for the aid agencies. Again, the Chinese, through their Canton trade fairs, have shown themselves to be shrewd, knowledgeable bargainers with companies willing to go through a certain amount of political charades first. There will probably always be a residual feeling that aid should go to non-profit bodies, but provided companies show that they have genuine technological knowledge to offer and stay respectable, there should be an increasing role for them as adjuncts to the official aid program.

Conclusion

Development is, above all, a social process, and any image of what constitutes a "healthy" society depends on personal political beliefs. Conservatives are impressed by rapid industrialization, which shows up in international trade statistics; if that is the critical factor, the multinationals have an undoubted role to play. Radicals and a growing number of development economists ask that development be broad enough to involve all sectors of the economy; they demand that attention also be paid to the rural sectors (and here technically sophisticated multinationals are badly equipped to help—even the agribusiness companies will have to forget much of their Western experience before they can make major contributions).

Most of the problems faced by the Third World have management aspects, requiring mixes of technology, finance, administration, and marketing know-how. The best sources for each of these factors may vary from case to case, and there is no reason why the multinationals have to contribute all of them. At the moment, it is true, there are few bodies as effective as the multinationals in dealing with complex international commercial problems, but they will in future have to compete with bodies like development banks, government research agencies, and other state enterprises.

An autarchic approach in which governments like China and Cuba try to do without the help of multinationals is certainly possible. There is, however, an economic cost involved. The effort used in rediscovering all the technical, managerial, and marketing innovations made by the multinationals could be spent in other ways. But provided a government is willing to accept a certain loss of growth, there can be beneficial side effects—its society as a whole has a chance of developing self-reliance and may pay more attention to the most relevant problems, rather than trying to become a pale imitation of the consumer-oriented societies found in the richer world. However, we should also note that the leading exponent of the autarchic approach, the U.S.S.R., has recently been compromising in favor of using multinational aid in key sectors of the economy, like autos, computers, and, possibly, mineral extraction. This suggests that it is confident that it can accept such aid and control the resulting social side effects.

The careless use of multinationals is dangerous. They can be an expensive way of getting products or processes that may well be available more cheaply in other ways. Moreover, multinationals like ITT still hark back to the days when they were major political forces in their own right. Those days are nearly over. The emergence of new multinationals, the growing knowledge and confidence of Third World governments, and the increasing attractiveness of the expanding Third World economies have shifted the balance of power firmly away from the multinationals. In addition, the combination of these new Third World capabilities and the revolutionary impact of transport technologies like air freight will allow the Third World's vast resources of cheap labor to be brought into the world economy for the first time. This will have a devastating effect on the American, and subsequently the European, economies, giving the Third World yet another bargaining counter. The multinationals themselves will survive by adapting to the changing international environment. They will move into technologies appropriate to an ecology-conscious economy. They will develop products and processes that are much more specifically tailored to the needs of the Third World. They will form alliances with new financial partners like governments and aid bodies. On the whole, they will be accepted by the Third World as one of the partners in its development, but multinationals will need handling with care. Multinational companies should be on tap—not on top.

Notes

1. David Brower in *Observer,* July 4, 1971.

2. Peccei was president of Fiat's subsidiary in Argentina at the time of the kidnapping of its general manager (see p. 130) by urban guerrillas. He was in telephone communication with the kidnappers, who asked him to call off the police, who came across the hiding place during routine street searches. Peccei got to the scene ten minutes too late. The Fiat hostage was dead.

ABBREVIATIONS

AEG   Algemeine Elektricitäts–Gesellschaft

ASECA   Association for Education and Cultural Advancement

BASF   Badische Analin–und Soda Fabrik A.G.

BLMC   British Leyland Motor Corporation

BP   British Petroleum

CACM   Central American Common Market

CARIFTA   Caribbean Free Trade Association

CEPAL   Economic Commission for Latin America

CGE   Compagnie Generale d'Électricité

CIPEC   Intergovernmental Committee of Copper-Exporting Countries

CPC   Corn Products Corporation

ECLA   Economic Commission for Latin America

ENI   Ente Nazionale Idrocarburi

GATT   General Agreement on Tariffs and Trade

GEC–AEI   General Electric Company–Associated Electrical Industries

IADB   Inter-American Development Bank

IATA   International Air Transport Association

IBEC   International Basic Economy Corporation

ICI   Imperial Chemical Industries

IOS   Investors Overseas Services

IPC   International Petroleum Corporation

LAFTA   Latin American Free Trade Association

MITI   Ministry of Internal Trade and Industry

MSA   Malaysia–Singapore Airlines

OAPEC   Organization of Arab Petroleum-Exporting Countries

OPEC   Organization of Petroleum-Exporting Countries

PAL   Philippine Airlines

PEMEX   Petroleos Mexicanos

RTZ   Rio Tinto-Zinc

SIAM   Sociedad Industrial Americana de Maquinarias Di Tella

SKF   Svenska Kullagerfabriken

UNCTAD   United Nations Conference on Trade and Development

UNIDO   United Nations Industrial Development Organization

BIBLIOGRAPHY

Adam, Gyorgy. "New Trends in International Business: World Wide Sourcing and De-domiciling." *Acta Oeconomica,* 7, 3–4 (1971), 349–67.

Adler, John H., ed. *Capital Movements and Economic Development.* London/New York: Macmillan/St. Martin's Press, 1967.

Advisory Committee on the Application of Science and Technology to Development. *Draft of World Plan of Action for Application of Science and Technology to Development.* United Nations, E/AC 52XIV/CRP 4 (1971).

Ady, Peter, ed. *Private Foreign Investment and the Developing World.* London/New York: Pall Mall/Praeger, 1972.

Amin, Samir. *L'Afrique de l'Ouest bloquée: l'économie politique de la colonisation 1880–1970.* Paris: Les éditions de minuit, 1971.

Amsden, Alice H. *International Firms and Labour in Kenya 1945–70.* London: Frank Cass, 1971.

Anderson, Charles W. "The Changing International Environment of Development in Latin America in the 1970s." *Inter-American Economic Affairs* 24, 2, (Autumn 1970), 65–87.

Arrighi, Giovanni. "International Corporations, Labour Aristocracies and Economic Development in Tropical Africa." In Rhodes, ed., pp. 220–80.

Avramovic, Dragoslav. "Latin American External Debt: A Study in Capital Flows and in Terms of Borrowing." *Journal of World Trade Law* 7, 2 (March/April 1970), 121–54.

Aymans, G. H. P. "Technology and Natural Resources: The Example of Latin America." *International Social Science Journal* 18, 3, (Autumn 1966), 345–61.

Balassa, Bela. "Industrial Policies in Taiwan and Korea." *Weltwirtschaftliches Archiv* 106, 1 (1971).

Baranson, Jack. *Manufacturing Problems in India: The Cummins Diesel Experience.* Syracuse University Press, 1967.

Baranson, Jack. "Will There Be an Auto Industry in the LDC's Future?" *Columbia Journal of World Business* 3, 3 (May/June 1968), 48–54.

———. *Automotive Industries in Developing Countries.* Baltimore: Johns Hopkins Press, 1969.

———. *Industrial Technologies for Developing Countries.* New York: Praeger, 1970.

Barkin, Solomon, et al, eds. *International Labor.* New York: Harper & Row, 1967.

Barnes, Leonard. *Africa in Eclipse.* London: Gollancz, 1971.

Barovick, Richard L., "Labor Reacts to Multinationalism." *Columbia Journal of World Business* 5, 4 (July/August 1970), 40–6.

Barr, Pat. *Foreign Devils: Westerners in the Far East.* London: Penguin, 1970.

Beckford, George. *Plantations and Poverty in the Third World.* Oxford University Press, 1972.

Behrman, Jack. *National Interests and the Multinational Enterprise.* Englewood Cliffs, N.J.: Prentice-Hall, 1970.

Bernstein, Marvin. *Foreign Investment in Latin America: Cases and Attitudes.* New York: Knopf, 1966.

Blashill, John. "The Proper Role of U.S. Corporations in South Africa." *Fortune* 86, (July 1972), 49–53, 89–91.

Boczek, Boleslaw Adam. *Flags of Convenience: An International Legal Study.* Cambridge, Mass.: Harvard University Press, 1962.

Bowman, Larry W. "South Africa's Southern Strategy and Its Implications for the United States." *International Affairs* 47, 1 (January 1971), 19–30.

Bredo, William. "The Industrial Estate Spreads the Development Risk." *Columbia Journal of World Business* 5, 2 (March/April 1970), 19–25.

Broehl, Wayne G., Jr. "The Company with a Cause." *Columbia Journal of World Business,* 3, 4 (July/August 1968).

———. "Venture in Venezuela." *The MBA* (November 1967).

Brown, Lester R. *Seeds of Change: the Green Revolution and Development in the 1970s.* London: Pall Mall, 1970.

Bryce, Murray D. *Industrial Development: A Guide for Accelerating Economic Growth.* New York: McGraw-Hill, 1960.

Business International. *Nationalism in Latin America: the Challenge and Corporate Response.* New York, 1970.

Business International. *Organizing for International Production.* Management Monograph 32, New York, 1966.

——. *The United Nations and the Business World.* New York, 1967.

Cartaino, T. F. *Technological Aspects of Contemporary and Future Civil Aircraft for the World's Less-developed Areas.* Santa Monica: Rand Corporation, 1962.

Ceceña, José Louis. *Los Monopolios en México.* Mexico, 1962.

Chandler, Geoffrey. "The Myth of Oil Power: International Groups and National Sovereignty." *International Affairs* 46, 4 (October 1970), 710–18.

Chenery, Hollis B. "Growth and Structural Change." *Finance and Development* 8, 3 (September 1971), 16–27.

Cilingiroglu, Ayhan. *The Manufacture of Heavy Electrical Equipment in Developing Countries.* Baltimore: Johns Hopkins Press, 1970.

Clarke, W. M. *Private Enterprise in Developing Countries.* Oxford: Pergamon, 1966.

Cochran, Thomas C., and Reina, Ruben E. *Capitalism in Argentine Culture: A Study of Torcuato di Tella and SIAM.* Philadelphia: University of Pennsylvania Press, 1962.

Cohen, Benjamin. *The Economic Impact of Foreign Investments for the Export of Manufactures: A Tentative Study of South Korea.* Economic Growth Center, discussion paper 136. New Haven: Yale University Press, 1972.

Cohen, Erik. "Arab Boys and Tourist Girls in a Mixed Jewish–Arab Community." *International Journal of Comparative Sociology* 12, 4 (1971), 217–33.

Collado, Emilio. "Economic Development through Private Enterprise." *Foreign Affairs* 4, 4 (July 1963), 708–20.

Committee of Returned Volunteers. *Gulf Oil: A Study in Exploitation.* New York: Africa Group, 1971.

Commoner, Barry. *The Closing Circle.* New York: Knopf, 1971.

Cooper, Charles, and Sercovitch, Francisco. *The Mechanisms for the Transfer of Technology from Advanced to Developing Countries.* Institute of Development Studies, Sussex University, 1970.

Copeland, Miles. *The Game of Nations.* London: Weidenfeld & Nicolson, 1969.

Council for Latin America. *Effects of United States and Other Foreign Investment in Latin America.* New York: 1970.

Cronon, E. David. *Josephus Daniels in Mexico*. University of Wisconsin Press, 1960.

Cross, Colin. *The Fall of the British Empire*. London: Hodder & Stoughton, 1968.

Daniel, James, ed. *Private Investment: The Key to International Industrial Development*. New York: McGraw-Hill, 1958.

Daniels, Josephus. *Shirt-sleeve Diplomat*. University of North Carolina Press, 1947.

Datis-Panero, José A. "Import Substitution." *Finance & Development* 8, 3 (September 1971), 34–9.

DeCubas, José. "It Pays to Speak Out." *Columbia Journal of World Business* 5, 5 (September/October 1970), 61–8.

De Kadt, Emmanuel, ed. *Patterns of Foreign Influence in the Caribbean*. Oxford University Press, 1969.

Denny, Ludwell. *America Conquers Britain: A Record of Economic War*. New York: Knopf, 1930.

Diaz Alejandro, Carlos F. "Direct Foreign Investment in Latin America." In Kindleberger, ed., *The International Corporation*, 1970.

Domhoff, William G. *Who Made American Foreign Policy 1945–63?* In Horowitz, ed., *Corporations and the Cold War*, 1969, 25–70.

———. *Who Rules America?* Englewood Cliffs, N.J.: Prentice-Hall, 1967.

Drucker, Peter F. *The Age of Discontinuity*. London: Heinemann, 1969.

Elkan, Walter. "Urban Unemployment in East Africa." *International Affairs* 46, 3 (July 1970), 517–28.

England, J. "Labour Policy in Hong Kong." *Venture* 22, 11 (December 1970), 23–6.

Ericson, Anna-Stina. "An Analysis of Mexico's Border Industrialization Program." *Monthly Labor Review* (May 1970), 33–46.

Ersmen, Sven, and Gardlund, Torsten. "In Sweden, Investment Abroad Is a Moral Issue." *Columbia Journal of World Business* 5, 1 (January/February 1970), 26–32.

Evans, Peter. "National Autonomy and Economic Development: Critical Perspectives on Multinational Corporations in Poor Countries." *International Organization* 35, 3 (Summer 1971), 675–92.

Fanon, Frantz. *The Wretched of the Earth*. New York/London: Grove Press/Penguin, 1963.

Ferrer, Esteban. "Peru: The General as Revolutionary." *Columbia Journal of World Business* 5, 6 (November/December 1970), 37–45.

Foggan, George. "Youth Aspects of Unemployment." Paper to Oxfam Conference, Cirencester. Summer 1971.

Forrester, Jay W. *World Dynamics*. Cambridge, Mass.: Wright-Allen Press, 1971.

Forster, J. "The Sociological Consequences of Tourism." *International Journal of Comparative Sociology* 5, 2 (1964), 217–27.

Frank, André Gunder. *Capitalism and Underdevelopment in Latin America*. New York: Monthly Review Press, 1967.

——. *Latin America: Underdevelopment or Revolution; Essays on the Development of Underdevelopment and the Immediate Enemy*. New York: Monthly Review Press, 1969.

Franko, Lawrence G. "Joint Venture Divorce in the Multinational Company." *Columbia Journal of World Business* 6, 3 (May/June 1971), 13–22.

Freeman, Orville L. *"The Challenge of the Seventies."* Keynote Address: 2nd International Conference on Cooperative Thrift and Credit. Paris, September 1970.

Friedmann, Wolfgang G., and Beguin, John Pierce. *Joint International Business Ventures in Developing Countries*. New York: Columbia University Press, 1971.

Friedmann, Wolfgang G., and Kalamanoff, George, eds. *Joint International Business Ventures*. New York: Columbia University Press, 1961.

Furtado, Celso. *Economic Development of Latin America: A Survey from Colonial Times to the Cuban Revolution*. Cambridge University Press, 1970.

Gabriel, Peter P. *The International Transfer of Corporate Skills: Management Contracts in Less Developed Countries*. Cambridge, Mass.: Harvard University Press, 1967.

Galenson, Walter. *Labour in Developing Economies*. Berkeley: University of California Press, 1962.

Geiger, Theodore. *The Conflicted Relationship*. New York: McGraw-Hill, 1967.

Gérard-Libois, J. "L'Affaire de l'Union Minière du Haut-Katanga." *Études Congolaises* 10, 2 (1967), 1–47.

Gerassi, John. *The Great Fear: The Reconquest of Latin America by Latin Americans*. London: Macmillan, 1963.

Glicksman, Martin. *Fabricated Foods* (mimeo). Tarrytown, N.Y.: General Foods, 1971.

González, Aguayo Leopoldo. *La Nacionalización de Bienes Extranjeros en América Latina.* Mexico City: Universidad Nacional Autónoma de México, 1969.

Gordon, Wendell C. *The Political Economy of Latin America.* New York: Columbia University Press, 1969.

Gray, H. Peter. *International Travel–International Trade.* Lexington, Mass.: Heath Lexington Books, 1970.

Günter, Hans, ed. *Transnational Industrial Relations.* London: Macmillan, 1972.

Hannigan, Tom, and Morganstern, Abe. *A Trade Union Program for Expansion of International Trade* (mimeo). New York: International Union of Electrical Workers, 1971.

Harrod, Jeffrey. "Multinational Corporations, Trade Unions and Industrial Relations: A Case Study of Jamaica." In Günter, ed.

Hartshorn, J. E. *Oil Companies and Governments.* London: Faber, 1967.

Hayter, Teresa. *Aid as Imperialism.* London: Penguin, 1971.

Helleiner, G. F. *Manufactured Exports from Less Developed Countries and Multinational Firms.* Paper presented to the Institute of Development Studies, Sussex University (mimeo), 1972.

Herbstein, Denis. "The Bridge Builders." *Sunday Times* (April 18, 1971).

Hero, Alfred O., Jr., and Starr, Emil. *The Reuther–Meany Foreign Policy Dispute: Union Leaders and Members View World Affairs.* New York: Oceans Publications, 1970.

Herring, Hubert. *A History of Latin America from the Beginnings to the Present.* London: Jonathan Cape, 1968.

Hirschman, Albert. *How to Divest in Latin America and Why.* Princeton University Press, 1969.

Hopkins, Keith, ed. *Hong Kong: The Industrial Colony.* Oxford University Press, 1971.

Horowitz, David. *From Yalta to Vietnam.* London: Penguin, 1969.

——, ed. *Corporations and the Cold War.* New York: Monthly Review Press, 1969.

Hoyt, Edwin P. *The Vanderbilts and Their Fortunes.* London: Frederick Muller, 1963.

Inter-American Development Bank. *Multinational Investment, Public and Private, in the Economic Development and Integration of Latin America.* Washington, D.C.: 1968.

International Labour Office. *Toward Full Employment: A Programme for Colombia.* Geneva, 1970.

Johnson, Harry G. "A Theoretical Model of Economic Nationalism in New and Developing States." *Political Science Quarterly* 80, 2 (June 1965), 169–85.

Kahn, Herman. *The Emerging Japanese Superstate: Challenge and Response.* Englewood Cliffs, N.J.: Prentice-Hall, 1970.

Kahnert, F.; Richards, P.; Stoutjespik, E.; Thomopoulos, P. *Economic Integration among Developing Countries.* Paris: OECD, 1969.

Kapoor, Ashok. "A Consortium That Never Was." *Columbia Journal of World Business* 4, 5 (September/October 1969) 63–70.

———. *"International Business–Government Negotiations in Developing Countries: The Asian Case."* Paper delivered to 1971 Annual Meeting of the Association for Asian Studies, Washington, D.C.

———. *International Business Negotiations: A Study in India.* New York University Press, 1971.

Kassalow, Everett M. "Trade Unionism and the Development Process in the New Nations: A Comparative View." In Barkin et al, 62–80.

Kay, G. B. *Political Economy of Colonialism in Ghana.* Cambridge University Press, 1972.

Kepner, Charles, and Soothill, Jay. *The Banana Empire: A Case Study in Economic Imperialism.* New York: Vanguard Press, 1935.

Kidron, Michael. *Foreign Investments in India.* Oxford University Press, 1965.

Kilby, Peter. *Industrialization in an Open Economy: Nigeria 1945–66.* Cambridge University Press, 1969.

Kindleberger, Charles P. *American Business Abroad: Six Lectures on Direct Investment.* New Haven: Yale University Press, 1969.

———, ed. *The International Corporation: A Symposium.* Cambridge, Mass.: MIT Press, 1970.

———. *Power and Money: The Politics of International Economics and the Economics of International Politics.* London: Macmillan, 1970.

Knowles, L. C. A. *The Economic Development of the British Empire.* London: Routledge & Kegan Paul, 1924.

Krieger, Ronald A. "Inflation and Growth: The Case of Latin America." *Columbia Journal of World Business* 5, 6 (November/December 1970), 46–53.

Kuznets, Simon. *Modern Economic Growth*. New Haven: Yale University Press, 1966.

Lary, Hal B. *Imports of Manufactures from Less Developed Countries*. New York: Columbia University Press, 1968.

Lefevre, Ernest W. *Uncertain Mandate: Politics of the UN Congo Operation*. Baltimore: Johns Hopkins Press, 1967.

Legum, Colin. *Congo Disaster*. London: Penguin, 1961.

Lemarchand, René. "The Limits of Self-Determination: The Case of the Katanga Secession." *American Political Science Review* 56, 2 (1962) 404–16.

Leontiades, James. "International Sourcing in the LDCs." *Columbia Journal of World Business* 6, 5 (September/October 1971), 24–30.

Levinson, Charles. *Capital, Inflation and the Multinationals*. London: Allen & Unwin, 1971.

Lipton, Michael. "The International Diffusion of Technology." In Seers and Joy, eds., 45–66.

Little, Ian; Scitovsky, Tibor; and Scott, Maurice. *Industry and Trade in Some Developing Countries*. Oxford: OECD Development Centre, 1970.

Litvak, I. A., and Maule, C. J. "Conflict Resolution and Extraterritoriality." *Journal of Conflict Resolution* XIII, 3 (September 1969), 305–19.

Livingstone, I., ed. *Economic Policy for Development: Selected Readings*. London: Penguin, 1971.

Lockhart, J. G., and Woodhouse, C. M. *Rhodes*. London: Hodder & Stoughton, 1963.

Lodge, George C. "U.S. Aid to Latin America: Funding Radical Change." *Foreign Affairs* 47, 4 (July 1969), 735–49.

Marchant, Douglas. "The Dam at Cabora Bassa." *Venture* 23, 4 (April 1971), 8–10.

Markensten, Klas. *Foreign Investment and Development: Swedish Companies in India*. Lund, Sweden: Studentlitteratur, 1972.

May, Herbert K. *See* Council for Latin America, 1970.

May, Stacy, and Plazo Lasso, Galo. *United Fruit Company in Latin America*. Washington, D.C.: National Planning Association, 1958.

McGrew, William W. "Litton's 'Noble Experiment.'" *Columbia Journal of World Business* 7, 1 (January/February 1972), 65–75.

Meadows, Donella; Meadows, Dennis L.; Randers, Jorgen; Behrens, William W. *The Limits to Growth*. New York: Universe Books, 1972.

Meads, Donald E. "The Task Force at Work on the New 'Ad-hoc-racy.' " *Columbia Journal of World Business* 5, 6 (November/December 1970), 30–6.

Meeker, Guy B. "Fade-out Joint Venture: Can It Work for Latin America?" *Inter-American Economic Affairs* 24 (Spring 1971).

Moussa, Pierre. *The Underprivileged Nations.* London: Sidgwick & Jackson, 1962.

Murray, Robin, and Stoneman, Colin. "Private Overseas Investment in Southern and Central Africa." Paper presented to Royal Institute of International Affairs seminar on Southern Africa. London, June 1970 (mimeo).

Myint, H. "The 'Classical Theory' of International Trade and Underdeveloped Countries." *Economic Journal* 68 (1958).

Myrdal, Gunnar. *Asian Drama.* London: Penguin, 1968.

——. *The Challenge of World Poverty.* Baltimore/London: Johns Hopkins Press/Penguin, 1970.

Nader, Claire, and Zahlen, A. B. *Science and Technology in Developing Countries.* Cambridge University Press, 1969.

Nehrt, Lee C. *Political Climate for Private Foreign Investment.* New York: Praeger, 1971.

Nkrumah, Kwame. *Challenge of the Congo.* London: Nelson, 1967.

Okita, Saburo, and Miki, Takeo. "Treatment of Foreign Capital on a Case Study for Japan." In Adler, ed.

Oldham, C. H. G. "Characteristics of the Process of Transfer of Technology." CIECC/Doc. 77, paper given to 2nd meeting of CIECC (Inter-American Council for Education, Science and Culture). Lima, Peru, 1971.

Ozawa, Terutomo. "Japan Exports Technology to Asian LDCs." *Columbia Journal of World Business* 6, 1 (January/February 1971), 65–71.

Panikkar, K. M. *Asia and Western Dominance.* London: Allen & Unwin, 1965.

Paul, James A. "Tourism and Development." *Venture* 23, 3 (March 1971).

Pearson Commission. *Partners in Development.* London: Pall Mall, 1969.

Penrose, Edith T. *The Large International Firm in Developing Countries; The International Petroleum Industry.* London: Allen & Unwin, 1968.

Perlmutter, Howard V. "Emerging East–West Ventures: The Transideological Enterprise." *Columbia Journal of World Business* 4, 5 (September/October 1969), 39–50.

Peters, Michael. *International Tourism: The Economics and Development of the International Tourist Trade.* London: Hutchinson, 1969.

Petras, James F., and La Porte, Robert, Jr. *"U.S. Response to Economic Nationalism in Chile"* (mimeo). Philadelphia: Pennsylvania State University, 1972.

Philip, Nicholas W. "Southeast Asia: Investment and Development." *Columbia Journal of World Business* 5, 6 (November/December 1970), 63–8.

Power, John H.; Sicat, Gerardo P.; Hsing, Mo Huan. *The Philippines: Taiwan. Industrialization and Trade Policies.* OECD Development Centre, 1971.

Prebisch, Raul. *Change and Development: Latin America's Great Task.* New York: Praeger, 1971.

Pugach, Noel H. "Standard Oil and Petroleum Development in Early Republican China." *Business History Review* (Winter 1971), 452–73.

Rhodes, John B. "The American Challenge Challenged." *Harvard Business Review* 47, 5 (September/October 1969), 45–57.

Rhodes, Robert I., ed. *Imperialism and Underdevelopment: A Reader.* New York: Monthly Review Press, 1970.

Rippy, J. Fred. *British Investments in Latin America 1822–1949: A Case Study in the Operations of Private Enterprise in Retarded Regions.* Minneapolis: University of Minnesota Press, 1959.

Rockefeller, Rodman C. "Turn Public Problems to Private Account." *Harvard Business Review* 49, 1 (January/February 1971), 131–8.

Roper, Penelope. *Investment in Latin America.* Economist Intelligence Unit, QER Special 6. 1970.

Rolfe, Sidney E. *The International Corporation.* Paris: International Chamber of Commerce, 1969.

Rose, Sanford. "The Poor Countries Turn from Buy-less to Sell-more." *Fortune* 81, 4 (April 1970), 90–3, 169–70.

Rosenstein-Rodan, P. N. "Multinational Investment in the Framework of Latin American Integration." See Inter-American Development Bank, 33–88.

Rouhani, Fuad. *A History of OPEC.* London/New York: Pall Mall/Praeger, 1972.

"Round Table: Foreign Investment in South Africa." *American Journal of International Law* 65, 4 (September 1971).

Salera, Virgil. "Liquidate U.S. Direct Investments?" *Inter-American Economic Affairs* 24, 4 (Spring 1971).

Sampredo, J. L. *Decisive Forces in World Economics.* London: Weidenfeld & Nicolson, 1967.

Sampson, Anthony. *The New Europeans.* London: Hodder & Stoughton, 1968.

Seers, Dudley, and Joy, Leonard, eds. *Development in a Divided World.* London: Penguin, 1971.

Servan-Schreiber, Jean-Jacques. *The American Challenge.* London: Penguin, 1968.

Shaw, Robert d'A. "Foreign Investment and Global Labor." *Columbia Journal of World Business* 6, 4 (July/August 1971), 52–62.

Shearer, John C. "Industrial Relations of American Corporations Abroad." In Barkin et al., eds., 109–31.

Shearman, Rodney P. "Recent Advances in Contraceptive Technology." *Proceedings of the Obstetrical and Gynaecological Society.* Singapore, 1971.

Shelton, William C. "The Relationship between Changes in Imports and Employment in Manufacturing in the United States 1960–65." Paper presented at annual meeting of American Statistical Association. Detroit, 1970.

Shulman, James. "When the Price Is Wrong by Design." In Stonehill, ed., 184–96.

Sigaux, G. *History of Tourism.* London: Leisure Arts, 1966.

Sigmund, Paul. *Ideologies of the Developing Nations.* New York: Praeger, 1968.

Singer, Hans W. "Dualism Revisited: A New Approach to the Problems of the Dual Society in Developing Countries." *Journal of Development Studies* 7 (October 1970), 60–76.

Sirota, David, and Greenwood, Michael J. "Understand Your Overseas Workforce." *Harvard Business Review* 49, 1 (January/February 1971), 53–60.

Skinner, Wickham. *American Industry in Developing Economies: The Management of International Manufacturing.* London: Wiley, 1968.

Smith, Timothy H. *The American Corporation in South Africa.* New York: Council for Christian Social Action, 1970.

Spender, J. A. *Weetman Pearson, First Viscount Cowdray 1856–1927.* London: Cassell, 1930.

Sperling, Jan Bodo. *The Human Dimension of Technical Assistance:*

The German Experience at Rourkela, India. Ithaca, N.Y.: Cornell University Press, 1969.

Stikker, Dirk U. *Expansion and Diversification of Exports of Manufactures and Semi-manufactures of Developing Countries: The Role of Private Enterprise in Investment and Promotion of Exports in Developing Countries.* A report for UNCTAD, TD/35/ Supp. 1. United Nations, 1967.

Stobaugh, Robert B. "The Multinational Corporation: Measuring the Consequences." *Columbia Journal of World Business* 6, 1 (January/February 1971), 59–64.

Stockholm International Peace Research Institute. *The Arms Trade with the Third World.* New York: Humanitarian Press, 1971.

Stonehill, Arthur I., ed. *Readings in International Financial Management.* California: Goodyear, 1970.

Streeten, Paul. *"The Contribution of Private Overseas Investment to Development."* Paper given to Columbia University conference on international economic development. February 1970.

——. "Obstacles to Private Foreign Investment in the LDCs." *Columbia Journal of World Business* 5, 3 (May/June 1970), 31–9.

Sussex Group. *Science, Technology and Underdevelopment: The Case for Reform* (mimeo). Institute of Development Studies, Sussex University, 1970.

Tanzer, Michael. *Political Economy of Oil and Underdeveloped Countries.* Boston: Beacon Press, 1969.

Taylor, Wayne Chatfield. *Firestone Operations in Liberia.* Washington, D.C.: National Planning Association, 1956.

Tomlinson, J. W. C. *A Model of the Joint Venture Process in International Business: British Joint Ventures in India and Pakistan.* Cambridge, Mass: MIT Press, 1970.

Tsurumi, Yoshi. "Myths That Mislead U.S. Managers in Japan." *Harvard Business Review,* 49, 4 (July/August 1971), 118–27.

Turner, Louis. *Invisible Empires: Multinational Companies and the Modern World.* London/New York: Hamish Hamilton/Harcourt Brace Jovanovich, 1970.

UNCTAD. *Handbook of International Trade and Development Statistics: Supplement 1970.* United Nations.

United Nations: Department of Economic and Social Affairs. *Panel on Foreign Investment in Developing Countries.* E.69.II.D.12. 1969.

Vaitsos, Constantine V. "Transfer of Resources and Preservation of

Monopoly Rents." Development Advisory Service: Economic Development Report 168. Cambridge, Mass.: Harvard University Press, 1970.

Van Dyke, Stuart H. "Who Is Aiding Whom?" *Columbia Journal of World Business* 5, 2 (March/April 1970), 7–18.

Vernon, Raymond. "Foreign Investors' Motivations in the Less Developed Countries." Development Advisory Service: Economic Development Report 172. Cambridge, Mass.: Harvard University Press, 1970.

——. "The Role of U.S. Enterprise Abroad." *Daedalus* 98, 1 (Winter 1969).

——, ed. *The Technology Factor in International Trade.* New York: National Bureau of Economic Research, 1970.

Ward, Richard J. "Long Think on Development: A United States View." *International Affairs* 46, 1 (January 1970), 11–22.

Watanabe, Susumu. "International Subcontracting, Employment and Skill Promotion." *International Labour Review* 105, 8 (May 1972), 425–49.

West, Richard. *Brazza of the Congo: Exploration and Exploitation in French Equatorial Africa.* London: Cape, 1972.

——. *River of Tears.* London: Earth Island, 1972.

Wharton, Clifton R. "The Green Revolution: Cornucopia or Pandora's Box?" *Foreign Affairs* 47, 3 (April 1969), 464–76.

Whitehead, Laurence. *The United States and Bolivia.* London: Haslemere Group, 1969.

Wilson, Charles. *The History of Unilever.* Vols. 1, 2. London: Cassell, 1954.

——. *Unilever 1945–65.* London: Cassell, 1968.

Young, Crawford. *Congo: Decolonization and Independence.* Princeton University Press, 1965.

INDEX

DATE DUE